I would like to dedicate this book to the students at Ferry Pass Middle School in Pensacola, FL. Their interest in App Inventor inspired me to think of apps and games that might be interesting to them.
−Dr. Lakshmi Prayaga

Dedicated to Amy Brosnaham, for reminding me to take a break every now and then and have some fun, and for being the best friend a man could hope for.
−Jeffrey Hawthorne

I would like to dedicate my work in this beginner's guide to the RILE Project, a continuing source of opportunity, work, and success. Only through groups like RILE and works like this book will higher education get the push it needs to prepare students for real-world computer science.
−Alex Whiteside

ACKNOWLEDGMENTS

I would like to thank my co-authors Jeffrey Hawthorne and Alex Whiteside for their contributions to the book. I wish to extend my thanks to the copy editor, Kate Shoup, and the tech editor, Dallas Sullivan, for their input and edits to ensure the accuracy of the content. Thanks, too, to Mitzi Koontz for keeping us on schedule. We would also like to acknowledge two groups, who contributed to Chapter 3, "Adventure Game: Ring of Fire." The first group is the Ring of Fire team, consisting of students from the art department at the University of West Florida. These students contributed the excellent art work for this chapter. The second group is the folks who maintain the Pura Vida Apps website (www.puravidaapps.com). The source for the optional section in Chapter 3 on embedding animated GIFs in an app is from this website. Finally, I would like to thank my family—my husband, Chandra Prayaga, and my mother, Indira Suri—for their patience and encouragement throughout this period.

–Dr. Lakshmi Prayaga

I'd like to thank Dr. Lakshmi Prayaga and Anthony Pinto for their support, assistance, and encouragement while pursuing my master's degree; my mother, Jacqueline Hawthorne, for supporting me through my higher education; and my doctors, for keeping me healthy while writing this book (a harder task than it sounds).

–Jeffrey Hawthorne

I would like to acknowledge my co-authors, Lakshmi and Jeff. In addition, I would like to thank our technical editor, Dallas Sullivan; copy editor, Kate Shoup; and acquisitions editor, Mitzi Koontz for making this textbook a reality. I would also like to acknowledge all of my friends here in Gainesville—namely, Travis Satiritz, Grant Felowitz, and Jensen Mendez-Wu—for their unrelenting encouragement and constant doses of reality.

–Alex Whiteside

Android™ App Inventor for the Absolute Beginner

Dr. Lakshmi Prayaga, Jeffrey Hawthorne, and Alex Whiteside

Cengage Learning PTR

CENGAGE
Learning™

Australia • Brazil • Japan • Korea • Mexico • Singapore • Spain • United Kingdom • United States

CENGAGE
Learning™

Android™ App Inventor for the Absolute Beginner: Dr. Lakshmi Prayaga, Jeffrey Hawthorne, and Alex Whiteside

Publisher and General Manager, Cengage Learning PTR: Stacy L. Hiquet

Associate Director of Marketing: Sarah Panella

Manager of Editorial Services: Heather Talbot

Senior Marketing Manager: Mark Hughes

Senior Acquisitions Editor: Mitzi Koontz

Project Editor: Kate Shoup

Technical Reviewer: Dallas Sullivan

Copy Editor: Kate Shoup

Interior Layout Tech: Value-Chain International

Cover Designer: Mike Tanamachi

Indexer: Kelly Talbot Editing Services

Proofreader: Kelly Talbot Editing Services

For product information and technology assistance, contact us at **Cengage Learning Customer & Sales Support, 1-800-354-9706**

For permission to use material from this text or product, submit all requests online at **cengage.com/permissions** Further permissions questions can be emailed to **permissionrequest@cengage.com**

Android is a trademark of Google Inc. All other trademarks are the property of their respective owners.

All images © Cengage Learning unless otherwise noted.

Library of Congress Control Number: 2013932041

ISBN-13: 978-1-285-73333-3
ISBN-10: 1-285-73333-9

Cengage Learning PTR
20 Channel Center Street
Boston, MA 02210
USA

Cengage Learning is a leading provider of customized learning solutions with office locations around the globe, including Singapore, the United Kingdom, Australia, Mexico, Brazil, and Japan. Locate your local office at: **international.cengage.com/region**

Cengage Learning products are represented in Canada by Nelson Education, Ltd.

For your lifelong learning solutions, visit **cengageptr.com**

Visit our corporate website at **cengage.com**

Printed in the United States of America
1 2 3 4 5 6 7 15 14 13

ABOUT THE AUTHORS

Dr. Lakshmi Prayaga is an assistant professor in the Department of Applied Sciences, Technology, and Administration at the University of West Florida. She has an interdisciplinary background with a master's in philosophy, a master's in business administration, a master's in software engineering, and a doctoral degree in instructional technology. Lakshmi has always been interested in teaching computing principles in an interesting manner that engages students. She has been a recipient of several local and national grants to accomplish these goals.

Jeffrey Hawthorne originally had no intention of becoming involved with computers in any way, shape, or form. Beginning with the goal of becoming an architect, he then shifted to a major in art, finding the flexibility of art more appealing than the structure of architecture. He eventually went back to architecture after a lengthy career as a veterinary assistant before the housing crisis drove him back to school and another career shift. He got his bachelor's degree in interdisciplinary information technology with a specialization in digital media (a fancy way of saying "Web design") at the University of West Florida in 2010. He then continued his studies there, acquiring a master's degree in software engineering in 2012. He currently works at Global Business Solutions as an open-source developer.

Alex Whiteside is a computer engineering student at the University of Florida in Gainesville. His technical background and interests range from low-level hardware-software interaction to high-level interface design and presentation. He has worked as a programmer for numerous agencies, including the U.S. Air Force Research Laboratory and American Express. He currently serves as the chief technology officer at RILE, Inc.

TABLE OF CONTENTS

INTRODUCTION

Designing mobile apps is exciting, but has historically been viewed as something that is nerdy and difficult. The App Inventor tool for the Android platform has changed this view by simplifying the process of app development and making it easy even for laypeople to design their own apps. This book, *Android App Inventor for the Absolute Beginner*, will introduce you to App Inventor. You will be amazed by this tool's simplicity and what you can do with it. After you set up your computer to use App Inventor, as discussed in Appendix A, "Setting Up Your System to Run App Inventor," it should take you 20 to 30 minutes to complete your first app.

WHAT YOU'LL FIND IN THIS BOOK

This book includes several concepts, from simple event-driven programming to using a mobile device to control robots. The book starts out with simple apps and increases in complexity as you move through the chapters. You will use components such as the following to design fun-filled apps:

- Various types of sensors
- Animations
- Multiple screens
- A TinyDB component

You will also build apps to interface with external devices such as NXT robots with Bluetooth and accelerometer sensors.

HOW THIS BOOK IS ORGANIZED

This book uses a step-by-step approach to build apps. Each chapter has specific instructions to design the graphical user interface, followed by a section on assembling the logic with the Blocks Editor, and finally, in some cases, instructions to test and deploy your app. The book has an advanced section that builds on ideas from previous chapters with the addition of new ideas. The advanced section contains chapters on robots, QR analyzers, and puzzle-based quizzes. This book contains the following chapters:

- **Chapter 1, "Introducing App Inventor":** This chapter provides an introduction to App Inventor. You will design a simple app that lights up a Christmas tree when a button is clicked.

- **Chapter 2, "See 'N' Say App":** The app in this chapter introduces the use of media elements such as sounds and images.

- **Chapter 3, "Adventure Game: Ring of Fire":** This chapter's app introduces the use of multiple screens to design an adventure game based on trivia. This chapter also has an optional section that provides instructions on including animated GIFs in your app.

- **Chapter 4, "Whack-a-Mole":** The app in this chapter illustrates the use of a random number generator to specify a random location on the screen where a new target appears each time an existing target is touched. The goal is to touch as many targets as possible within a given time.

- **Chapter 5, "Car Racing Game":** The car racing game app discussed in this chapter uses a timer, an orientation sensor, animated image sprites, collision detection, a countdown timer, and global variables. The goal is to hit or miss other obstacles on the racing track within a given time.

- **Chapter 6, "Trivia Quiz":** The app in this chapter illustrates the use of the TinyDB and option buttons to design a quiz and check the answers submitted.

- **Chapter 7, "The Jigsaw Puzzle":** This chapter's app demonstrates moving objects by touch and collision detection.

- **Chapter 8, "Physics-Based Animation: Brick Breaker":** This chapter explores simple physics concepts of trajectory and velocity to design a brick-breaker game. You will again see the use of collision detection.

- **Chapter 9, "Using Persistent Databases: Tracking Your Weight":** This chapter applies concepts you've learned so far, including TinyDB and storing values. You will use these concepts to design a practical application that helps you track your weight.

- **Chapter 10, "The Quizzler":** This chapter applies the principles you learned in Chapter 6 and Chapter 7 to design a picture puzzle. The pieces of the puzzle are revealed with each correct response to a quiz question.

- **Chapter 11, "Controlling NXT Robots":** This chapter illustrates how to use your Android mobile device to connect to an NXT robot via Bluetooth, send commands, and receive data.

- **Chapter 12, "Virtual Reality: Using QR Codes":** In this chapter, you will create a program to launch a QR code reader; wait for the result; determine whether the QR code contains a phone number, URL, or message; and, depending on the data type, call the number, open the webpage, or display the message.

WHO THIS BOOK IS FOR

This book is designed for anyone who wishes to explore and have fun with mobile app development. Because of the wide variety of topics introduced in this book, it has something for everyone, from the novice programmer to the programmer hobbyist.

COMPANION WEBSITE

The companion website for this book can be found at www.cengageptr.com/downloads. The website contains the source code and assets used for each app.

CHAPTER 1

INTRODUCING APP INVENTOR

CHAPTER OBJECTIVES

- What is App Inventor?
- Prepare your computer to use App Inventor
- Concepts used in this chapter
- Design your first app, Light Me Up

WHAT IS APP INVENTOR?

App Inventor is a tool to design apps for the Android platform. It was developed by Google and is now maintained by MIT. App Inventor provides a very easy drag-and-drop user interface, and makes it very easy for people with no programming experience to develop apps. The learning curve on this tool is not steep, as you will see when you complete your first app.

PREPARE YOUR COMPUTER AND PHONE TO USE APP INVENTOR

Before you begin to use App Inventor, you must check that your computer system meets the requirements suggested by appinventor.mit.edu. Some of the basic requirements are listed here. Detailed, step-by-step instructions to install the necessary software and set up your computer and phone may be found at http://appinventor.mit.edu/teach/curriculum/setup-instructions.html.

- **A gmail account.** Before you start setting up your system to use App Inventor, make sure you have a gmail account. If you don't have one, now is a good time to set one up. Type "`setup gmail account`" in Google and follow the link to set up a gmail account.
- **Computer and operating system.** You can run App Inventor on a Macintosh, Windows, or GNU/Linux machine. If you use a Mac, it must have an Intel processor, and must run Mac OS X 10.5, 10.6, 10.7, and up. If you use a Windows machine, it must run Windows XP, Windows Vista, or Windows 7. GNU/Linux machines must run Ubuntu 8+ or Debian 5+.
- **Browser.** This can be Mozilla Firefox 3.6 or higher, Apple Safari 5.0 or higher, Google Chrome 4.0 or higher, or Microsoft Internet Explorer 7 or higher.
- **Java 6.** Your computer needs to run Java 6 (also known as Java 1.6). You can download Java from http://www.java.com.

Before you run App Inventor, test your Java configuration. Visit the Java test page. You should see a message that Java is working and that the version is Java 1.6. (You need to allow your computer to run Java when a pop-up message appears at the top corner of the page.) Run the App Inventor Java test by clicking on this message. This will check that your browser is properly configured to run Java, and that your computer can launch applications with Java Web Start.

- **App Inventor Setup software.** Before you can use App Inventor, you need to install some software on your computer. The software you need is provided in a package called App Inventor Setup. Follow the instructions for your operating system to do the installation, and then go on to set up your Android phone.
- **App Inventor software.** You must also install the App Inventor software.

Visit the URL at the beginning of this section for detailed instructions on installing the required software and setup of your phone to use App Inventor.

Check out the accompanying website for this text book to download resources including images and sound files used in the chapters.

Concepts Used in This Chapter

The concepts used in this chapter are basic ideas pertaining to event-driven programming. With event-driven programming, an event in the program triggers an action. For example, if you look at buttons, checkboxes, drop-down lists, etc., you will see that each of these components has several events attached to it, including clicking, double-clicking, mouse-overs, etc. These events trigger actions, such as opening a page or providing more details about a product in an online shopping cart.

In this chapter, you look at a Button component and its click event, which triggers a set of actions in an app. You also use the Image component to display the appropriate image and manipulate its visible properties.

Designing Your First App: Light Me Up

The best way to learn about App Inventor is to dig into it and start using it, so let's get started designing your first app. This app will enable you to click a button to light up a Christmas tree and click another button to turn off the lights. When designing this app, you will use the screen and will import pictures, sound files, and buttons. You will also look at the properties and methods for each of these elements.

To begin, follow these steps:

1. After you have set up your computer and installed all the necessary files, open your Web browser and visit http://appinventor.mit.edu/. Your screen should look like Figure 1.1.

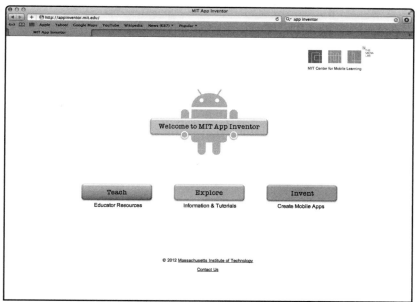

Source: Massachusetts Institute of Technology.

FIGURE 1.1

The App Inventor home page.

2. Click the Invent button. A screen with options to create a new project appears. If necessary go to My projects at the top of the screen and then click New Project.
3. Click the New button to create a new project.
4. In the Project Name text box, type LightMeUp. Your screen should be similar to the one shown in Figure 1.2. Notice that the layout has four panels: Palette, Viewer, Components, and Properties.

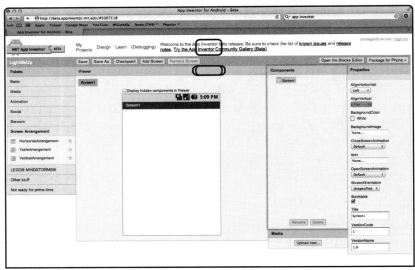

FIGURE 1.2

Creating a new
project.

This is the graphical user interface (GUI) window. You will use this window to place all the components that will be used for your app, such as images, sound files, buttons, drop-down boxes, etc. This same window also has tabs to package the app for your phone.

The other window that will be used is the Blocks Editor, which enables you to assemble the blocks that contain the code to run your app and a tab to test your app in an Emulator or transfer the app to your phone. You will go back and forth between these windows to complete your app.

The Design Phase

The center part of your screen, the Viewer, is the area on which you will have access to the screen and place all the components of your app, such as buttons, image holders, sound files, checkboxes, drop-down lists, and so on. For this app, you will add buttons and images to the screen and work with their properties. Follow these instructions to set up the GUI for your app:

1. The first item to add to your interface is an alignment option. To begin, click the Screen Arrangement tab in the Palette panel. Then drag the HorizontalArrangement component to the screen1 in the Viewer panel. This component will help retain the position of the controls you place on the screen and prevent them from being shifted at runtime. Your screen should now be similar to the one shown in Figure 1.3.

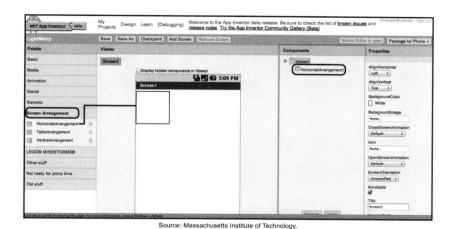

Source: Massachusetts Institute of Technology.

FIGURE 1.3

Setting the screen arrangement.

2. In the Palette panel, click the Basic tab. Then drag a Button component and drop it in the HorizontalArrangement component.

3. Click the button. Then, in the Properties panel on the right, click the button's Text property and type `Lights On`. See Figure 1.4.

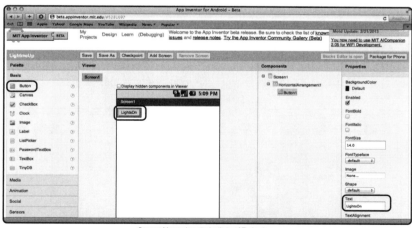

Source: Massachusetts Institute of Technology.

FIGURE 1.4

Button Text property.

NOTE If you like, you can change the shape of the button, the button's background color, the color of the text, etc. Feel free to experiment with those properties in the Properties panel.

4. Drag another Button component and drop it in the HorizontalArrangement component. Change the text of this button to read "Lights Off."

5. Click the Image component in the Basic tab and drag it to screen 1. In the Properties tab for the image component, click the Picture tag, click Upload New, browse to open the appropriate folder on your computer, and choose the image you want to use. In this case, find the image of the tree without the lights from the resources you downloaded and saved for this chapter. (See Figure 1.5.)

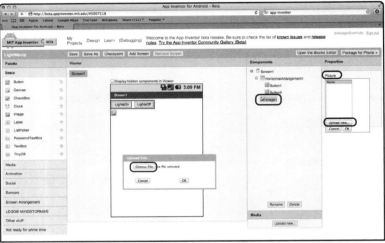

FIGURE 1.5

Choosing an image.

6. In the Properties panel, click the Visible drop-down list and choose Showing. (See Figure 1.6.) Also set the Width and Height properties to 200 pixels.

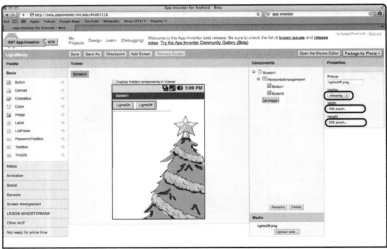

FIGURE 1.6

The Image component.

7. Drag a second Image component to the screen. Locate its Source tag, click its Picture tag, and click Upload New to open the appropriate folder on your computer to choose the image you want to use. In this case, from the resources downloaded and saved for this chapter, choose the image of the tree with the lights. In the Properties window, click the Visible drop-down list and choose Hidden. Also set the Width and Height properties to 200 pixels.

8. It's a good idea to give your components more meaningful names. That way, you can identify them more easily when you start to code them. To begin, click the Button1 component in the Components panel; then click Rename. In the New Name text box, type `LightsOn`. Repeat this step for the Button2 component, renaming it LightsOff. Similarly, rename the Image1 and Image2 components treeLightsOff and treeLightsOn, respectively. Notice that the image tags are placed in reverse order: Image 2, and Image 1. That should not matter as long as you name them correctly. Also note that when you name your files, App Inventor does not allow spaces and special characters.

This completes the GUI for the app. The completed GUI should look like Figure 1.7. This completes the first phase of the project, the design phase. At this point, it's a good idea to click on the Save button to save your project. The Save button is located on the top panel of the Viewer tab. Now you move on to the second phase, which is the code phase.

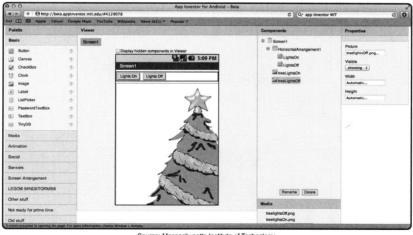

Source: Massachusetts Institute of Technology.

FIGURE 1.7

The completed GUI.

The Code Phase

App Inventor has a very easy, user-friendly interface for coding your apps. In this interface you associate events with the components you added in the design phase by choosing from a set of available events that trigger specific behaviors. A Button component, for example, is associated with several events, including clicking, double-clicking, mouse-overs, etc.

In this chapter, you will code a click event. That way, when the user clicks the LightsOn button, the lights on the tree will be turned on, and when the user clicks the LightsOff button, the lights on the tree will be turned off. The point to remember here is that clicking a button triggers an event that results in an action. You, as the programmer, can choose the event and the action that follows from this trigger. In this project, there are two buttons that must be coded: the LightsOn button and the LightsOff button.

The LightsOn Button

When the user clicks the LightsOn button, the program should do three things:

- Show the image with the lights on.
- Hide the image with the lights off.
- Enable the LightsOff button so it can be clicked.

The LightsOff Button

When the user clicks the LightsOff button, the program should do three things (the opposite of what happens when the LightsOn button is clicked):

- Show the image with the lights off.
- Hide the Image with the lights on.
- Enable the LightsOn button so it can be clicked.

Code the Buttons

To code the buttons, first open the Blocks Editor. To do so, click the Open Blocks Editor button in the top-right corner of the screen. When the Blocks Editor is open, your screen should be similar to the one shown in Figure 1.8.

FIGURE 1.8

The Blocks Editor.

Source: Massachusetts Institute of Technology.

If you are working on a Mac, you will find AppInventorforCodeBlocks.jnlp in the Downloads folder. Double-click that file to open the Blocks Editor. The Finder folder is the very first square icon, with a face on it, at the bottom of the screen on a Mac computer. In some cases, you may need to right-click the file and choose Show in Finder. The Finder opens and shows this file in it. Once it appears in the Finder, you can double-click it to open the Blocks Editor.

On the left panel, you'll see three tabs: Built-In, My Blocks, and Advance. You will learn about the Built-In and Advanced tabs in the later chapters. In this chapter, we will be working with the My Blocks tab.

To code the buttons, follow these steps:

1. Click the My Blocks tab. You will see all the components you added in the design phase—LightsOff, LightsOn, treeLightsOff, treeLightsOn, and other system-related components including My Definitions and Screen1. (See Figure 1.9.)

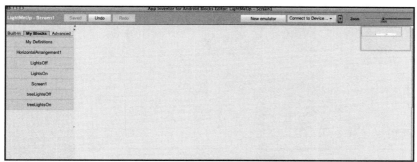

Source: Massachusetts Institute of Technology.

FIGURE 1.9

The My Blocks tab.

2. Click the LightsOn component. A bunch of events and settings (properties) for the LightsOn button will become available on the left panel.
3. Click the LightsOn.Click event and drag it to the center area, or screen1. This is your work area, where the code resides. As you can see in Figure 1.10, this is a little like setting up a picture puzzle piece!

Source: Massachusetts Institute of Technology.

FIGURE 1.10

The LightsOn.Click event.

4. Click the treeLightsOn component. You will find a set of options available for the image, including Visible, Width, Height, Picture, etc. (See Figure 1.11.)

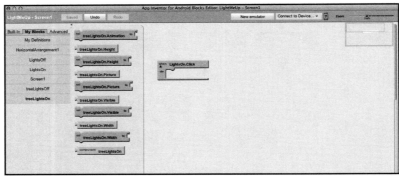

Source: Massachusetts Institute of Technology.

FIGURE 1.11

Image properties.

5. Click the set treeLightsOn.Visible property and drag it to fit the LightsOn.Click puzzle piece, or block, as shown in Figure 1.12.

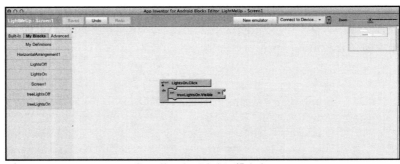

Source: Massachusetts Institute of Technology.

FIGURE 1.12

The treeLightsOn.Visible property.

6. Now you need to set the treeLightsOn.Visible property to true. To do so, click an empty area on the screen to reveal more options, in the form of tabs. Then click the Logic tab and choose True, as shown in Figure 1.13.

FIGURE 1.13

Setting the treeLightsOn. Visible property.

Source: Massachusetts Institute of Technology.

7. Drag the true block to fit the set treeLightsOn.Visible block, as shown in Figure 1.14.

FIGURE 1.14

Fitting the True piece to the treeLightsOn. Visible piece.

Source: Massachusetts Institute of Technology.

8. Click the treeLightsOff component.
9. Click the set treeLightsOff.Visible property and drag it to fit the LightsOn.Click block.
10. Click an empty area on the screen to reveal more options. Then click the Logic tab and choose False.
11. Drag the false block to fit the treeLightsOff.Visible block.
12. Click LightsOff component.
13. Click the set LightsOff.Visible property and drag it below the treeLightsOff.Visible piece.
14. Click an empty area, click the Logic tab, choose True, and drag the true block to fit the treeLightsOff.Visible block.

This completes the coding of the LightsOn button. Your screen should now be similar to the one shown in Figure 1.15.

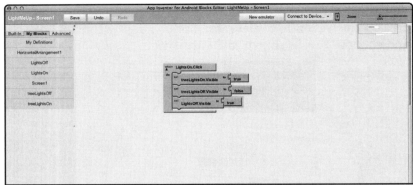

FIGURE 1.15

The complete code
for the LightsOn
button.

The next set of instructions are to code the LightsOff button, to turn off the lights:

1. Click the LightsOff button in the My Blocks tab. A bunch of events and settings (properties) for LightsOff button will become available on the left panel.
2. Click the `LightsOff.Click` event and drag it to the center area, below the `LightsOn.Click` block. See Figure 1.16.

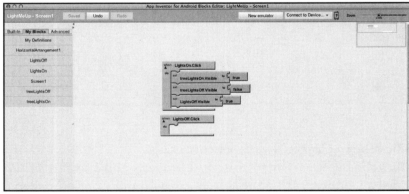

FIGURE 1.16

The LightsOff.Click
event.

3. Click the treeLightsOff component. You will find a set of options available for the image, including Visible, Width, Height, Picture, etc.
4. Click the `set treeLightsOff.Visible` property and drag it to fit the `LightsOff.Click` block, as shown in Figure 1.17.

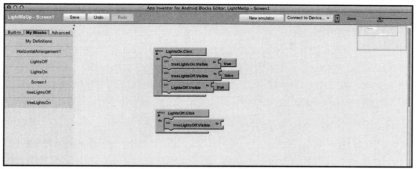

Source: Massachusetts Institute of Technology.

FIGURE 1.17

The `treeLightsOff.Visible` property.

5. Now you need to set the `treeLightsOff.Visible` property to true. To do so, click an empty area on the screen to reveal more options, in the form of tabs. Then click the Logic tab and choose True.

6. Drag the `true` block to fit `treeLightsOff.Visible` block.

7. Click the treeLightsOn component.

8. Click the `set treeLightsOn.Visible` property and drag it to fit the `LightsOff.Click` block.

9. Click an empty area on the screen to reveal more options. Then click the Logic tab and choose False.

10. Drag the `false` block to fit the `treeLightsOff.Visible` block. Your screen should now be similar to the one shown in Figure 1.18.

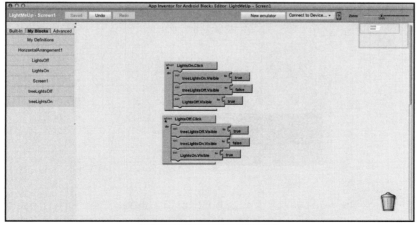

Source: Massachusetts Institute of Technology.

FIGURE 18

The complete code for the LightsOff button.

Testing Phase

Now it's time for the third and final phase of your app development: the testing phase. This phase will implement your code and provide a run-time version of it, enabling you to visualize how your audience will view your app. This phase also gives you an opportunity to fix any errors or make changes before you deploy the app to your audience. The App Inventor also has a built-in Emulator, on which you can test your app virtually before loading it to your phone. Follow these steps to test your app:

1. In the Blocks Editor, click the New Emulator button. (Note that it takes a while to open the Emulator, so be patient.) When the process of opening the Emulator is initiated a green Android icon will appear on the bottom panel of your screen to identify the Emulator. (See Figure 1.19.) When the Emulator is open, you will see an image of an Android phone on your screen. (See Figure 1.20.) If it is hidden, click the green Android icon to bring the Emulator to the front. The Emulator will appear in the taskbar for Windows and Linux users.

Source: Massachusetts Institute of Technology.

FIGURE 1.19

The Android icon.

FIGURE 1.20

The Emulator.

Source: Massachusetts Institute of Technology.

2. In the Blocks Editor, click the Connect to Device button and choose 544. Again, be patient while your program connects to the Emulator. During this process, you'll see a flashing yellow phone icon next to the Connect to Device button. Once it is connected, the flashing yellow phone changes to a solid green icon. (See Figure 1.21.)

Source: Massachusetts Institute of Technology.

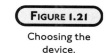

FIGURE 1.21

Choosing the device.

3. When you see the solid green phone icon, slide the lock on the Emulator (that is, on the image of the phone) to the right to unlock the phone. You should then be able to see the app on the Emulator, as shown in Figure 1.22.

Source: Massachusetts Institute of Technology.

FIGURE 1.22

Unlock the phone to see the app on the Emulator.

4. To test the app, click on each of the buttons to check if the correct image appears on the screen. The LightsOn button should turn the tree lights on and the LightsOff button should turn the tree lights off. That's it! You've created your first app for the Android phone.

Deployment Phase

The deployment phase is the final phase of any software development. Once the testing is completed and your application is error free, it can be deployed or made available for live testing and usage by the general public. Industry software is tested widely by many people before it becomes available to public. Beta testing is precisely this part of software development.

In your application, the emulator provides you an opportunity to make changes before you deploy it. The App Inventor has three ways in which you can deploy your app, manual transfer via the USB port, create an APK file which can be shared with other users, and a WiFi mode. The steps listed below provide instructions to deploy your app using the USB port.

1. Close the Emulator and make sure the Blocks Editor is still open.
2. Using the USB port, connect your phone to your computer.
3. In the Blocks Editor, click the Connect to Device button and choose the ID number shown in the drop-down list. (Mine, for example, is MS80edf1544f.)
4. Return to the App Inventor GUI window and click the Package for Phone button. If you don't see it, check your browser and as long as you did not close the App Inventor browser you should find it in the browser. If you accidentally closed it, then you go back to the App Inventor website and go to Invent and you'll find your project in the Projects tab. Open your project to access the GUI for your project.
5. Choose Download to the Connected Phone. When the installation is complete, the system displays a message indicating that the application was installed successfully. (This can take a couple minutes, so be patient.)
6. Check the apps on your phone. You should find the app installed. Test it, and enjoy your very first app!

 A recent contribution from MIT is a wireless option to install apps on your phone. Basically, you download a barcode scanner to your phone and use it to scan the barcode generated for your app by the App Inventor. For details, visit http://appinventor.mit.edu/explore/content/setup-device-wifi.html.

Sharing Your App

To share your app with friends, go back to the GUI designer page of the App Inventor. This is a good time to also check if you would like to make any additional changes. You can open the project, make modifications, and save it again before packaging the application. Click the Package for Phone button and choose Download to the Computer.

A ZIP file containing the assets used in your app, such as image files, sound files, etc., will be downloaded to your computer. You can then e-mail the ZIP file to your friends, who can access the app by opening this e-mail from their phone. For more options on packaging and sharing your app, visit the App Inventor site hosted by MIT at http://appinventor.mit.edu/teach/curriculum/packaging-apps.html.

SUMMARY

This chapter introduced the App Inventor, for building apps for the Android platform. The App Inventor was originally designed by Google and is presently owned by MIT. The chapter described the tool's user interface, the Blocks Editor (for assembling the logic for the app), and testing and deployment options. The main concepts covered in the chapter included the idea of event-driven programming, basic components such as buttons, and image containers to build the GUI and assemble the code blocks. Future chapters will look into the use of more advanced components to build interesting apps.

CHAPTER 2

SEE 'N' SAY APP

CHAPTER OBJECTIVES

- Design a multi-media app using images and sound files
- Use the if conditional statement
- Use the accelerometer sensor

INTRODUCTION

This app will provide a user interface with several pictures of animals and prompt the user to click each picture to hear what it says. This is accomplished through the use of the Button component's click event, which you saw in Chapter 1, "Introducing App Inventor." You'll add a fun aspect to this app by implementing an accelerometer. Three of the pictures will respond to the Button component's click event, but the picture of the lion will require that you tilt the phone to hear it roar. The accelerometer's change event will be used to play the sound of the lion's roar. You can download the images and sound files used for this chapter from www.cengageptr.com/downloads.

THE DESIGN PHASE

The GUI for this app will consist of a TableArrangement component, Button components, and Sound components. The following sections contain the instructions to set up your graphical user interface.

To get started, do the following:

1. In App Inventor, click Invent. You should find the projects you have created so far. To start a new project, click the New button and type SeeNSay in the dialog box that opens to name your project.
2. Click the Screen Arrangement tab and drag the TableArrangement component to the screen.
3. In the Properties tab on the far right, type 2 in the Columns field and 2 in the Rows field. Your screen should look like Figure 2.1.

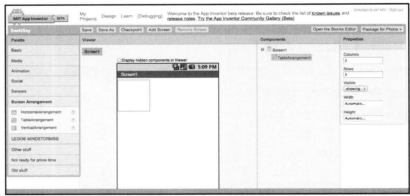

Table properties.

Source: Massachusetts Institute of Technology.

Add the Buttons for the App

In this section, you will add buttons to provide the interactivity for the app. You will add four buttons and set the buttons' properties to display an image.

1. In the Palette, click Basic, and drag a Button component to the TableArrangement component.
2. In the Properties panel, change the Button component's Width and Height settings to 100 pixels.
3. In the Properties panel, in the Text field, type What does the cat say? to change the button's text.

4. In the Properties panel, click the Image Source field. A Browse dialog box opens; browse to the folder on your computer where you have stored the images and sound files for this app, and choose kitten1.jpg. Your screen should be similar to the one shown in Figure 2.2.

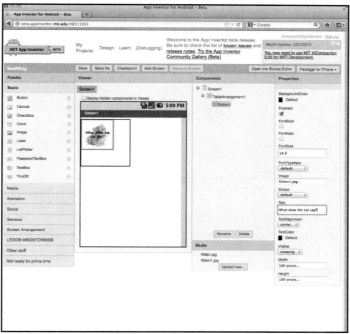

Source: Massachusetts Institute of Technology. Kitten image ©iStockphoto.com/kadmy.

FIGURE 2.2

Choose an image for the button.

5. Click the button in the Components panel, and click the Rename button at the bottom of the panel. Then type btnCat to change the name of the button accordingly.
6. Drag another Button component from the Palette and drop it next to the btnCat button in the TableArrangement component. Change its Width and Height settings to 100 pixels. Then type What does the puppy say? in the Properties panel's Text field to change the text on the button.
7. Click the Image Source field. A Browse dialog box opens; browse to the folder on your computer where you have stored the images and sound files for this app, and choose the puppy1.jpg image. Your screen should be similar to the one shown in Figure 2.3.
8. Rename this button to btnPuppy, as shown in Figure 2.3.

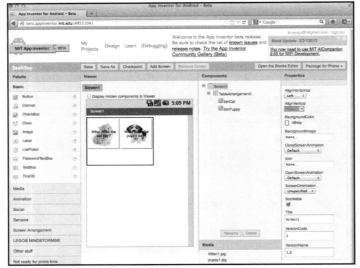

FIGURE 2.3

Add the second button.

Source: Massachusetts Institute of Technology. Kitten image ©iStockphoto.com/kadmy. Puppy image ©iStockphoto.com/sankai.

9. Drag another Button component from the Palette and drop it below the btnCat button in the TableArrangement component. Change its Width and Height settings to 100 pixels and its text to What does the goat say?.

10. Click the Image Source field. A Browse dialog box opens; browse to the folder on your computer where you have stored the images and sound files for this app, and choose the goat1.jpg image.

11. Rename this button to btnGoat.

12. Drag another Button component from the Palette and drop it below the btnPuppy button in the TableArrangement component. Change its Width and Height settings to 100 pixels and its text to What does the lion say?.

13. Click the Image Source field. A Browse dialog box opens; browse to the folder on your computer where you have stored the images and sound files for this app, and choose the lion1.jpg image.

14. Rename the button to btnLion. Your screen should be similar to the one in Figure 2.4.

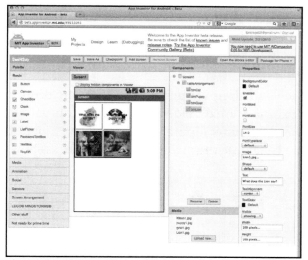

Source: Massachusetts Institute of Technology. Kitten image ©iStockphoto.com/kadmy. Puppy image ©iStockphoto.com/sankai. Goat image ©iStockphoto.com/NikiTaxidis Photography. Lion image ©fotosearch.com.

FIGURE 2.4

Four buttons added to the table.

15. Drag a Label component from the Palette and drop it below the table on the screen.
16. In the Properties panel, type `Tilt me to hear me roar` in the Text field.
17. In the Properties panel, click the Visible drop-down list (it's currently set to Showing, as in Figure 2. 5) and choose Hidden.

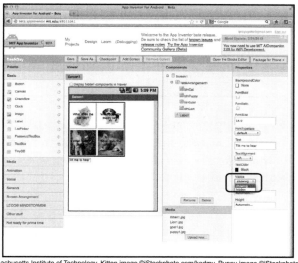

Source: Massachusetts Institute of Technology. Kitten image ©iStockphoto.com/kadmy. Puppy image ©iStockphoto.com/sankai. Goat image ©iStockphoto.com/NikiTaxidisPhotography. Lion image ©fotosearch.com.

FIGURE 2.5

Add a Label component and Visible property.

18. Rename the label to lblTilt.

Add the Sound Components

A Sound component is an invisible component. It will not be added to the screen. Rather, it will be listed below the screen. It will not be visible at run time. To add the Sound components needed for this app, follow these steps:

1. In the Palette, open the Media tab, drag a Sound component, and drop it on the screen.
2. In the Properties panel, click the Source field for the Sound component, click Upload New and browse to the folder on your computer where you have stored the images and sound files for this app. Finally, choose the meow.wav sound file, as shown in Figure 2.6.

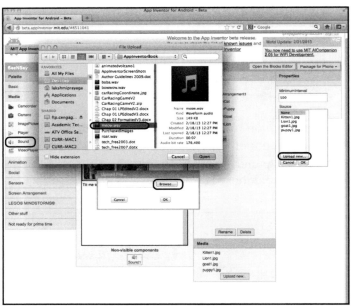

FIGURE 2.6

Choose the sound file.

Source: Massachusetts Institute of Technology.

3. Click the Sound1 component, then click Rename and type `meow` to rename the Sound1 component. Your screen will look like the one shown in Figure 2.7.

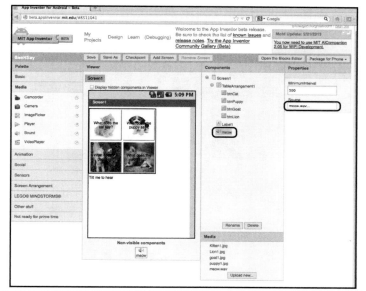

FIGURE 2.7

Rename the
Sound I
component.

4. Repeat steps 1–3 to add a second Sound component, this time choosing the bowwow.wav sound file. Rename the sound component to bowwow.

5. Repeat steps 1–3 to add a third Sound component, this time choosing the baba.wav sound file. Rename the sound component to baba.

6. Repeat steps 1–3 to add a fourth Sound component, this time choosing the roar.wav sound file. Rename the sound component to roar. Your screen should be similar to the one shown in Figure 2.8.

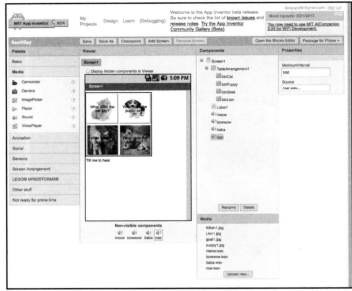

Add the Accelerometer

The App Inventor provides three types of sensors: the accelerometer sensor, the orientation sensor, and the location sensor. In this chapter, you will use the accelerometer sensor. The accelerometer sensor is used to measure acceleration in three directions: the vertical direction (Z) and two perpendicular directions in the horizontal plane (X and Y).

 TIP For further details on the sensor, visit http://beta.appinventor.mit.edu/learn/ reference/components/sensors.html.

To add an accelerometer, click the Sensors tab in the Palette and drag an AccelerometerSensor component onto the screen. As with the Sound component, this component is also invisible. It will not show up at run time when you run your application.

This completes the GUI portion of the app. Your screen should now look like the one shown in Figure 2.9.

Source: Massachusetts Institute of Technology. Kitten image ©iStockphoto.com/kadmy. Puppy image ©iStockphoto.com/sankai.
Goat image ©iStockphoto.com/NikiTaxidisPhotography. Lion image ©fotosearch.com.

FIGURE 2.9

Completed GUI.

THE CODE PHASE

The idea behind this app is to play a sound when a button is clicked or the phone is tilted. Before you start coding, note the list of the steps required for this app.

When the btnCat button is clicked:

- Play the meow file.
- Stop the bowwow sound file.
- Stop the baba sound file.
- Stop the roar sound file.

When the btnPuppy button is clicked:

- Play the bowwow sound file.
- Stop the meow sound file.
- Stop the baba sound file.
- Stop the roar sound file.

When the btnGoat button is clicked:

- Play the baba file.
- Stop the bowwow sound file.
- Stop the meow sound file.
- Stop the roar sound file.

When the btnLion button is clicked:

- Show the "Tilt me to hear me roar" label.
- Stop the bowwow sound file.
- Stop the baba sound file.
- Stop the meow sound file.

The following sections contain the instructions to set up the blocks for this app. Before you begin, make sure the Blocks Editor is open. (Click the Open the Blocks Editor button in the top-right corner of the App Inventor window.) You will code the buttons and the accelerometer to play the appropriate sound.

Assemble the Button-Click Events

In this section, you will assemble the blocks for the action phase. This is where you specify instructions for the button-click events for the four buttons you placed on the screen. The steps listed here will guide you to complete assembly of the blocks for the four button-click events.

1. Click the My Blocks tab.
2. Click the btnCat component.
3. Drag the `when btnCat.Click do` block to the center of the screen.
4. Click the meow component and drag `meow.Play` under the `btnCat.Click` event.
5. Click the bowWow component and drag `bowWow.Stop` under the `btnCat.Click` event.
6. Click the baba component and drag `baba.Stop` under the `btnCat.Click` event.
7. Click the roar component and drag `roar.Stop` under the `btnCat.Click` event. (See Figure 2.10.)

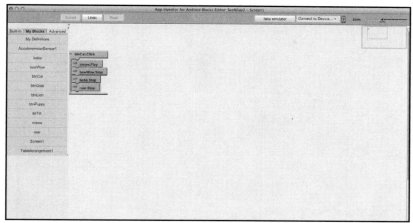

Source: Massachusetts Institute of Technology.

FIGURE 2.10

Assemble btnCat.

8. Click the My Blocks tab.
9. Click the btnPuppy component.
10. Drag the when btnPuppy.Click do block to the center of the screen.
11. Click the bowWow component and drag bowWow.Play under the btnPuppy.Click event.
12. Click the meow component and drag meow.Stop under the btnPuppy.Click event.
13. Click the baba component and drag baba.Stop under the btnPuppy.Click event.
14. Click the roar component and drag roar.Stop under the btnPuppy.Click event.
15. Click the My Blocks tab.
16. Click the btnGoat component.
17. Drag the when btnGoat.Click do block to the center of the screen.
18. Click the baba component and drag baba.Play under the btnGoat.Click event.
19. Click the bowWow component and drag bowWow.Stop under the btnGoat.Click event.
20. Click the meow component and drag meow.Stop under the btnGoat.Click event.
21. Click the roar component and drag roar.Stop under the btnGoat.Click event.
22. Click the My Blocks tab.
23. Click the btnLion component.
24. Drag the when btnLion.Click do block to the center of the screen.
25. Click the lblTilt component and drag set lblTilt.Visible under the btnLion.Click event.
26. Click an empty area on the screen and click Logic. Then click True and drag the true block so it fits the slot of lblTilt.Visible. See Figure 2.11.

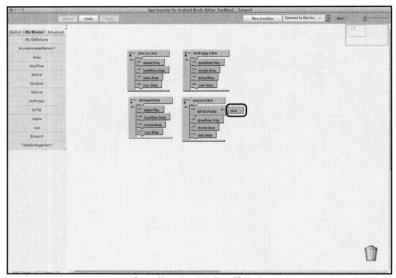

FIGURE 2.11

Set Visible
property of the
label to true.

Source: Massachusetts Institute of Technology.

27. Click the bowWow component and drag bowWow.Stop under the btnLion.Click event.
28. Click the baba component and drag baba.Stop under the btnLion.Click event.
29. Click the meow component and drag meow.Stop under the btnLion.click event.
30. Click the roar component and drag roar.Stop under the btnLion.Click event.

Assemble the Accelerometer Sensor

As documented by App Inventor, the accelerometer sensor senses when the phone is shaking and measures acceleration in three dimensions. It produces three values:

- **XAccel:** This is a positive value when the phone is tilted to the right and a negative value when the phone is tilted to the left.
- **YAccel:** This is a positive value when the top is raised and a negative value when the bottom is raised.
- **ZAccel:** This is a positive value when the display is facing up and a negative value when the display is facing down.

Follow these instructions to assemble the blocks for the accelerometer sensor using the tilt value:

1. Click the My Blocks tab.
2. Click the AccelerometerSensor1 component and drag the when AccelerometerSensor1. AccelerationChanged block to an empty area on the screen. Notice that the xAccel, yAccel, and zAccel pieces are automatically added to this block.

3. Click the Built-In tab.
4. Click Control.
5. Click the `if test then-do` block (see Figure 2.12) and drag it to the `do` section of the `when AccelerometerSensor1.AccelerationChanged` block (see Figure 2.13).

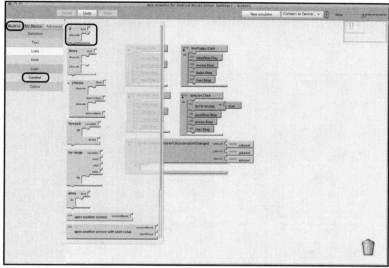

Source: Massachusetts Institute of Technology.

FIGURE 2.12

Locating the `if test then-do` block.

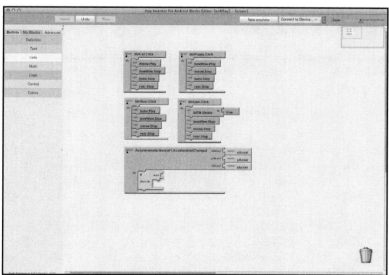

Source: Massachusetts Institute of Technology.

FIGURE 2.13

Inserting the if-then-do block.

6. If-then-do is a programming construct available in all programming languages. It allows you to test for a certain condition in your program and, if that condition turns out to be true, to make your program execute an action. In this case, you will test to see whether the sensor's Y acceleration is greater than 5. If so, the app will play the lion's roar sound file. To begin, click the Built-In tab.

7. Click Math.

8. Click the greater-than (>) sign, shown in Figure 2.14, and drag it to fit the slot nearest the test condition, as shown in Figure 2.15.

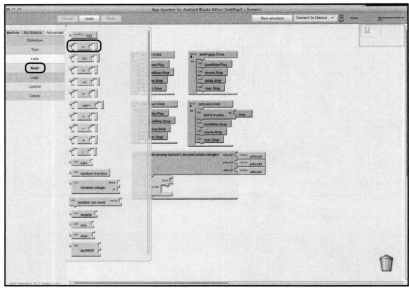

FIGURE 2.14

Locate the math functions.

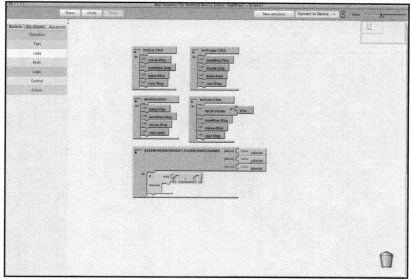

Source: Massachusetts Institute of Technology.

FIGURE 2.15

Insert the greater-than (>) math function.

9. Click the My Blocks tab.

10. Click `AccelerometerSensor1.YAccel` and drag it to the first blank area of the greater-than (>) block, as shown in Figure 2.16.

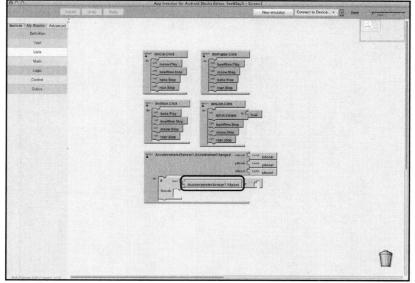

Source: Massachusetts Institute of Technology.

FIGURE 2.16

Add `AccelerometerSensor1.YAccel`.

11. Click a blank area of the screen and choose Math. Then click the number 123, shown in Figure 2.17, and type 5.

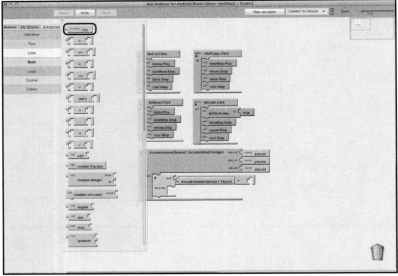

FIGURE 2.17

Locate the Math library.

12. Drag the number tag (5) and drop it in the second blank area of the > block. Your screen should look like the one in Figure 2.18.

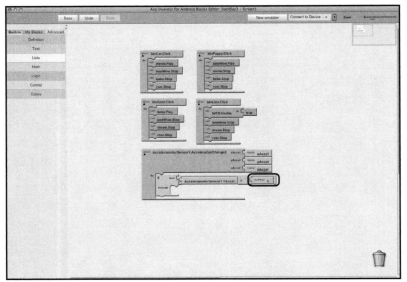

FIGURE 2.18

Change value of number to 5.

13. Click My Blocks.
14. Click the roar component and drag roar.Play to the then-do section of the
if test then-do block, as shown in Figure 2.19.

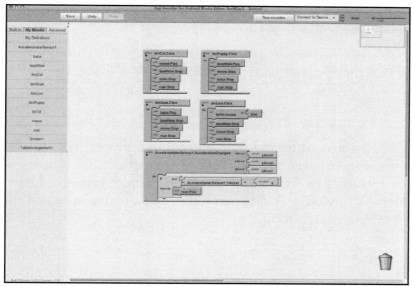

Source: Massachusetts Institute of Technology.

FIGURE 2.19

Add the roar.Play
sound file.

The test condition used here is that the acceleration in the Y direction should be greater than
5 m/s². As a comparison, the acceleration of a freely falling object is 9.8 (also called 1g) m/s²
in the Z direction. If the acceleration is greater than 5 m/s², then you can hear the lion roar.
This completes the design and code phases.

NOTE You can change the parameters and experiment with the app you just completed.
Try changing the values of the number from 5 to 8, from 5 to 2, and so on to see
how it affects your app. You can also change the direction to X acceleration and
tilt your phone sideways instead of forward and backward.

THE TESTING AND DEPLOYMENT PHASE

To test your newly designed app, try it out in the Emulator. Note that for this app, you can
use the Emulator to test the three buttons—btnCat, btnPuppy, and btnGoat—by clicking them
and listening to the sound.

For the btnLion button, you can see that the label becomes visible when you click the button. However, you cannot hear the sound because you cannot tilt the Emulator. To test this option, you should have a physical device, such as an Android phone. Tilt the phone and listen to the sound of the lion roar! To port the app to the phone, use the Wi-Fi option or download the code to your phone via a USB port. Because you are using Y acceleration, tilt your phone forward to hear the lion roar.

Once you have checked that the app runs on the Emulator, you can install the app to your phone through the USB port. Refer to Chapter 1 for help packaging it for the phone.

SUMMARY

In this chapter, you learned about using multiple buttons and proper logic to assemble buttons that carry out multiple instructions. You learned about the accelerometer and its use. You also learned about the if-then programming construct, which is used in many more chapters throughout this book. This chapter has given you an introduction to several building blocks that are essential to create interesting apps.

ADVENTURE GAME: RING OF FIRE

CHAPTER OBJECTIVES

- Design an app with multiple screens
- Use the if-else construct
- Use a comparison with the = operator
- Use a ListPicker component
- Set user-defined variables
- Use the "make a list" construct

INTRODUCTION

This app will illustrate the use of multiple screens through an adventure game, called *Ring of Fire*. In this game, the player must stop a volcano, Mt. Labadoo, from erupting in order to save Macadoo Island. To complete this task, the player must visit four screens and answer trivia questions in each one. If the player answers correctly, he or she gets a token. When the player brings all four tokens to the mountain, he or she can stop the volcano from erupting.

To keep the game simple and to help you understand the concepts presented in this chapter, you have only one trivia question for each screen. Later, you can use the TinyDB presented in Chapter 6, "Trivia Quiz," and Chapter 9, "Using Persistent

Databases: Tracking Your Weight," to include more trivia questions to make the game more interesting.

You can download the images and sound files used for this chapter from www.cengageptr.com/downloads.

 This app requires that you have a physical Android mobile device. At the present time, the Emulator does not support multiple screens, and this app uses multiple screens.

THE DESIGN PHASE

The graphical user interface (GUI) for this app will consist of several screens, buttons, labels, and a list picker. This section includes the instructions to set up your GUI.

 This app requires you to create a lot of screens with various components. Remember that screen names, variable names, and other component names are case sensitive. So type exactly as the instructions direct you to do.

Design the Title Screen

To design the title screen, follow these steps:

1. Open the App Inventor site, click My Projects, and click New Project. Type Adventure as the name for the new project. In the Palette, click Basic, and drag a Canvas component to the screen. Change the Width and Height settings of the Canvas component to 300 pixels.

2. Click the Background Image field in the Properties panel. In the dialog box that opens, locate the folder where you saved the images for this app. Then locate and select the title ScreenV2.png image. At this point, your screen should look like the one in Figure 3.1.

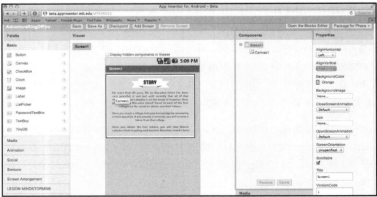

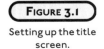

FIGURE 3.1

Setting up the title screen.

3. From the Basic palette, drag a Label component to the screen, dropping it below the Canvas component. In the Label component's Properties panel, in the Text field, type `The pirate here will accompany you.`

4. From the Basic palette, drag an Image component to the screen, dropping it below the Label component. In the Image component's Properties panel, click the Picture box field, and then locate and select the pirate.png image from the downloaded resources for this chapter.

5. From the Basic palette, drag a Button component to the screen, placing it below the Canvas component. In the Button component's Properties panel, change the Width and Height settings to 100. In the Text field, type `Click to continue...` See Figure 3.2.

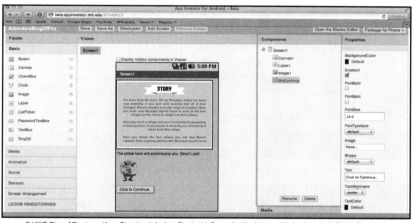

FIGURE 3.2

The completed title screen.

Design the Docks screen

To design the Docks screen, follow these steps:

1. Click the Add Screen button, found above the Viewer panel.

2. The New Form dialog box opens. Type `Docks` in the Form Name field. Then click the OK button. (See Figure 3.3.)

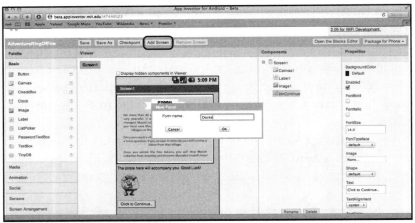

FIGURE 3.3

Add a screen.

3. In the Palette, click Basic, and drag a Canvas component to the screen. In the Canvas component's Properties panel, change the Width setting to 300 pixels and the Height setting to 280 pixels.

4. Click the BackgroundImage field. In the dialog box that opens, locate the folder where you saved the resources for this chapter. Then locate and select the Docks-01.png image. Your screen should be similar to the one in Figure 3.4.

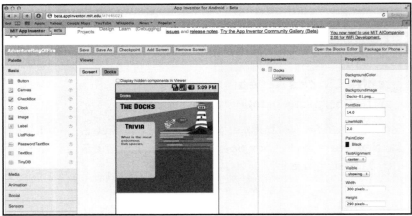

FIGURE 3.4

The Docks screen.

5. In the Palette, click Screen Arrangement, drag a TableArrangement component to the screen, dropping it below the Canvas component. Set it to three columns and two rows. Change the Width setting to 300 pixels and the Height setting to 90 pixels.

6. In the Palette, click Basic, and drag a ListPicker component to the screen, dropping it in the first column and first row of the table. Your screen should be similar to the one in Figure 3.5.

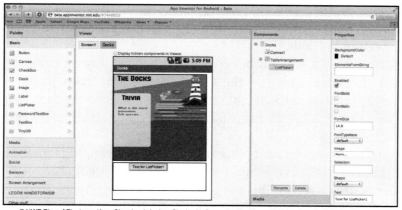

FIGURE 3.5

Adding a list picker to the table.

7. Delete the text for the ListPicker component. Then click the BackgroundImage field. In the dialog box that appears, locate the folder where you saved the resources for this chapter. Then locate and select the dock_token-01.png image as the source for the ListPicker component. Change its Width setting to 100 pixels and its Height setting to 50 pixels.

8. From the Basic palette, drag a Label component to the screen, dropping it in the second column of the table. In the Properties panel, change the Label component's Width setting to 80 pixels and its Height setting to 50 pixels. In the Text field, type Correct. Change the Label component's Visible property to Hidden. See Figure 3.6.

FIGURE 3.6

Change the Label component's Visible property to Hidden.

9. From the Basic palette, drag a second Label component to the screen, dropping it in the third column of the table. In the Properties panel, change its Width setting to 100 pixels and its Height setting to 50 pixels. In the Text field, type `Aw incorrect`. Click Reset and then click the token to try again. If the text does not fit, you can adjust the size of the label. Try increasing the Width setting to 120 pixels and the Height setting to 60 pixels. You can also try to reduce the font size. Use your discretion to accommodate the text.

10. Change the Visible setting to Hidden.

11. From the Basic palette, drag a third Label component to the screen, dropping it in the first column of the second row of the table. In the Properties panel, change its Width setting to 100 pixels and its Height setting to 40 pixels. In the Text field, type `Click on token above for trivia choices`. Change the Visible setting to Showing and the FontSize setting to 12.

12. From the Basic palette, drag a Button component to the screen, dropping it in the second row of the second column. In the Properties panel's Text field, type `Next`.

13. From the Basic palette, drag a second Button component to the screen, dropping it in the third column of the second row. In the Properties panel's Text field, type `Reset`. Your screen should be similar to the one in Figure 3.7.

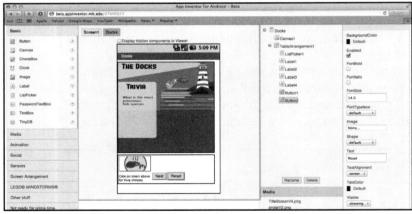

FIGURE 3.7

Completed Docks screen.

14. In the Properties panel, change the Visible setting for both Button components to Hidden.

15. Rename the components on the screen as follows:

- Rename Label 1 to lblCorrect.
- Rename Label 2 to lblIncorrect.
- Rename Label 3 to lblCaption.

- Rename Button 1 to btnNext.
- Rename Button 2 to btnReset.

Design the Farms Screen

You will repeat the steps for Docks screen to set up three more screens: Farms, Mills, and Mines. Here are the steps for the Farms screen:

1. Click the Add screen button, found above the Viewer panel.
2. The New Form dialog box opens. Type Farms in the Form Name field. Then click the OK button.
3. In the Palette, click Basic, and drag a Canvas component to the screen. In the Canvas component's Properties panel, change the Width setting to 300 pixels and the Height setting to 280 pixels.
4. Click the BackgroundImage field. In the dialog box that opens, locate the folder where you saved the resources for this chapter. Then locate and select the Farms-01.png image. Your screen should be similar to the one in Figure 3.8.

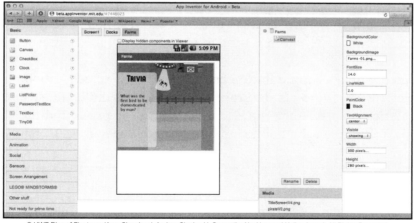

FIGURE 3.8

The Farms screen.

5. In the Palette, click ScreenArrangement, drag a TableArrangement component to the screen, dropping it below the Canvas component. Set it to three columns and two rows. Change the Width setting to 300 pixels and the Height setting to 90 pixels.
6. In the Palette, click Basic, and drag a ListPicker component to the screen, dropping it in the first column and first row of the table.
7. Delete the text for the ListPicker component. Then click the Image field. In the dialog box that appears, locate the folder where you saved the resources for this chapter. Then locate and select the farm_token-01.png image as the source for the ListPicker component. Change its Width setting to 100 pixels and its Height setting to 50 pixels.

8. From the Basic palette, drag a Label component to the screen, dropping it in the second column of the table. In the Properties panel, change the Label component's Width setting to 80 pixels and its Height setting to 50 pixels. In the Text field, type `Correct`. Change the Label component's Visible setting to Hidden.

9. From the Basic palette, drag a second Label component to the screen, dropping it in the third column of the table. In the Properties panel, change its Width setting to 100 pixels and its Height setting to 50 pixels. In the Text field, type `Aw incorrect`. Click Reset and then click the token to try again. If the text does not fit, you can adjust the size of the label. Try increasing the Width setting to 120 pixels and the Height setting to 60 pixels. You can also try to reduce the font size. Use your discretion to accommodate the text.

10. Change the Visible setting to Hidden.

11. From the Basic palette, drag a third Label component to the screen, dropping it in the first column of the second row of the table. In the Properties panel, change its Width setting to 100 pixels and its Height setting to 40 pixels. In the Text field, type `Click on token above for trivia choices`. Change the Visible setting to Showing and the FontSize setting to 12.

12. From the Basic palette, drag a Button component to the screen, dropping it in the second row of the second column. In the Properties panel, click the Text field, and type `Next`. In the Properties panel, change the Width setting to 100 pixels and the Height setting to 40 pixels.

13. From the Basic palette, drag a second Button component to the screen, dropping it in the third column of the second row. In the Properties panel, click the Text field and type `Reset`. In the Properties panel, change the Width setting to 100 pixels and the Height setting to 40 pixels. Your screen should be similar to the one in Figure 3.9.

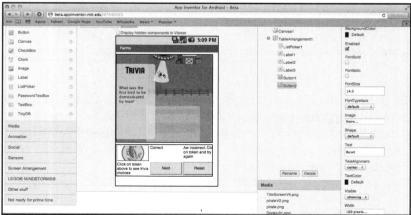

FIGURE 3.9

Completed Farms screen.

14. In the Properties panel, change the Visible setting for both Button components to Hidden.
15. Rename the components on the screen as follows:

   • Rename Label 1 to lblCorrect.

   • Rename Label 2 to lblIncorrect.

   • Rename Label 3 to lblCaption.

   • Rename Button 1 to btnNext.

   • Rename Button 2 to btnReset.

Design the Mills Screen

Here are the steps for the Mills screen:

1. Click the Add screen button, found above the Viewer panel.
2. The New Form dialog box opens. Type Mills in the Form Name field. Then click the OK button.
3. In the Palette, click Basic, and drag a Canvas component to the screen. In the Canvas component's Properties panel, change the Width setting to 300 pixels and the Height setting to 290 pixels.
4. Click the BackgroundImage field. In the dialog box that opens, locate the folder where you saved the resources for this chapter. Then locate and select the Mills-01.png image. Your screen should be similar to the one in Figure 3.10.

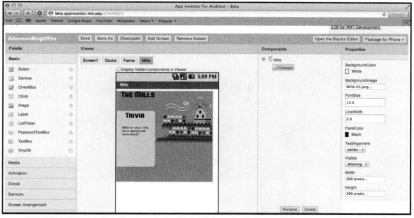

FIGURE 3.10

The Mills screen.

5. In the Palette, click ScreenArrangement, and drag a TableArrangement component to the screen, dropping it below the Canvas component. Set it to three columns and two rows. Change the Width setting to 300 pixels and the Height setting to 90 pixels.

6. In the Palette, click Basic, and drag a ListPicker component to the screen, dropping it in the first column and first row of the table.

7. Delete the text for the ListPicker component. Then click the Image field. In the dialog box that appears, locate the folder where you saved the resources for this chapter. Then locate and select the mills_token-01.png image as the source for the ListPicker component. Change its Width setting to 100 pixels and its Height setting to 50 pixels.

8. From the Basic palette, drag a Label component to the screen, dropping it in the second column of the table. In the Properties panel, change the Label component's Width setting to 80 pixels and its Height setting to 50 pixels. In the Text field, type Correct. Change the Label component's Visible setting to Hidden.

9. From the Basic palette, drag a second Label component to the screen, dropping it in the third column of the table. In the Properties panel, change the Width setting to 100 pixels and the Height setting to 50 pixels. In the Text field, type Aw incorrect. Click Reset and then click the token to try again. If the text does not fit, you can adjust the size of the label. Try increasing the Width setting to 120 pixels and the Height setting to 60 pixels. You can also try to reduce the font size. Use your discretion to accommodate the text.

10. Change the Visible setting to Hidden.

11. From the Basic palette, drag a third Label component to the screen, dropping it in the first column of the second row of the table. In the Properties panel, change its Width setting to 100 pixels and its Height setting to 40 pixels. In the Text field, type Click on token above for trivia choices. Change the Visible setting to Showing and the FontSize setting to 12.

12. From the Basic palette, drag a Button component to the screen, dropping it in the second row of the second column. In the Properties panel's Text field, type Next.

13. From the Basic palette, drag a second Button component to the screen, dropping it in the third column of the second row. In the Properties panel locate the Text field, type Reset. Your screen should be similar to the one in Figure 3.11.

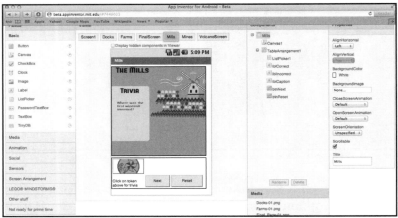

FIGURE 3.11

Completed Mills screen.

14. In the Properties panel, change the Visible setting for both Button components to Hidden.
15. Rename the components on the screen as follows:

- Rename Label 1 to lblCorrect.
- Rename Label 2 to lblIncorrect.
- Rename Label 3 to lblCaption.
- Rename Button 1 to btnNext.
- Rename Button 2 to btnReset.

Design the Mines screen

Here are the steps for the Mines screen:

1. Click the Add screen button, found above the Viewer panel.
2. The New Form dialog box opens. Type Mines in the Form Name field. Then click the OK button.
3. In the Palette, click Basic, and drag a Canvas component to the screen. In the Canvas component's Properties panel, change the Width setting to 300 pixels and the Height setting to 290 pixels.
4. Click the BackgroundImage field. In the dialog box that opens, locate the folder where you saved the resources for this chapter. Then locate and select the mines-01.png image. Your screen should be similar to the one in Figure 3.12.

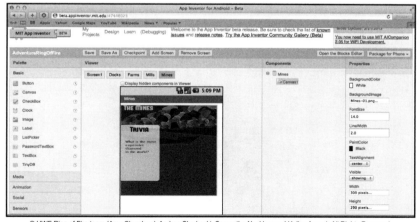

FIGURE 3.12

The Mines screen.

5. In the Palette, click ScreenArrangement, and drag a TableArrangement component to the screen, dropping it below the Canvas component. Set it to three columns and two rows. Change the Width setting to 300 pixels and the Height setting to 90 pixels.

6. In the Palette, click Basic, and add a ListPicker component to the screen, dropping it in the first column and first row of the table.

7. Delete the text for the ListPicker component. Then click the Image field. In the dialog box that appears, locate the folder where you saved the resources for this chapter. Then locate and select the mines_token-01.png image as the source for the ListPicker component. Change its Width setting to 100 pixels and its Height setting to 50 pixels.

8. From the Basic palette, drag a Label component to the screen, dropping it in the second column of the table. In the Properties panel, change the Label component's Width setting to 80 pixels and its Height setting to 50 pixels. In the Text field, type `Correct`. Change the Label component's Visible setting to Hidden.

9. From the Basic palette, drag a second Label component to the screen, dropping it in the third column of the table. In the Properties panel, change the Width setting to 100 pixels and the Height setting to 50 pixels. In the Text field, type `Aw incorrect`. Click Reset and then click the token to try again. If the text does not fit, you can adjust the size of the label. Try increasing the Width setting to 120 pixels and the Height setting to 60 pixels. You can also try to reduce the font size. Use your discretion to accommodate the text.

10. Change the Visible setting to Hidden.

11. From the Basic palette, drag a third Label component to the screen, dropping it in the first column of the second row of the table. In the Properties panel, change its Width setting to 100 pixels and its Height setting to 50 pixels. In the Text field, type `Click on token above for trivia choices`. Change the Visible setting to Showing and the FontSize setting to 12.

12. From the Basic palette, drag a Button component to the screen, dropping it in the second row of the second column. In the Properties panel's Text field, type `Next`.

13. From the Basic palette, drag a second Button component to the screen, dropping it in the third column of the second row. In the Properties panel's Text field, type `Reset`. Your screen should be similar to the one in Figure 3.13.

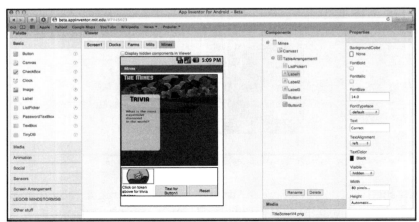

FIGURE 3.13

Completed Mines screen.

14. In the Properties panel, change the Visible setting for both Button components to Hidden.

15. Rename the components on the screen as follows:

- Rename Label 1 to lblCorrect.
- Rename Label 2 to lblIncorrect.
- Rename Label 3 to lblCaption.
- Rename Button 1 to btnNext.
- Rename Button 2 to btnReset.

Design the Final Screen

To design the final screen, follow these steps:

1. Click the Add Screen button, found above the Viewer panel.
2. The New Form dialog box opens. Type FinalScreen in the Form Name field. Then click the OK button.
3. In the Palette, click Basic, and drag a Canvas component to the screen. In the Canvas component's Properties panel, change the Width setting to 300 pixels and the Height setting to 330 pixels.
4. Click the BackgroundImage field. In the dialog box that opens, locate the folder where you saved the resources for this chapter. Then locate and select the Final_Page-01.png image.
5. From the Basic palette, drag a Button component below the Canvas component. In the Button component's Properties panel, in the Text field, type Click here to play again. Your screen should be similar to the one in Figure 3.14. Rename the button to btnReplay. This completes the GUI for the *Ring of Fire* adventure game.

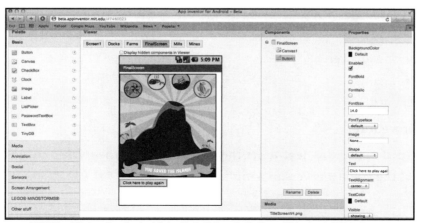

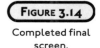

FIGURE 3.14

Completed final screen.

THE CODE PHASE

As mentioned, the idea behind this game is that the player must stop a volcano from erupting and destroying Macadoo Island. To accomplish this, the player visits four areas (Docks, Farms, Mills, and Mines) and answers trivia questions. If the player answers the trivia question correctly, that person is given a token that accompanies him or her through the journey. When the player gets all four tokens, he or she lands in the final scene, at the volcano, and stops the eruption.

Because the objective of this lesson is for you to learn about multiple screens and the use of the ListPicker component, the player will be given multiple chances to answer the trivia question correctly. Every time the player gets the question wrong, he or she can press the Reset button and try again. When the player gets the answer right, he or she can progress to the next area. When you are comfortable with App Inventor, you can change the functionality of the game to include points for getting the question right, reduce points for a wrong answer, and so on.

Steps for Completing the Game

Before you start assembling the blocks in the Blocks Editor, here are the steps required for this app:

When btnContinue is clicked:

- Call the `show another screen` procedure.

When btnRest is clicked:

- Set labels 1, 2, and 3 to `hidden`.

When btnNext is clicked:

- Call the `show another screen` procedure.

When btnReset is clicked:

- Hide the label "Wrong answer."
- Hide the label "Try again."
- Hide the label "Correct."

Define variables and procedures:

- Define a user-defined variable as `text` to set the right answer to the trivia question.
- Make a list to hold the trivia answers in a multiple choice.
  - Set choice 1.
  - Set choice 2.

- Set choice 3.
- Set choice 4.
- Define a user-defined variable as `list` to take the trivia answers as its data type.

Before the player clicks the list picker:

- Call the List of Trivia choices.
- Display the score on the label.

After the player clicks the list picker:

- Use an `if` condition to check whether the player's choice is the same as the answer defined in the variable.
  - If the choice is equal, or correct:
    - Show the label "Correct answer."
    - Show the next button.
  - If choice is not correct:
    - Show the label "Incorrect answer."
    - Show the label "Try again."

Set Up the Blocks

Here are the instructions to set up the blocks for this app. Make sure the Blocks Editor is open. (Click the Open the Blocks Editor button in the top-right corner of the App Inventor GUI design window.) You will assemble the following blocks:

- User-defined variables
- `ListPicker.BeforePicking`
- `ListPicker.AfterPicking`
- Button-click events

Assemble the Title Screen

To assemble the title screen, follow these steps:

1. Make sure that Screen1 is selected. Click the My Blocks tab, click btnContinue, and drag a `when btnContinue.Click do` block to the screen.
2. Click the Built-In tab, click Control, and drag a `call open another screen` block to the screen. This built-in block enables you to navigate from one screen to another. It requires

the name of the screen to go to, which is supplied to it as a text argument. See Figure 3.15.

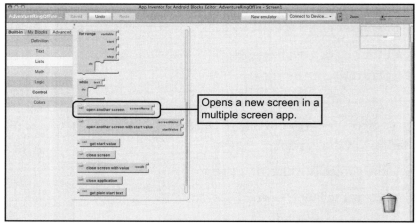

FIGURE 3.15

The `call open another screen` block.

3. In the Built-In tab, click Text, and drag a `text` block to the empty slot of the `call open another screen` block. Double-click the `text` block and type `Docks`. The names used here are case sensitive, so make sure to type the word `Docks` exactly as you typed it when you named your screen. This tells the program that when btnNext is clicked, it should go to the Docks screen. (See Figure 3.16.)

FIGURE 3.16

Instruct the program to open the Docks screen.

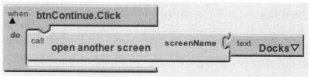

Assemble the Docks Screen

Just below the Viewer panel, click the Docks screen to open that screen. See Figure 3.17.

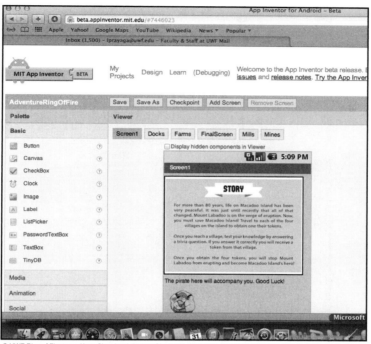

FIGURE 3.17

Locate the Docks screen.

Coding this screen requires the use of variables. A *variable* is similar to a placeholder that can hold a value. You can define a variable and set it to hold values of specific types—for example, numbers, text, and so on. For this app, you will define two variables for each of the trivia screens: one to hold the correct answer and one to hold the multiple choice answers. The variables for the Docks screen will be named FishAns and FishList, respectively.

Set Up User-Defined Variables

To set up the user-defined variables for the Docks screen, starting with the fishAns variable, follow these steps:

1. Click the Built-In tab, click Definition, and drag a def variable block to the screen. See Figure 3.18.

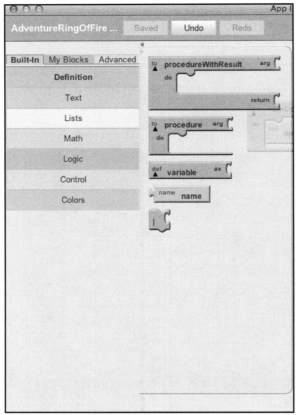

FIGURE 3.18.

Defining a user-defined variable.

2. Double-click the word `variable` and change it to `FishAns`.
3. In the Built-In tab, click Text, and drag a `text` block into the empty slot of the `def FishAns` block.
4. Double-click the word `text` and change it to `Puffer Fish`. The answer to the trivia question listed on the Docks screen is Puffer Fish. See Figure 3.19.

FIGURE 3.19

Define the `FishAns` variable as Puffer Fish.

5. To create a list for the ListPicker component, in the Built-In tab, click Lists, and drag a call make a list block to the screen. Your screen should be similar to the one in Figure 3.20.

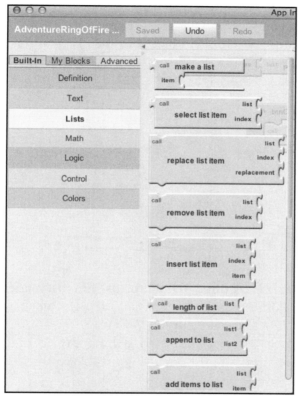

FIGURE 3.20

Create a list picker.

NOTE A list construct is used to hold a number of values of a data type—for example, a list of numbers, a list of names, a list of places, etc. For this app, you will create a list to hold names that vary depending on the screen you are in.

6. For the Docks screen, you will create a list of types of fish, so the data type used will be text. In the Built-In tab, click Text, and drag a text block to the empty item slot. See Figure 3.21.

FIGURE 3.21.

Add text values as
items to list.

7. Double-click the text block and type Snail Fish.
8. Repeat steps 6 and 7 to add three more text blocks to the call make a list block. For each text block, replace the word text with Puffer Fish, Rice Fish, and Needle Fish. Your screen should be similar to the one in Figure 3.22.

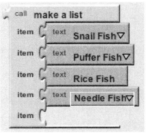

FIGURE 3.22

Completed list
with text items.

9. A second user-defined variable is required to hold the list you just made. To create this, click the Built-In tab, click Definitions, and drag a def variable block to the screen.
10. Double-click the word variable and change it to FishList.
11. Drag the call make a list block you just completed to the empty slot of the def FishList block. Your screen should be similar to the one in Figure 3.23.

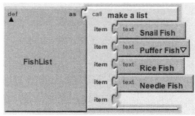

FIGURE 3.23

FishList variable.

Assemble the List Picker

The next step is to assemble the list picker. The list picker has ListPicker.BeforePicking and the ListPicker.AfterPicking events. You will use the ListPicker.BeforePicking event to populate the component with the FishList variable you just created. The ListPicker.AfterPicking event will be used to compare the item selected by the player from the `FishList` variable with the correct answer for the trivia question. Here are the steps to achieve these goals:

1. Click the My Blocks tab, click ListPicker1, and drag the `when ListPicker1.BeforePicking do` block to the screen.
2. In the My Blocks tab, from ListPicker1, drag the `set ListPicker1.Elements` block to the `when ListPicker1.BeforePicking do` block.
3. In the My Blocks tab, click My Definitions, and drag the `global FishList` block to the empty slot of the `set ListPicker1.Elements` block. See Figure 3.24.

©2013 Lakshmi Prayaga, All Rights Reserved.

4. In the My Blocks tab, click ListPicker1, and drag the `when ListPicker1.AfterPicking do` block to the screen.
5. Click the Built-In tab, click Control, and drag an `ifelse then-do else-do` block to the screen. See Figure 3.25.

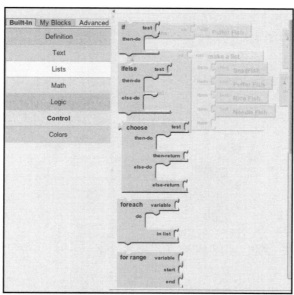

©2013 Lakshmi Prayaga, All Rights Reserved.

FIGURE 3.25

Add `ifelse` then
do block.

The ifelse statement is very powerful in any programming language. This construct tests for a condition. If that condition is satisfied, then one block of actions get executed. If the condition is not satisfied, then another block of actions get executed. In this case, you will test to see if the player's choice agrees with the correct answer for the trivia question. If so, the player gets a "correct answer" message. If not, then the player sees a "wrong answer" message and a prompt to try again.

6. In the Built-In tab, click Logic, and drag a = connector to the empty test slot of the ifelse then-do else-do block. The = connector compares two values and checks if the two values are the same. See Figure 3.26.

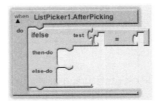

FIGURE 3.26

Add a comparison
(=) connector.

©2013 Lakshmi Prayaga, All Rights Reserved.

7. Click the My Blocks tab, click ListPicker1, and drag the ListPicker1.Selection block to the first empty slot of the = connector.
8. In the My Blocks tab, click My Definitions, and drag the global FishAns block to the second slot of the = connector. See Figure 3.27.

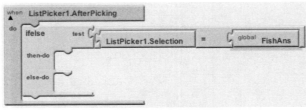

FIGURE 3.27

A completed
comparison block.

©2013 Lakshmi Prayaga, All Rights Reserved.

9. In the My Blocks tab, click lblCorrect, and drag the set lblCorrect.Visible block to the empty then-do slot of the ifelse then-do else-do block.
10. Click the Built-In tab, click Logic, and drag a true block to the empty slot of the set lblCorrect.Visible block.
11. Click the My Blocks tab, click btnNext, and drag the set btnNext.Visible block below the set lblCorrect.Visible block.
12. Click the Built-In tab, click Logic, and drag a true block to the empty slot of the set btnNext.Visible block. See Figure 3.28.

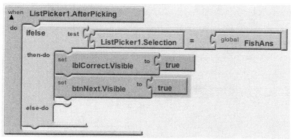

FIGURE 3.28

A completed
`then-do` block.

13. Click the My Blocks tab, click lblInCorrect, and drag a `set lblInCorrect.Visible` block to the `else-do` slot of the `ifelse then-do else-do` block.

14. Click the Built-In tab, click Logic, and drag a `true` block to the empty slot of the `set lblInCorrect.Visible` block. See Figure 3.29.

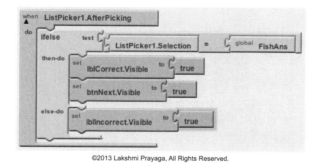

FIGURE 3.29

Assemble the
`else-do` part.

Assemble the Button-Click Events for the Docks Screen

To assemble the button-click events for the Docks screen, follow these steps:

1. Click the My Blocks tab, click btnNext, and drag a `when btnNext.Click do` block to the screen.

2. Click the Built-In tab, click Control, and drag the `call open another screen` block to the `when btnNext.Click do` block. See Figure 3.30.

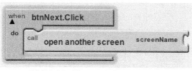

FIGURE 3.30

The `call open
another screen`
block.

3. In the Built-In tab, click Text, and drag a `text` block to the empty slot of the `call open another screen` block.
4. Double-click the word `text` and type `Farms`. See Figure 3.31.

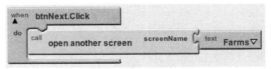

5. In the My Blocks tab, click btnReset, and drag a `when btnReset.Click do` block to the screen.
6. In the My Blocks tab, click lblCorrect, and drag a `set lblCorrect.Visible` block to the `when btnReset.Click do` block.
7. Click the Built-In tab, click Logic, and drag a `false` block to the empty slot of `set lblCorrect.Visible` block. See Figure 3.32.

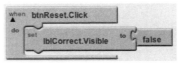

8. In the My Blocks tab, click lblInCorrect, and drag a `set lblInCorrect.Visible` block below the `set lblCorrect.Visible` block.
9. Click the Built-In tab, click Logic, and drag a `false` block to the empty slot of the `set lblInCorrect.Visible` block. This completes the Docks screen. See Figure 3.33.

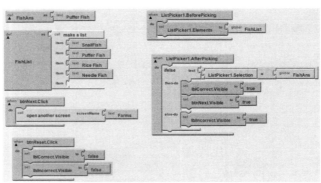

You will repeat these steps for the next three screens (Farms, Mills, and Mines). However, you can test this at this stage. Check that your app works when you choose the correct answer and asks you to try again when you select the incorrect answer.

Assemble Farms Screen

To assemble the Farms screen, follow these steps:

 NOTE Because most of the steps are repeated from the Docks screen, you can refer to Figures 3.18 through 3.33. You can also look ahead to Figure 3.34, which is a complete listing of the blocks required for the Farms screen.

1. In the App Inventor screen, on the Viewer tab, locate the Farms screen in the top panel and double-click it to open it.
2. You'll set up two user-defined variables for the Farms screen: BirdAns and BirdList. To define the BirdAns variable, click the Built-In tab, click Definition, and drag a def variable block to the screen.
3. Double-click the word variable and change it to BirdAns.
4. In the Built-In tab, click Text, and drag a text block into the empty slot of the def BirdAns block.
5. Double-click the word text and change it to Goose. The answer to the trivia question listed in the Farms screen is Goose.
6. To create a list for the ListPicker component, in the Built-In tab, click Lists, and drag a call make a list block to the screen.
7. For the Farms screen, you will create a list of different types of birds, so the data type used will be text. In the Built-In tab, click Text, and drag a text block to the empty item slot.
8. Double click the text block and type Swan.
9. Repeat steps 7 and 8 to add three more text blocks to the call make a list block. For each text block, replace the word text with Goose, Hummingbird, and Duck.
10. A second user-defined variable is required to hold the list you just made. To create this, click the Built-In tab, click Definitions, and drag a def variable block to the screen.
11. Double-click the word variable and change it to BirdList.
12. Drag the call make a list block you just completed to the empty slot of the def BirdList block.
13. Click the My Blocks tab, click ListPicker1, and drag the when ListPicker1.BeforePicking do block to the screen.
14. In the My Blocks tab, from ListPicker1, drag the set ListPicker1.Elements block to the empty slot of the when ListPicker1.BeforePicking do block.

15. In the My Blocks tab, click My Definitions, and drag the `global BirdList` block to the empty slot of the `set ListPicker1.Elements` block.
16. In the My Blocks tab, click ListPicker1, and drag the `when ListPicker1.AfterPicking do` block to the screen.
17. Click the Built-In tab, click Control, and drag the `ifelse then-do else-do` block to the screen.
18. In the Built-In tab, click Logic, and drag a = connector to the empty test slot of the `ifelse then-do else-do` block.
19. Click the My Blocks tab, click ListPicker1, and drag the `ListPicker1.Selection` block to the first empty slot of the = connector.
20. In the My Blocks tab, click My Definitions, and drag the `global BirdAns` block to the second slot of the = connector.
21. In the My Blocks tab, click lblCorrect, and drag the `set lblCorrect.Visible` block to the empty `then-do` slot of the `ifelse then-do else-do` block.
22. Click the Built-In tab, click Logic, and drag a true block to the empty slot of the `set lblCorrect.Visible` block.
23. Click the My Blocks tab, click btnNext, and drag the set btnNext.Visible block below the `set lblCorrect.Visible` block.
24. Click the Built-In tab, click Logic, and drag a `true` block to the empty slot of the `set btnNext.Visible` block.
25. Click the My Blocks tab, click lblInCorrect, and drag a `set lblInCorrect.Visible` block to the `else-do` slot of the `ifelse then-do else-do` block.
26. Click the Built-In tab, click Logic, and drag a `true` block to the empty slot of the `set lblInCorrect.Visible` block.
27. Click the My Blocks tab, click btnNext, and drag a `when btnNext.Click do` block to the screen.
28. Click the Built-In tab, click Control, and drag the `call open another screen` block to the `when btnNext.Click do` block.
29. Click the Built-In tab, click Text, and drag a `text` block to the empty slot of the `call open another screen` block.
30. Double-click the word `text` and type `Mills`.
31. In the My Blocks tab, click btnReset, and drag a `when btnReset.Click do` block to the screen.
32. In the My Blocks tab, click lblCorrect, and drag a `set lblCorrect.Visible` block to the `when btnReset.Click do` block.
33. Click the Built-In tab, click Logic, and drag a `false` block to the empty slot of the `set lblCorrect.Visible` block.

34. In the My Blocks tab, click lblInCorrect, and drag a set lblInCorrect.Visible block below the set lblCorrect.Visible block.

35. Click the Built-In tab, click Logic, and drag a false block to the empty slot of the set lblInCorrect.Visible block. This completes the Farms screen. See Figure 3.34.

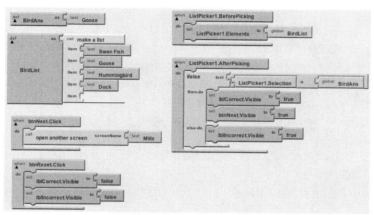

©2013 Lakshmi Prayaga, All Rights Reserved.

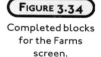

FIGURE 3.34

Completed blocks for the Farms screen.

Assemble the Mills Screen

To assemble the Mills screen, follow these steps:

1. In the App Inventor screen, on the Viewer tab, locate the Mills screen in the top panel and double-click it to open it.

2. You'll set up two user-defined variables for the Mills screen: MillsAns and MillsList. To define the MillsAns variable, click the Built-In tab, click Definition, and drag a def variable block to the screen.

3. Double-click the word variable and change it to MillsAns.

4. In the Built-In tab, click Text, and drag a text block into the empty slot of the def MillsAns block.

5. Double-click the word text and change it to China. The answer to the trivia question listed in the Mills screen is China.

6. To create a list for the ListPicker component, in the Built-In tab, click Lists, and drag a call make a list block to the screen.

7. For the Mills screen, you will create a list of names of countries, so the data type used will be text. In the Built-In tab, click Text, and drag a text block to the empty item slot.

8. Double-click the text block and type Holland.

9. Repeat steps 7 and 8 to add three more text blocks to the call make a list block. For each text block, replace the word text with China, Scotland, and Russia.

10. A second user-defined variable is required to hold the list you just made. To create this, click the Built-In tab, click Definitions, and drag a `def variable` block to the screen.

11. Double-click the word `variable` and change it to `MillsList`.

12. Drag the `call make a list` block you just completed to the empty slot of the `def MillsList` block.

13. Click the My Blocks tab, click ListPicker1, and drag the `when ListPicker1.BeforePicking do` block to the screen.

14. In the My Blocks tab, from ListPicker1, drag the `set ListPicker1.Elements` block to the empty slot of the `when ListPicker1.BeforePicking do` block.

15. In the My Blocks tab, click My Definitions, and drag the `global MillsList` block to the empty slot of the `set ListPicker1.Elements` block.

16. In the My Blocks tab, click ListPicker1, and drag the `when ListPicker1.AfterPicking do` block to the screen.

17. Click the Built-In tab, click Control, and drag the `ifelse then-do else-do` block to the screen.

18. In the Built-In tab, click Logic, and drag a = connector to the empty `test` slot of the `ifelse then-do else-do` block.

19. In the My Blocks tab, click ListPicker1, and drag the `ListPicker1.Selection` block to the first empty slot of the = connector.

20. In the My Blocks tab, click My Definitions, and drag the `global MillsAns` block to the second slot of the = connector.

21. In the My Blocks tab, click lblCorrect, and drag the `set lblCorrect.Visible` block to the empty `then-do` slot of the `ifelse then-do else-do` block.

22. Click the Built-In tab, click Logic, and drag a `true` block to the empty slot of the `set lblCorrect.Visible` block.

23. Click the My Blocks tab, click btnNext, and drag the `set btnNext.Visible` block below the `set lblCorrect.Visible` block.

24. Click the Built-In tab, click Logic, and drag a `true` block to the empty slot of the `set btnNext.Visible` block.

25. Click the My Blocks tab, click lblInCorrect, and drag a `set lblInCorrect.Visible` block to the `else-do` slot of the `ifelse then-do else-do` block.

26. Click the Built-In tab, click Logic, and drag a `true` block to the empty slot of the `set lblInCorrect.Visible` block.

27. Click the My Blocks tab, click btnNext, and drag a `when btnNext.Click do` block to the screen.

28. Click the Built-In tab, click Control and drag the `call open another screen` block to the `when btnNext.Click do` block.

29. Click the Built-In tab, click Text, and drag a `text` block to the empty slot of the `call open another screen` block.

30. Double-click the word `text` and type `Mines`.

31. In the My Blocks tab, click btnReset and drag a `when btnReset.Click do` block to the screen.

32. In the My Blocks tab, click lblCorrect, and drag a `set lblCorrect.Visible` block to the `when btnReset.Click do` block.

33. Click the Built-In tab, click Logic, and drag a `false` piece to the empty slot of `set lblCorrect.Visible` block.

34. In the My Blocks tab, click lblInCorrect, and drag a `set lblInCorrect.Visible` block below the `set lblCorrect.Visible` block.

35. Click the Built-In tab, click Logic, and drag a `false` block to the empty slot of the `set lblInCorrect.Visible` block. This completes the Mills screen. See Figure 3.35.

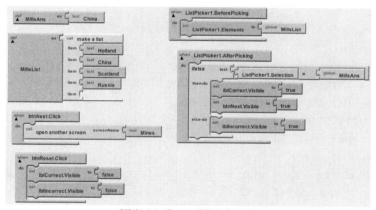

FIGURE 3.35

Completed blocks for the Mills screen.

Assemble the Mines Screen

To assemble the Mines screen, follow these steps:

1. In the App Inventor screen, on the Viewer tab, locate the Mines screen in the top panel and double-click it to open it.

2. You'll set up two user-defined variables for the Mines screen: `MinesAns` and `MinesList`. To define the `MinesAns` variable, click the Built-In tab, click Definition, and drag a `def variable` block to the screen.

3. Double-click the word `variable` and change it to `MinesAns`.

4. In the Built-In tab, click Text, and drag a `text` block into the empty slot of the `def MinesAns` block.

5. Double-click the word `text` and change it to `Koh-i-Noor Diamond`. The answer to the trivia question listed on the Mines screen is Koh-i-Noor Diamond.

6. To create a list for the ListPicker component, click the Built-In tab, click Lists, and drag a `call make a list` block to the screen.

7. For the Mines screen, you will create a list of names of diamonds, so the data type that will be used is text. In the Built-In tab, click Text, and drag a `text` block to empty `item` slot.

8. Double-click the `text` block and type `Sandy Diamond`.

9. Repeat steps 7 and 8 to add three more `text` blocks to the `call make a list` block. For each `text` block, replace the word text with `Koh-i-Noor Diamond`, `Hope Diamond`, and `Alnatt Diamond`.

10. A second user-defined variable is required to hold the list you just made. To create this, click the Built-In tab, click Definitions, and drag a `def variable` block to the screen.

11. Double-click the word `variable` and change it to `MinesList`.

12. Drag the `call make a list` block you just completed to the empty slot of the `def MinesList` block.

13. Click the My Blocks tab, click ListPicker1, and drag the `when ListPicker1.BeforePicking do` block to the screen.

14. In the My Blocks tab, from ListPicker1, drag the `set ListPicker1.Elements` block to the empty slot of the `when ListPicker1.BeforePicking do` block.

15. In the My Blocks tab, click My Definitions, and drag the `global MinesList` block to the empty slot of the `set ListPicker1.Elements` block.

16. In the My Blocks tab, click ListPicker1, and drag the `when ListPicker1.AfterPicking do` block to the screen.

17. Click the Built-In tab, click Control, and drag the `ifelse then-do else-do` block to the screen.

18. In the Built-In tab, click Logic, and drag a = connector to the empty test slot of the `ifelse then-do else-do` block.

19. In the My Blocks tab, click ListPicker1, and drag the `ListPicker1.Selection` block to the first empty slot of the = connector.

20. In the My Blocks tab, click My Definitions, and drag the `global MinesAns` block to the second slot of the = connector.

21. In the My Blocks tab, click lblCorrect, and drag the `set lblCorrect.Visible` block to the next empty `then-do` slot of the `ifelse then-do else-do` block.

22. Click the Built-In tab, click Logic, and drag a `true` block to the empty slot of the `set lblCorrect.Visible` block.

23. Click the My Blocks tab, click btnNext, and drag the `set btnNext.Visible` block below the `set lblCorrect.Visible` block.

24. Click the Built-In tab, click Logic, and drag a `true` block to the empty slot of the `set btnNext.Visible` block.

25. Click the My Blocks tab, click lblInCorrect, and drag a set lblInCorrect.Visible block to the else-do slot of the ifelse then-do else-do block.

26. Click the Built-In tab, click Logic, and drag a true block to the empty slot of the set lblInCorrect.Visible block.

27. Click the My Blocks tab, click btnNext, and drag a when btnNext.Click do block to the screen.

28. Click the Built-In tab, click Control, and drag the call open another screen block to the when btnNext.Click do block.

29. Click the Built-In tab, click Text, and drag a text block to the empty slot of the call open another screen block.

30. Double-click the word text and type FinalScreen.

 NOTE There is no space between the words "Final" and "Screen." This is because App Inventor does not allow you to include spaces when you name screens.

31. In the My Blocks tab, click btnReset, and drag a when btnReset.Click do block to the screen.

32. In the My Blocks tab, click lblCorrect, and drag a set lblCorrect.Visible block to the when btnReset.Click do block.

33. Click the Built-In tab, click Logic, and drag a false block to the empty slot of the set lblCorrect.Visible block.

34. In the My Blocks tab, click lblInCorrect, and drag a set lblInCorrect.Visible block below the set lblCorrect.Visible block.

35. Click the Built-In tab, click Logic, and drag a false block to the empty slot of the set lblInCorrect.Visible block. This completes the Mines Screen. See Figure 3.36.

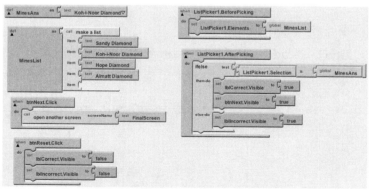

FIGURE 3.36

Completed blocks for Mines screen.

Assemble the Final Screen

This screen requires the assembly of only one button, btnReplay, to allow the player to play again. Follow these steps:

1. In the App Inventor screen, on the Viewer tab, locate the Final screen in the top panel and double-click it to open it.
2. Click the My Blocks tab, click btnReplay, and drag a when btnReplay.Click do block to the screen.
3. Click the Built-In tab, click Control, and drag a call open another screen block to the when btnReplay.Click do block.
4. In the Built-In tab, click Text, and drag a text block to the empty slot of the call open another screen block.
5. Double-click the word text and type Screen1. See Figure 3.37.

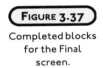

FIGURE 3.37

Completed blocks for the Final screen.

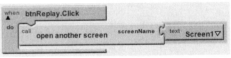

©2013 Lakshmi Prayaga, All Rights Reserved.

Optional Section

This section shows you how to include animated GIFs in your apps. You use the webViewer component to open an HTML page in which the animated GIF is embedded. The animated GIF and the HTML page must be uploaded into the app before they can be used.

 NOTE   This section is based on code snippets from the following website: http://puravidaapps.com/snippets.php.

Follow these steps:

1. In the App Inventor interface, add another Button component to the final screen. Rename the button btnVolcano. In the Properties panel, in the button's Text field, type Click here to see an active volcano.
2. Click the Add Screen button to add another screen to your app. Name this screen VolcanoScreen. See Figure 3.38.

FIGURE 3.38

VolcanoScreen.

3. In the Palette, click Not Ready for Prime Time, and drag the webViewer component to the Volcano screen. See Figure 3.39.

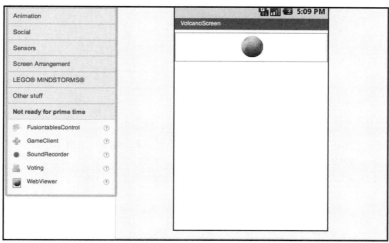

FIGURE 3.39

The WebViewer component.

4. Upload the animated GIF and the HTML file that refers to the volcano.gif image. To begin, click the Upload New button at the bottom of the Components panel, where all the media uploaded for your app is listed. Locate the folder where you saved the resources for this app, and then locate and select the volcano.gif image.

5. Open a text editor, type the following code, and save the file as volcano.html.

```
<html>
<body>
<img src="volcano.gif" width="100%" alt="" title="">
</body>
</html>
```

6. Click the Upload New button again and upload the volcano.html file. You should see the two files you just uploaded listed in the Media tab. See Figure 3.40.

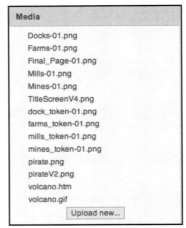

Media

Docks-01.png
Farms-01.png
Final_Page-01.png
Mills-01.png
Mines-01.png
TitleScreenV4.png
dock_token-01.png
farms_token-01.png
mills_token-01.png
mines_token-01.png
pirate.png
pirateV2.png
volcano.htm
volcano.gif

Upload new...

FIGURE 3.40

Uploaded files.

To code the animated GIF to work in your app, follow these steps:

1. In the App Inventor screen, on the Viewer tab, locate the Final screen in the top panel and double-click it to open it.
2. Click the My Blocks tab, click btnVolcano, and drag a when btnVolcano.Click do block to the screen.
3. In the My Blocks tab, click Control, and drag a call open another screen block to the when btnVolcano.Click do block.
4. Click the Built-In tab, click Text, and drag a text block to the empty slot of the call open another screen block.
5. Double-click the text block and type VolcanoScreen. This tells the program to open the Volcano screen when the player clicks this button.
6. Open the Volcano screen.
7. Click the My Blocks tab and drag a when VolcanoScreen.Initialize do block to the screen.
8. In the My Blocks tab, click Web Viewer1, and drag the call WebViewer1.GoToUrl block to the when VolcanoScreen.Initialize do block. See Figure 3.41.

9. Click the Built-In tab, click Text, and drag a `text` block to the empty slot of the `when VolcanoScreen.Initialize do` block.

10. Double click `text` and type the following URL to refer to the HTML file you uploaded: `file:///mnt/sdcard/AppInventor/assets/volcano.htm`. See Figure 3.42.

NOTE During development, you use this path to refer to the files you added to the app. Before packaging and uploading the app to your phone, however, you should change this path to the following: file:///android_asset/ani.htm. See Figure 3.43.

11. Upload the app to your phone and test this feature. When you go to the Volcano screen, you should see an animated GIF of a volcano.

THE TESTING AND DEPLOYMENT PHASE

To test this app fully, you will need a physical Android mobile device. If you want to test one screen at a time, however, you can test it on the Emulator. Refer to Chapter 1, "Introducing App Inventor," for instructions to test and deploy your completed app. If you get errors, make sure your screen names and variable names have all been typed exactly as they appear in the instructions. Enjoy!

Summary

This chapter looked at designing apps with multiple screens and navigating through these screens. It also demonstrated how to create user-defined variables and to use the comparison operator to check whether two values are equal. The ListPicker component was introduced, along with its various available properties. An important programming structure, `ifelse then-do else-do`, was also discussed in this chapter. With these introductory concepts, you have a good foundation to learn other concepts in future chapters and build interesting and fun apps.

WHACK-A-MOLE

CHAPTER OBJECTIVES

- Implement a random number generator
- Use a clock to function as a timer
- Use a clock to manipulate objects
- Use multiple screens
- Use the Canvas component
- Use image sprites
- Use fixed coordinates to place images
- Keep track of the score

TESTING YOUR REFLEXES

You may remember as a child going to the arcade and playing *Whack-A-Mole*, in which players used a padded mallet to hit the moles on the head as they popped up through the holes, the goal being to hit as many as you could within a given timeframe. In this chapter, you will learn how to create a mobile application that mimics this game.

You're going to do something a little different in this chapter: You'll be making two apps instead of one to learn two different methods of implementing the same game. In one method, the player clicks the mole and the mole vanishes before reappearing at a random point on the screen. The other method uses fixed locations like the more traditional version of the game.

THE DESIGN PHASE

As mentioned, the first app you're going to create will use completely random points. This is actually easier to implement than using fixed locations. The app will consist of three screens, with the game played on the second screen. Let's go!

Create the App

To create the app, follow these steps:

1. Create a new project in App Inventor and name it MoleWhacker. If you have created other projects, you may find that the software forwards you to the project screen before you are able to create a new project. If this happens, click My Projects at the top of the window and then create your project. After your project has been created, your screen should look like the one in Figure 4.1.

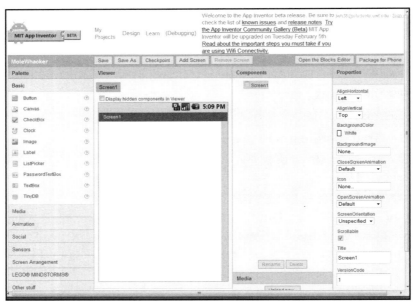

FIGURE 4.1

Created app screen.

2. Click the Add Screen button to create a new screen. Name the new screen Game and click OK.

3. Click the Add Screen button again to create another new screen. Name this screen Victory and click OK. You should now have three screens, with the last one displayed. (See Figure 4.2.)

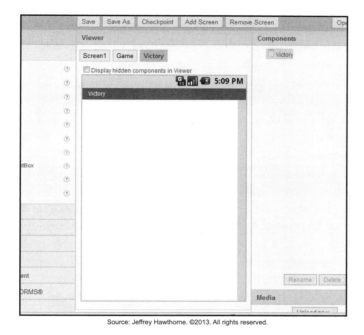

Source: Jeffrey Hawthorne. ©2013. All rights reserved.

FIGURE 4.2

The app now has three screens created.

Add Components

With your screens created, it's now time to add the components to the screens to create the buttons and images for your app. In this section you'll also change the screen settings to make them a little easier on the eyes.

Add Screen1 Components

Screen1 will be a simple welcome screen that explains to the user how to play the game, shows some animation, and allows the user to advance to the next screen, where the game will actually be played.

To add the necessary components to Screen1, follow these steps:

1. Click the Screen1 button in the Viewer.
2. Change the background color to dark gray. To do so, click Screen1 under Components; then click the BackgroundColor drop-down list in the Properties panel and choose the dark gray option.
3. Repeat step 2 for the Game and Victory screens.

4. Back on Screen1, with nothing selected, change the AlignHorizontal setting to Center. This will center your components within the screen.

5. Add a Label component to the screen. Change the FontSize setting to 24, the FontTypeFace setting to Sans Serif, the TextAlignment property to Center, the Width property to Fill Parent, and the TextColor property to yellow.

6. In the Text field, delete the existing text and type `Welcome to Whack-A-Mole!`.

7. Add another Label component below Label1. Then click it under Components. In the Text field in the Properties panel, type `How to play: use your finger to tap the mole. The mole will move to a new position. Keep tapping the mole until the timer runs out`. Then change the label's Width setting to Fill Parent, the FontTypeFace setting to Sans Serif, the FontSize setting to 16, the TextAlignment setting to Center, and the TextColor setting to green.

8. Next, you're going to create a little animation to play when the app is loaded. (You may notice a great deal of similarity between the implementation of the animation and the game itself on the second screen.) To begin, drag a Canvas component from the Basic section of the Palette onto the screen. A *canvas* is a special kind of component that enables you to draw on the screen. Drawing is also used for dynamic images, as the app must redraw an image when it has been moved. If you are familiar with the Java programming language and graphical user interfaces, this should make sense to you. A more detailed explanation of the Canvas component can be found here: developer.android.com/reference/android/graphics/Canvas.html.

9. Change the Canvas component's Width setting to Fill Parent and the Height setting to 150 pixels. Then change the BackgroundColor property to none. Your screen should now look like the one in Figure 4.3.

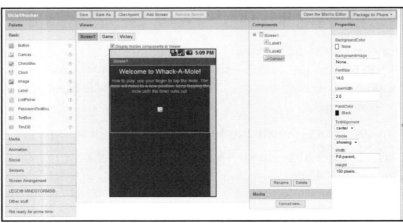

FIGURE 4.3

Screen1 with three added components: Label1, Label2, and Canvas1.

NOTE You may notice the canvas overlaps the preceding text. Don't worry about that. When the app is loaded, the components will be stacked like they're supposed to be.

10. Expand the Animation section of the Palette and drag an ImageSprite component onto the Canvas1 component (directly on the component, not above or below it). An ImageSprite component is very similar to an Image component, but an Image component cannot be used inside a canvas and cannot be dynamically moved around the screen—a function you need for this app. An ImageSprite component can do both of these things, but cannot be used outside of the canvas.

11. In the ImageSprite component's Properties panel, click the Picture field, choose Upload New, and select the whackamole.png file included with this book. (Its placement within the canvas doesn't matter.)

12. The last two components you need for this screen are a Button component, which you will use to advance to the next screen, and a Clock component, to create automatic events. Drag both of these components from the Basic section of the Palette to the canvas. The Button component should appear centered underneath the screen. The Clock component should appear below the screen, listed as a non-visible component. Non-visible components add functionality but can't actually be seen by the user.

NOTE The word "clock" is a bit of a misnomer here. Although the Clock component can be used to tell time and has a number of blocks to get hours, minutes, and seconds, most devices have built-in clocks you would use for these functions. So the most common use of a Clock component is as a timer, or stopwatch. Often, you'll have functions that, once started, need to end on their own, not because someone clicked something. To accomplish this, you use a timer. The key characteristic of a timer is that it fires automatically. That is, after a specified number of milliseconds has passed, the timer does something. The number of milliseconds between firing events is called an *interval*. You can define how long an interval is (the default is one second, or 1,000 milliseconds) and what actions occur when it fires. For example, if you want to use a countdown clock (which you will be using later in this chapter), you want the label showing the number of seconds left to change. So every 1,000 milliseconds, an event will go off that updates the text displayed by the label.

13. In the Button component's Properties panel, type `Play Game` in the Text field. Your screen should look like the one in Figure 4.4.

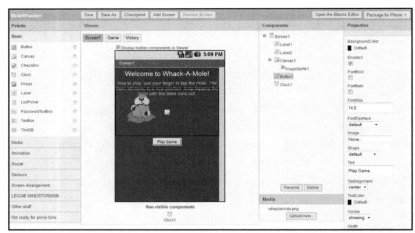

FIGURE 4.4

Screen 1 with all the added components.

Add Game Screen Components

To add the necessary components to the Game screen, follow these steps:

1. Click the Game button in the Viewer.
2. From the Screen Arrangement section of the Palette, drag a HorizontalArrangement component onto the screen. Change the Width property to Fill Parent and the AlignHorizontal property to Center.
3. Drag two Label components from the Basic palette into the HorizontalArrangement component. The labels should appear side by side. The first label will be used to display the score and the second will display countdown created by the game timer (the clock). For both Label components, change the TextColor property to yellow and the Width property to 150 pixels. Do this for both Label1 and Label2.
4. Drag a Canvas component onto the screen. Change BackgroundColor property to None, the Width property to Fill Parent and the Height property to 400 pixels.
5. From the Animation section of the Palette, drag an ImageSprite component onto the Canvas1 component just as you did for Screen1 in step 10 of the previous section.

> **NOTE** You may notice these last two steps are nearly identical to how you added the Canvas component on Screen1. The only real difference is the height of the canvas. As with Screen1, the position of the sprite within the canvas doesn't matter at this point.

6. Click the Picture field and choose whackamole.png. This time, you won't need to upload it; the file should already appear in the list when you click the field. Simply select it and click OK.

7. Add a Clock component to the Game screen from the Basic palette. Remember, this will show up as a non-visible component below the main window. When you're finished, your screen should look like the one in Figure 4.5. You don't need a button on this screen; it will advance when the Clock's timer runs out. More on timers later in the chapter.

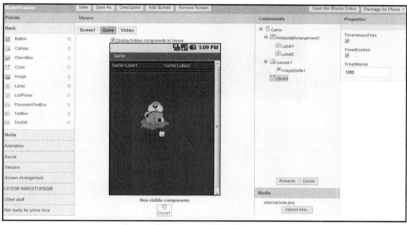

FIGURE 4.5

The Game screen with its components added.

Add Victory Screen Components

For this screen you merely need two labels and a button. Do the following:

1. Click the Victory button to move to the next screen.
2. Make sure the screen's AlignHorizontal property is set to Center.
3. Drag two Label components and a Button component onto the screen.
4. For both labels, change the TextColor property to yellow and the Width property to Fill Parent.
5. For the first label, change the FontSize property to 30 and the FontTypeface property to Sans Serif. Then, in the Text field, type CONGRATULATIONS! YOU WHACKED A BUNCHA MOLES!!. Make sure the TextAlignment property is set to Center.
6. For the second label, change the FontSize property to 20. As with the first screen, don't worry about the text and button overlapping. For this label, you don't need to change the Text field, but you do need to make sure the TextAlignment property is set to Center.
7. Click the Button1 component. In the Text field, type PLAY AGAIN?. When you're finished, your screen should look like the one in Figure 4.6.

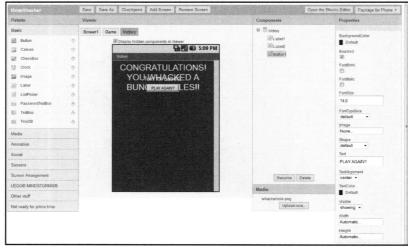

Figure 4.6

The Victory screen with its components added.

The Code Phase

Now you're ready to do the coding. Before you begin, let's take another look at the Clock component. As mentioned, this component has a great many methods related to date and time, but the one you'll be focusing on for this app is the timer function. By necessity, timers are among the most commonly used components in all games. Without a timer, simple games such as this one could theoretically go on forever. To make them stop, developers could use the score, but if the game ended when a certain score was reached, then players wouldn't be able to improve their scores and, as a result, would get bored very quickly. The better solution is to limit the amount of time the player has to play the game. In that scenario, players are limited only by their own ability (and perhaps some technical limitations) and always have the hope of improving their score. Given that games such as these can often be used for self improvement, such as improving memory or hand/eye coordination (lumosity.com, for example, uses games to help measure cognitive functions), this is a very effective technique.

To code the app, including configuring the clock to work as a timer, follow these steps:

1. Return to Screen1 and open the Blocks Editor.
2. In the My Blocks tab of the Blocks Editor, click Clock1. Then drag the when Clock1.Timer do block onto the workspace in the Blocks Editor.
3. In the My Blocks tab, click ImageSprite1. Then scroll down to the bottom of the list and drag a set ImageSprite1.X block and a set ImageSprite1.Y block onto the workspace. Attach both blocks to the when Clock1.Timer do block.
4. Click the Built-In tab and click Math. Part of the fun of an app like this—indeed, a requirement of it—is to make the movement of the mole unpredictable, or random. Fortunately, randomization is built-in in the form of the call random integer block. Drag

two of these blocks from the Math menu onto the workspace, attaching one to the set ImageSprite1.X block and the other to the set ImageSprite1.Y block.

5. Each of the two call random integer blocks covers a range from one number to another number. There should be two number blocks pre-attached to the call random integer blocks' from and to sockets. If not, you'll need to drag four number blocks from the Math menu to the workspace and attach them to the from and to sockets of each call random integer block. ImageSprite1.X and ImageSprite1.Y represent grid coordinates (in pixels), just as X and Y do in math. Assuming that (1,1) represents the top-left corner, if both ImageSprite.X and ImageSprite.Y equal 1, that places the top-left corner of the picture in the top-left corner of the canvas. That represents the low end of your range. In the call random integer block, the low end of the range is represented by the from socket, which is already set to 1 if the blocks came pre-attached. If you had to add number blocks, set the value for the ones attached to the from sockets to 1.

6. Figuring out the upper end of the range is a little trickier. The mole image for this game is 100 pixels square, and the canvas is approximately 300 pixels wide. Therefore, if you set the X coordinate to 200, that would put the right edge of the picture roughly at the right edge of the canvas (100 + 200 = 300). The upper end of the range is represented by the to socket of the call random integer block. Set the value of the number block attached to the to socket of the call random integer block attached to set ImageSprite1.X to 200.

7. The height of the canvas is 150 pixels, so the Y coordinate needs to be set to 50. Set the value of the number block attached to the to socket of the call random integer block attached to set ImageSprite1.Y to 50. Your screen should look like the one in Figure 4.7.

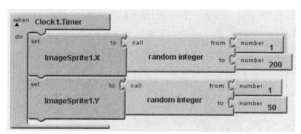

Source: Jeffrey Hawthorne. ©2013. All rights reserved.

FIGURE 4.7

Randomly moving an image sprite based on a timer.

8. The last thing you need to do for this screen is to code the button to open the Game screen. From the Button1 menu under the My Blocks tab, select a when Button1.Click do block.

9. From the Control menu under the Built-In tab, select the call open another screen block.

10. While in the Built-In tab, open the Text menu and select a text block. Set the text to Game, attach it to the call open another screen block, and then attach that block to the when Button1.Click do block. (See Figure 4.8.)

FIGURE 4.8

Setting the button function to advance to another screen.

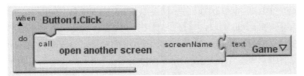

 TIP

If you'd like to see this in action, start the Emulator and run your app in it. Switching screens doesn't work in the Emulator at this time, but you'll be able to see the animation working on the first screen. If you'd like to test that the button works, you can download the APK and install it manually on your device.

11. In App Inventor, switch to the Game screen. If the Blocks Editor doesn't update to the new screen, you may need to close it and reload the Web page before reopening it.

12. Back in the Blocks Editor, refer to Figure 4.7 and bring over to the workspace a when Clock1.Timer do and two call random integer blocks. (See steps 2 and 4 for more information.) Instead of blocks to set ImageSprit1.X and ImageSprite1.Y, you need a call ImageSprite1.MoveTo block from the ImageSprite1 menu under the My Blocks tab. Attach the call random integer blocks to the call ImageSprite1.MoveTo block. This time, however, change the range on the Y coordinate to 300 rather than 50 because the Canvas component on this screen is much longer than the previous one. Do not attach the call ImageSprite1.MoveTo block to the when Clock1.Timer do block.

13. Now you'll code the movement of the mole. When the mole is tapped, it should move to a new, random location, and the score should be incremented and displayed. From the ImageSprite1 menu, drag a when ImageSprite1.Touched do block to the workspace. The when ImageSprite1.Touched do block should come populated with two name blocks, one for X and one for Y. Don't mess with them. Assemble the blocks as shown in Figure 4.9. Now, whenever the mole is touched, it will move.

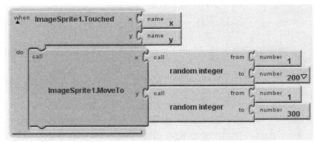

FIGURE 4.9

Random movement tied to a touch event.

14. Set the text for displaying the score to the user. Begin by initializing the text for the first label. In the Built-In tab, click Definition, and drag two `def variable` blocks onto the workspace. Name one `def variable` block `score` and the other `label`. Then, from the Text menu, drag a `text` block onto the workspace and set it to `Score:` (be sure to add a space at the end). Finally, from the Math menu, drag a `number` block to the workspace and set it to 0. Attach the `text` block to `def label` and the `number` block to `def score`.

15. From the Text menu, drag a `join` block onto the workspace. Then, click the My Blocks tab, click Game, and drag a `when Game.Initialize do` block onto the workspace. Next, from the Label1 menu, drag a `set Label1.Text` block, and from the My Definitions menu, drag over a `global label` and `global score` block. Attach them as shown in Figure 4.10.

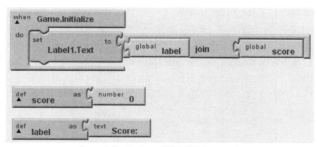

Source: Jeffrey Hawthorne. ©2013. All rights reserved.

FIGURE 4.10

Initializing label text when the screen loads.

16. It's time to add more blocks to the `when ImageSprite1.Touched do` cluster. First, to increment the score, drag over a `set global score` block and a `global score` block from the My Definitions menu. Then, from the Math menu, drag over a `number` block and a + (plus) block. Set the value of the `number` block to 1. Attach them as shown in Figure 4.11.

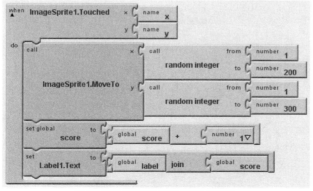

Source: Jeffrey Hawthorne. ©2013. All rights reserved.

FIGURE 4.11

Fully implemented ImageSprite1. Touched block.

17. To display the updated score, replicate the cluster within the Game.Initialize block (refer to Figure 4.10). To do so, simply click the set Label1.Text block and press Ctrl+C to copy it and the blocks attached to it. Then press Ctrl+V to paste the copied block. Finally, move the whole group down to the ImageSprite.Touched block. (Refer to Figure 4.11.)

18. Now you need to set the timer to allow the game to end. By default, your timer is set to an interval of 1,000 milliseconds, or 1 second. Leave this alone. Make sure that both TimerAlwaysFires and TimerEnabled are checked in the Properties panel for the Clock1 component in App Inventor. (You may need to minimize the Blocks Editor so you can refer back to your Web browser.)

19. Pull up the Blocks Editor again and create two more definitions as you did for score and label, using two def variable blocks from the Definitions menu under the Built-In tab. Name them countdown and label2. Set the value for countdown to 30 using a number block from the Math menu. (This enables you to create a 30-second game; you can change this number later for a longer or shorter game.) Then set the value for label2 to Time Remaining: using a text block from the Text menu. (Don't forget the space after the colon.)

20. Review Figure 4.10 and add a similar set of blocks using global label2 and global countdown to Game.Initialize for set Label2.Text so it resembles Figure 4.12. (You'll need a set Label2.Text block, a join block, a global label2 block, and a global countdown block.)

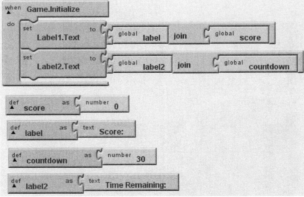

Source: Jeffrey Hawthorne. ©2013. All rights reserved.

FIGURE 4.12

Completed Game.Initialize block, initializing both labels upon loading.

21. The timer itself does not have a built-in function to stop it. Therefore, you must program an instruction to make it stop, or in this case, tell it to move on to the next screen. Take a look at the when Clock1.Timer do block you placed in the workspace in step 2 of this section. From the Control menu under the Built-In tab, drag an ifelse then-do else-do block inside the when Clock1.Timer do block. You'll be using the global

countdown variable to tell the timer when to stop. If the countdown has reached 0, then the timer code will do one thing. If the countdown hasn't reached 0 yet, then the timer code will do something else.

22. In the test socket of the ifelse then-do else-do block, place an = block from the Math menu. For the first half of the condition, drag a global countdown block from the My Definitions menu under the My Blocks tab. For the second half of the condition, add a number block from the Math menu under the Built-In tab and set the value to 0. Your test should read test: global countdown = number 0.

23. There are two tasks for the then-do portion of the block. First, you need to stop the timer, so place a set Clock1.TimerEnabled block from the Clock1 menu under the My Blocks tab in the then-do slot; then, from the Logic menu under the Built-In tab, drag a false block to the to socket. Next, if the global countdown variable is equal to 0, you want to move on to the next screen. From the Control menu, drag a call open another screen with start value block. You need the start value part as a way to carry the score variable over to the final screen. With a text block from the Text menu, tell it the screenName is Victory. Finally, from the My Definitions menu under the My Blocks tab, drag over a global score block for the start value. Place these blocks in the then-do slot below the set Clock1.TimerEnabled block.

24. In the else-do slot, you need to increment countdown downward (or else it will never reach 0 and the game will go on forever), and you need to update the Time Remaining label. Start with a set global countdown block from the My Definitions menu under the My Blocks tab. Then, using a - block from the Math menu under the Built-In tab, create the condition of global countdown - 1. The cluster should read: set global countdown to global countdown - 1. Attach that to the else-do slot.

25. Below that, add a set Label2.Text block from the Label2 menu under the My Blocks tab. Using a join block from the Text menu under the Built-In tab, create the condition of combining the Label2 text and the countdown variable. The cluster should read: set Label2.Text to global label2 join global countdown. See Figure 4.13.

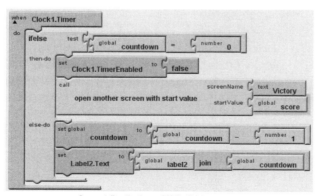

FIGURE 4.13

Creating a countdown timer.

26. In App Inventor, switch to the Victory screen. This screen requires very little in the way of code blocks. If the Blocks Editor does not reset for the new screen, close the Blocks Editor, reload the webpage, and restart the Blocks Editor.
27. In the Blocks Editor, add a `when Victory.Initialize do` block from the Victory menu under the My Blocks tab. You will use this block to set the text for the second label.
28. From the Label2 menu, drag over a `set Label2.Text` block. Attach to this a `join` block from the Text menu. In the first socket of the `join` block, place a `call get start value` block, found in the Control menu under the Built-In tab. In the second socket, place a `text` block from the Text menu under the Built-In tab, and change the text to `Moles Whacked`. (Note the space before the letter M. This is so the sentence will read, "25 Moles Whacked" rather than "25Moles Whacked.") See Figure 4.14.

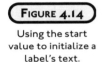

FIGURE 4.14

Using the start value to initialize a label's text.

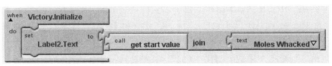

29. Add a `when Button1.Click do` block from the Button1 menu under the My Blocks tab. Then, from the Control menu under the Built-In tab, drag over a `call open another screen` block. Add a `text` block from the Text menu and change the text to `Screen1`. Attach them as shown in Figure 4.15. Now, when the button is clicked, it will take the player back to the first screen.

FIGURE 4.15

Button coded to return to the first screen.

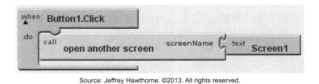

30. Click the Save button in the Blocks Editor. Your app is finished! You should be able to download the APK file and install and play it on your phone now. Next, you're going to make some changes to this app to make it more like a traditional *Whack-A-Mole* game.

WHACK-A-MOLE VERSION 2.0

Much of this app is going to be the same as version 1.0, so you have a choice to make before you begin this section:

- If you're not yet comfortable with the process, you can create a new app and work through all of the steps again.

- You can use your existing app and make the changes outlined in the following section (not recommended).

- You can create a new project using the source code from the preceding project (recommended).

The steps in this section are based on the last option. Do the following:

1. Close the Blocks Editor and click the My Projects link at the top of App Inventor to open your project list. Then select the MoleWhacker checkbox (or whatever you named your game), open the More Actions menu, and choose Download Source.

2. There should now be a ZIP folder in your download location for the app. Change the name of the ZIP folder to MoleWhacker2.zip.

3. Click the MoleWhacker checkbox in the list to uncheck it. Then choose Upload Source from the More Actions menu. Browse to your download location, select the renamed file, and click OK. In a few moments, you should have a new entry in the list, and it should automatically load the new project.

 NOTE Bear in mind, App Inventor is run on the Massachusetts Institute of Technology's (MIT) Web servers, so connectivity may be sporadic. If you get an error when you try to upload your project source code, try again.

4. The first and last screens don't require any changes. This section focuses on the second screen, Game. When you load the Game screen, you should see two labels inside a HorizontalArrangement component, a Canvas component, and an ImageSprite component. The ImageSprite component should have the picture of your mole attached to it. There should also be a Clock component listed under non-visible components.

5. Add six ImageSprite components from the Animation palette. Place them in a grid pattern: three across and two down. Don't worry if the placement isn't perfect; you'll use the code blocks to fix them.

6. In the Components panel to the right of the screen, under Media heading at the bottom, click the Upload New button, select the molehole.png file that came with this book (you should already see whackamole.png listed), and click OK.

7. For ImageSprite2 through ImageSprite7, change the Picture property to molehole.png.

8. In this version of the app, you'll stack image sprites. To do this, use the third dimension: depth. You've used X and Y coordinates up to this point; now you'll use the Z coordinate. Z enables you to place one element in front of another element. Right now, all the image sprites have the same Z coordinate: 1. While it may display correctly in the builder, you'll need to change this to guarantee the mole properly overlays the holes when the game

is actually played. To experiment with this before you code the app, drag your mole over one of the holes. (See Figure 4.16.)

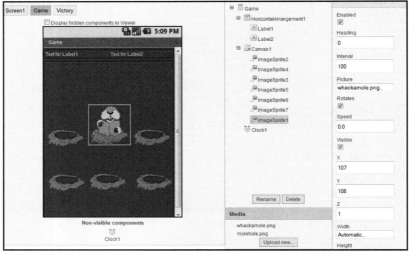

FIGURE 4.16

Traditional layout for
Whack-A-Mole.

9. Change the Z coordinate of ImageSprite1 to 0 and tab or click out of the selection box. Your mole should now appear *behind* the hole, as shown in Figure 4.17. If you were to have that happen in the live app, the mole would be untouchable, which would frustrate players and ruin their score.

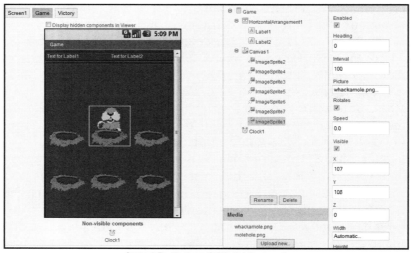

FIGURE 4.17

The mole is behind the second hole instead of on top of it because of the Z coordinate.

10. Now change the Z coordinate for ImageSprite1 to 2. It should again appear in front of the hole, as in Figure 4.16.

11. Drag a second Clock component onto your screen from the Basic palette. This timer will run separately from the countdown timer and will be used to move the mole around (rather than the player clicking the mole to move it). Clicking it will still increment the score, but movement will be controlled differently.

12. Open the Blocks Editor. Your code blocks should be organized into four different clusters: four variable definitions (not connected to anything else), a when Clock1.Timer do cluster, a when ImageSprite1.Touched do cluster, and a when Game.Initialize do cluster. You don't need to make any changes to the definitions or the when Clock1.Timer do cluster. You do, however, need to modify the other two clusters. In addition, you'll need to add another cluster of blocks for Clock2.

13. First, let's deal with the Game.Initialize cluster. Leave the two set Label.Text blocks where they are; those parts aren't changing. You do, however, need to initialize the positions of the six image sprites you added earlier. For each ImageSprite component (2 through 7), drag over a set ImageSprite.X block and a set ImageSprite.Y block from the corresponding ImageSprite menu in the My Blocks tab. This will add 12 new blocks to the when Game.Initialize do cluster. For each of these blocks, set the following values by placing a number block from the Math menu under the Built-In tab to the to socket of each set ImageSprite.X and set ImageSprite.Y block. (Note that these values can also be set for each component on the main screen to make sure the images don't shift when the screen is opened. Also remember you can drag over one number block then copy/paste it 11 times to make this go faster.) See Figure 4.18.

- ImageSprite2
  - X = 1
  - Y = 100

- ImageSprite3
  - X = 105
  - Y = 100

- ImageSprite4
  - X = 210
  - Y = 100

- ImageSprite5
  - X = 1
  - Y = 230

- ImageSprite6
  - X = 105
  - Y = 230
- ImageSprite7
  - X = 210
  - Y = 230

14. Do the same for ImageSprite1, setting it to the same value as one of the other sprites (for example, 1, 230). Additionally, drag over a `set ImageSprite1.Visible` block from the ImageSprite1 menu under the My Blocks tab and set it to `false` using a `false` block from the Logic menu under the Built-In tab. That way, all the player will see when the screen loads is the holes. See Figure 4.18.

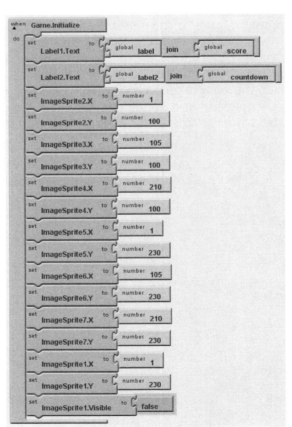

FIGURE 4.18

Expanded when Game. Initialize do block used to set sprite locations and visibility.

15. The easiest cluster to fix is the `when Image1.Touched do` cluster. The movement of the mole will no longer be tied to the touch event, so the `call ImageSprite1.MoveTo` block with the random integers can go away. Throw it in the trash can. But be careful! When you pull out the `call ImageSprite1.MoveTo` block, the `set global score` and `set Label1.Text` block clusters will come out with it. Make sure you detach those before trashing the `MoveTo` block. You need the `set global score` and `set Label1.Text` blocks, plus one more block: the `set ImageSprite1.Visible to false` cluster that you attached to the `when Game.Initialize do` block in step 14. That block can be copied and pasted to the `when Image1.Touched do` cluster and placed below the `set Label1.Text` block. (See Figure 4.19.)

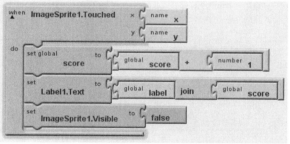

FIGURE 4.19

Modified `when ImageSprite1.Touched` block used to control visibility rather than movement.

16. Now you need a `when Clock2.Timer do` block, so drag one over from the Clock2 menu under the My Blocks tab. This block will have quite a bit of code in it to cover two recurring sequences of events. First, the mole will vanish and reappear each second. Second, the mole needs to randomly move from one hole to another. For the first part, you'll need an `ifelse then-do else-do` block. The visibility of the mole will change each second. To make this happen, you will use a second countdown variable and the visibility will be governed by that countdown. If you haven't already, from the Control menu, drag an `ifelse then-do else-do` block to the `when Clock2.Timer do` block.

17. You want the mole to vanish and reappear without outside intervention. An easy way to accomplish this is to tie it to a countdown and have it change based on whether the countdown variable is even or odd. The check for this is easier than it may sound. You're used to the terms multiply, divide, subtract, and add, but there is a fifth term that non-programmers are likely not familiar with: modulo. The modulo returns only the remainder of a division operation. As an example, if you divide 5 by 2, you get 2 with a remainder of 1. If you put in the operation 5 modulo 2, you get just the remainder: 1. In this fashion, you can check whether numbers are even or odd, because an even number divided by 2 will always have a remainder of 0, while an odd number divided by 2 will always have a remainder of 1. To implement this, first create a new variable definition exactly like `countdown` by dragging to the workspace a `def variable` block from the

Definition menu under the Built-In tab, but name this one countdown2. You'll keep this one separate because you can change the speed of the game by adjusting the timer interval. (If it were tied to the same countdown as Clock1, then changing the interval of Clock2 would have an impact on Clock1.) Don't forget to add a number block to your new variable definition and set it to 30.

18. Create the condition for your ifelse then-do else-do block. You'll need an = block, two number blocks, and a call modulo block, all from the Math menu. You'll also need a global countdown2 block from My Definitions. Assemble these as shown in Figure 4.20, with the first number set to 2 and the second number set to 1.

19. In the then-do slot, place a set ImageSprite1.Visible block from the ImageSprite1 menu, and in the to socket place a false block from the Logic menu under the Built-In tab. In the else-do slot, place a set ImageSprite1.Visible block and set it to true.

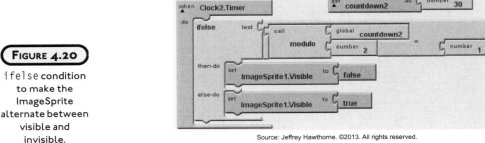

FIGURE 4.20

ifelse condition to make the ImageSprite alternate between visible and invisible.

20. Below the else-do slot, outside of the ifelse then-do else-do block, place a set global countdown2 block from the My Definitions menu under the My Blocks tab and set the value to countdown2 - 1 using a - block from the Math menu under the Built-In tab with a global countdown2 block from the My Definitions menu under the My Blocks tab in the first socket, and a number block from the Math menu in the second socket. Set the value of the number block to 1. It's important that the countdown not be inside a decision. If it's in an if or else decision, then it will not decrement properly, which means the sprite will vanish, never to appear again!

21. Create another definition called rand by dragging a def variable block from the Definitions menu and renaming it rand. Add a call random integer block from the Math menu under the Built-In tab to the def rand block you just created and set the range to 2 through 7. See Figure 4.21. Add a set global rand block from the My Definitions menu under the My Blocks tab (this block is created automatically when you created the definition). Then add a call random integer block from the Math menu to it and set the range from 2 to 7. See Figure 4.22.

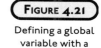

FIGURE 4.21

Defining a global variable with a random value.

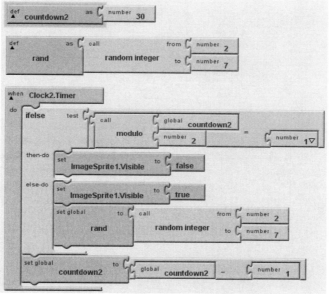

FIGURE 4.22

Decrementing the countdown2 variable and creating a new random integer.

22. The last section for the when Clock2.Timer do block requires six if then-do blocks. Each time the timer fires, the random number will be changed to something between two and seven by the set global rand block. You will set the X and Y coordinate of ImageSprite1 to the same location as one of the holes based on the random integer. To achieve this, first set a comparison between rand and a number from two to seven (rand = 2, rand = 3, rand = 4, etc.) in the test condition for each if block. So starting with the number 2, drag over an if then-do block from the Control menu under the Built-In tab. Place an = block from the Math menu in the test socket. Place a global rand block from the My Definitions menu under the My Blocks tab in the first socket of the = block. Place a number block from the Math menu in the second socket and change the value to 2.

23. Repeat step 22 five more times. You can save time by copying and pasting the if then-do block. Change the value of each number block so that you have a test for numbers 2, 3, 4, 5, 6, and 7.

24. In the then-do slot of each if then-do block, place a set ImageSprite1.X block and a set ImageSprite1.Y block from the ImageSprite1 menu under the My Blocks tab. Then attach a number block to each one and set the value to the X and Y coordinates of the

image sprite that corresponds to the number in the test condition. For example, if rand = 6, set ImageSprite1.X to 105 and ImageSprite.Y to 230. Use the list between steps 13 and 14 to get the appropriate values. This cluster of blocks should now look like Figure 4.23.

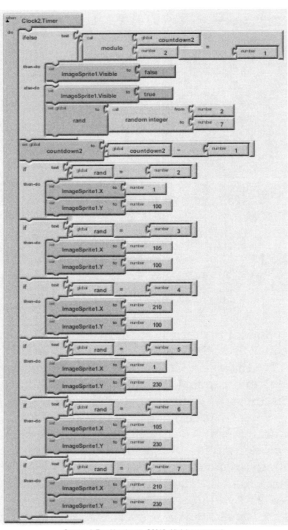

FIGURE 4.23

Completed
Clock2.Timer
block.

The third screen requires no changes, so you're finished! Download the app and test it out. You've now made two different applications that share much of the same code, demonstrating a programming principle common to object-oriented design that is reflected in the App Builder: reuse. Traditional Android apps are written in Java, an object-oriented language that breaks down code into files called classes. For your apps, you can consider each screen a class. Because they are separate and unique, you can make changes to one screen without affecting the other screens, as long as you take care to carry over any required data, such as score, from one screen to the next.

SUMMARY

This chapter deals with randomizing movement. You learned two different ways to control that movement: manually, using a touch event; and automatically, using a timer. You can experiment with timers by changing the TimerInterval setting in the App Builder Properties panel. Some other items you should take away from this chapter are using touch events to change a score and using the Canvas and ImageSprite components. App Inventor relies a great deal on these last two components for its graphics capabilities.

CAR-RACING GAME

CHAPTER OBJECTIVES

- Design an app with a collision-detection mechanism
- Use a timer
- Use a random-number generator
- Use an orientation sensor
- Use the Notifier component

This app will provide a user interface to play a car-racing game. In this app, you will use collision detection, a timer, and random-number generator. This app is also very generic, with all the necessary functionality built into it, and allows plenty of scope for extensibility and modification. You can download the images and sound files used for this chapter at www.cengageptr.com/downloads.

THE DESIGN PHASE

The GUI for this app will consist of a canvas, a table arrangement, buttons, a clock/timer, and sound components.

Throughout this chapter, specific instructions to change the color, font size, font style are left to your discretion. The screen shots simply give you some guidance for these aspects.

Design the Race Track

Here are the instructions to set up your graphical user interface:

1. Go to the App Inventor site, click My Projects, and click New Project. Type CarRacing as the name for the new project. In the Palette, click Basic, click a Canvas component, and drag it to the screen.
2. In the Properties panel, change the Canvas component's Width and Height settings to 300 pixels.
3. Click the BackgroundImage field in the Properties panel. Then browse to the folder where you saved the images for this app and select the racingTrack.png image. At this point, your screen should look like Figure 5.1.

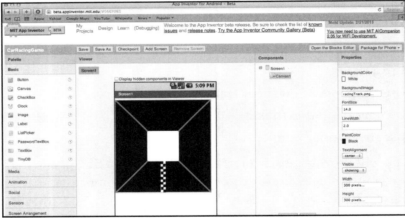

FIGURE 5.1

The racing track set up on the canvas.

4. In the Palette, from the Animation section, drag an ImageSprite component onto the canvas.
5. In the Properties panel, change the Interval setting to 10, change the Speed setting to 3.0, and deselect the Enabled checkbox.
6. Click the Picture field in the Properties panel. Then browse to the folder where you saved the images for this app and choose the car1.jpg image.
7. In the Palette, from the Animation section, drag a second ImageSprite component onto the canvas. In the Properties panel, change the Interval setting to 10, change the Speed setting to 0.0, and deselect the Enabled checkbox.

8. Click the Picture field in the Properties panel. Then browse to the folder where you saved the images for this app and choose the greenCar.jpg image. Your screen should now be similar to the one in Figure 5.2.

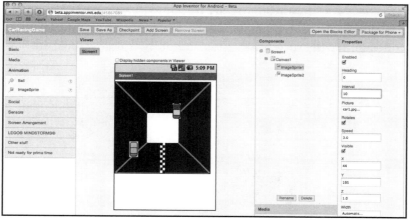

Source: Lakshmi Prayaga. ©2013. All Rights Reserved.

FIGURE 5.2

The racing car on the track.

9. In the Palette, from the Animation section, drag a Ball component and drop it anywhere on the canvas. Notice that by default the name of the ball is Ball1. You can leave this as it is.

10. In the Properties panel, change the Ball component's PaintColor setting to Cyan and change the Radius setting to 8 pixels. Make sure that both the Visible and Enabled checkboxes are checked. See Figure 5.3.

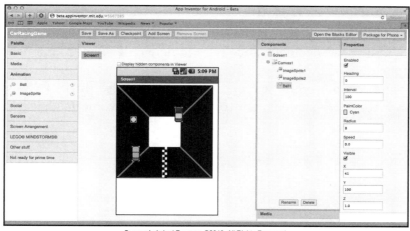

Source: Lakshmi Prayaga. ©2013. All Rights Reserved.

FIGURE 5.3

An animated ball on the canvas.

11. Drag three more Ball components from the Animation section of the Palette to the canvas. Change their PaintColor settings to Green, Magenta, and Red, and their Radius settings to 8. (You may increase or decrease the Radius setting based on your preference. If you like larger sizes, increase the Radius setting; if you like smaller sizes, then reduce the Radius settings.) The balls will automatically be named Ball2, Ball3, and Ball4.

12. In the Palette, click Sensors, and drag an OrientationSensor component to the screen. This completes the design for the race track. Your screen should now look similar to the one in Figure 5.4.

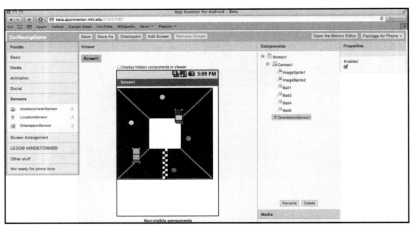

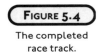

FIGURE 5.4

The completed race track.

Source: Lakshmi Prayaga. ©2013. All Rights Reserved.

Design the Control Panel

In the control panel, you will lay out the navigation controls, the score card, and the timer components for the user to interact with. Follow these steps:

1. In the Palette, click Screen Arrangement, and drag a TableArrangement component onto the screen, below the canvas.

2. In the Properties panel, change both the Columns and the Rows settings to 3, as shown in Figure 5.5. Change the TableArrangement component's Width and Height settings to Fill parent.

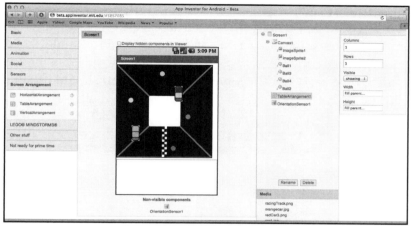

FIGURE 5.5

A TableArrangement component on the screen.

3. In the Palette, click Basic, and drag a Label component to the first row and first column of the table.

4. In the Properties panel, change the Label component's Width setting to 18 pixels and its Height setting to 14 pixels. Choose any color you like for the BackgroundColor setting. Change the FontSize setting to 14. Name the label TimerValue. Your screen should look like the one in Figure 5.6.

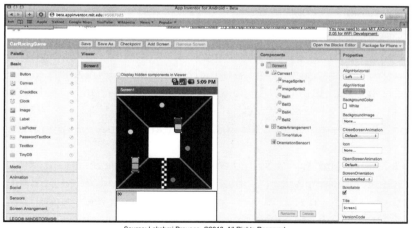

FIGURE 5.6

A Label component on the screen.

5. Repeat steps 3 and 4, placing two more Label components in the first row of the table. Name the second label TimerRunning and the third label Score. Change the Label

components' Width settings to 60 pixels and their Height settings to 30 pixels. You can choose to set any font size and any color you like for the labels.

6. In the Palette, from the Basic section, drag a Button to the second row and first column of the table. Name the button btnReSet.

7. In the Properties panel, type `Replay` in the Text field. Your screen should be similar to the one in Figure 5.7.

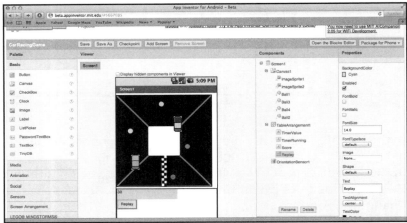

FIGURE 5.7

A Button component on the screen.

Source: Lakshmi Prayaga. ©2013. All Rights Reserved.

8. Repeat steps 6 and 7, placing two more Button components in the second row of the table. Name the second button btnLeft and change its Text setting to Left. Name the third button btnRight and change its Text setting to Right.

9. In the Palette, from the Basic section, drag one more Button component to the last row of the table, in the first column. Name this button btnStart and change its Text setting to Start.

10. In the Palette, from the Sensors section, drag an OrientationSensor component to the screen.

11. In the Palette, click Media, and drag a Sound component to the screen.

12. In the Properties panel, click the Sound component's source field. Then browse to the folder where you saved the resources for this app and choose car-beep.mp3.

13. In the Palette, click Other Stuff, and drag a Notifier component to the screen. This will be used to notify the player when the time is up for the game.

14. From the palette, drag a Clock component and drop it on the screen. This completes the GUI for the car-racing game. Your screen should look similar to the one in Figure 5.8.

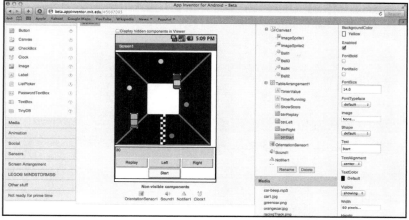

FIGURE 5.8

The completed
graphical user
interface.

THE CODE PHASE

The idea behind this app is to enable you to drive a car on a race track and hit or miss as many obstacles as you can. The GUI enables you to control the car with the left and right buttons. You also have the option to drive the car by changing the orientation of the phone. Both options are discussed in this section; you can choose the one you prefer to use. Before you start coding, here is the list of the steps required for this app:

When btnStart is clicked:

- Call the ReSet button.

When btnLeft is clicked:

- Turn the image sprite to the left.

When btnRight is clicked:

- Turn the image sprite to the right.

When btnReset is clicked:

- Set the clock timer to Enabled.
- Set the image sprite to Enabled.
- Set the balls at random positions.
- Reset the counter to 30 seconds.
- Reset the score to 0.

When the clock timer starts:

- Decrease the timer value.
- Show the timer value on a label.
- If the timer value = 0, stop the timer.
- Set `ImageSprite1.Enabled` to `false`.
- Notify the player that time is up!

When the image sprite collides with another object:

- Set the score to `score` +1.
- Display the score on the label.

When the image sprite reaches the edge of the screen:

- Call the built-in `ImageSprite1.Bounce` procedure.

Optionally, if you want to play on the device itself, you can make full use of the available sensors. You can assemble the orientation sensor so that when the orientation sensor is tilted you set the image direction to the angle the phone was tilted by and the speed to the magnitude * 10.

Set Up the Blocks

Open the Blocks Editor. (If you need to refresh your memory as to how to open the Blocks Editor, refer to Chapter 1, "Introducing App Inventor.") You will assemble the following blocks:

- User-defined variables
- User-defined procedures
- Other built-in procedures
- Button-click events
- Optional: the orientation sensor

Assemble User-Defined Variables

A variable is similar to a placeholder that can hold a value. You can define the variable and set it to hold values of specific types, numbers, text, etc. For this app, you will define two variables, counter and score.

1. Make sure the Blocks Editor is open. To define the counter variable, click the Built-In tab, and click Definition.

2. Drag the `def variable` block to the screen. See Figure 5.9.

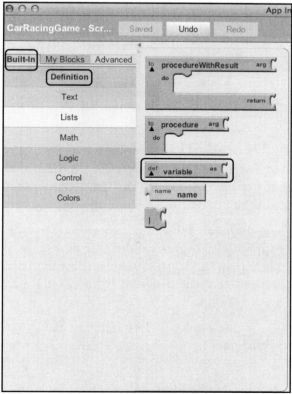

Source: Lakshmi Prayaga. ©2013. All Rights Reserved.

FIGURE 5.9

Defining a user-defined variable.

3. Change the word `variable` to `score`.
4. In the Built-In tab, click Math, and drag a `number` block to the `as` slot of the variable. Double click the 123 value and change it to 0. See Figure 5.10.

Source: Lakshmi Prayaga. ©2013. All Rights Reserved.

FIGURE 5.10

User-defined variable: `score`.

5. To define the `score` variable, click Definition in the Built-In tab.
6. Drag the `def variable` block to the screen.
7. Change the word `variable` to `counter`.

8. Click Math in the Built-In tab and drag a number block to the as slot of the variable. Change the value to 30. See Figure 5.11.

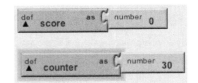

FIGURE 5.11

User-defined variable: counter.

Assemble the Blocks for User-Defined Procedures

All programming languages have procedures, or functions. A procedure, or function, is a construct that executes a set of instructions. Procedures can execute a set of instructions and give back a result, or simply execute the instructions without giving any result.

Procedures can be built-in or user-defined. A built-in procedure is something that the programming language provides for you. Examples are the true and false attributes in the Logic tab and the call min and call max in the Math tab. A user-defined procedure is one in which you provide a set of instructions that the program has to execute and either give a result or not, depending on the need.

The main idea in using a procedure is that once you define it, you can use it as many times as is necessary in a program. Procedures make your code modular; you can design it once and use it many times.

In this app, you will use both built-in procedures and user-defined procedures. In this program, you will define a procedure called ReSet, which will be used in the btnStart and btnReset.

Assemble the User-Defined Reset Procedures

To assemble the user-defined ReSet procedures, follow these steps:

1. In the Blocks Editor, click the Built-In tab and click Definition.
2. Click the to procedure do block and drag it to the screen to assemble the code.
3. Double-click the word procedure and type ReSet. Your screen should look like the one in Figure 5.12.

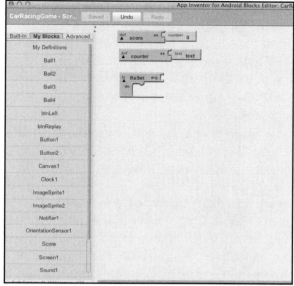

FIGURE 5.12

Procedure block.

4. Click the My Blocks tab, click Clock, and drag the `set Clock1.TimerEnabled` block to the `to ReSet do` block.
5. Click the Built-In tab and click Logic.
6. Click `true` and drag it to the `set Clock1.TimerEnabled` block's to slot. See Figure 5.13.

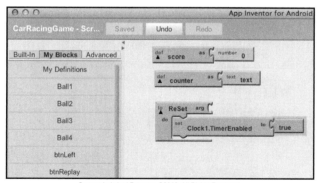

FIGURE 5.13

User-defined `ReSet` procedure.

7. Click the My Blocks tab, click ImageSprite1, and drag the `set ImageSprite1.Enabled` block under the `set ImageSprite1.Enabled to` instruction.
8. Click the Built-In tab and click Logic.
9. Click `true` and drag it to fit the `set ImageSprite1.Enabled` block's to slot.

10. Click the My Blocks tab, click My Definitions, and drag a `set global counter` block under the `set ImageSprite1.Enabled` instruction.
11. Click the Built-In tab, click Math, and drag a `number` block to the `set global counter` block's empty slot. Then double-click the `number` block and change its value to 30 to set the counter to start counting down from 30 seconds.
12. Click the My Blocks tab, click My Definitions, and drag the `set global score` piece under the `set global counter` instruction.
13. Click the Built-In tab, click Math, and drag a `number` block to the `set global score` block's empty slot. Then double-click the `number` block and change its value to 0. This will set the value of the score to 0 whenever the `ReSet` procedure is called.

Set the Four Balls to Appear at Random Locations

The next part of the `ReSet` procedure is to set the balls at random positions within the canvas each time `ReSet` is called. The `Ball1.MoveTo` block takes two parameters: X and Y coordinates. When those parameters are given, the ball will be moved to that location on the canvas. The idea here is to place the four balls at random positions on the 300×300 canvas. To accomplish this, you use the random-number generator to generate a random number for X and Y and use that to place the ball on the canvas. The random-number generator takes `range from` and `range to` boundaries and generates an integer between those two values. In this case, you can use any integers between 0 and 300 for X and 0 and 300 for Y for the random-number generator so it can generate a number within that range. For example, if you specify 100, 200 for X, the random-number generator will generate a number within the range of these two numbers. This is what is used in this section to place the four balls on the canvas.

To set the balls at random positions, complete the following steps:

1. Click the My Blocks tab. Then click Ball1 and drag the `call Ball1.MoveTo` procedure to the screen below the `global score` block within the `ReSet` procedure. See Figure 5.14.

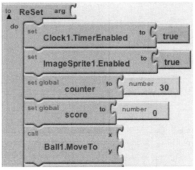

FIGURE 5.14

Random–number generator block.

2. Click the Built-In tab, click Math, and drag two `call random integer` parameters with `from` and `to` slots to the `call Ball1.MoveTo` block, adding one to the x slot and one to the y slot.

3. In the Built-In tab, click Math. Drag a `number` block to the `from` slot for the first `call random integer` block (the X parameter). Change the value from 123 to 50.

4. In the Math section of the Built-In tab, drag a `number` block to the `to` slot for the first `call random integer` block (the X parameter). Change the value from 123 to 100. This will generate a random number between 50 and 100 each time the `ReSet` procedure is called.

5. Repeat steps 3 and 4 to add two more `number` pieces for the Y parameter. Your screen should be similar to the one in Figure 5.15.

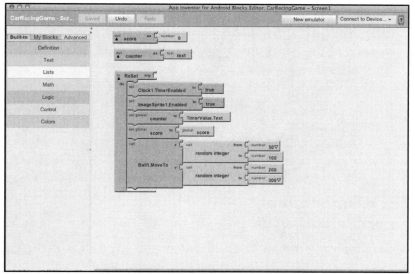

Source: Lakshmi Prayaga. ©2013. All Rights Reserved.

FIGURE 5.15

Random-number generator for X and Y values.

6. Repeat steps 1 through 5 to move the three remaining balls. In the My Blocks tab, click Ball2, and drag the `Ball2.MoveTo` block to the screen. Assemble the block like you did `Ball1.MoveTo`. You may use any values you like as long as they are within 0 and 300 for both X and Y, as that is the width and height of the canvas and you want to place the ball within the canvas. See Figure 5.16 for the completed `ReSet` procedure.

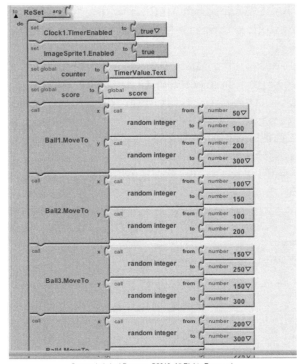

FIGURE 5.16

Completed ReSet
procedure.

Assemble the Clock Timer Event

This block is responsible for the following tasks:

1. For each timer click (which was set to 1 second), decrease the value of the counter by one.
2. Show this new value on the label.
3. If the counter value = 0, then notify the player that the time is up.
4. Show the final score to the player.
5. Set Clock1.Enabled to false.
6. Set ImageSprite1.Enabled to false.

To assemble this, do the following steps:

1. Click the My Blocks tab, click Clock1, and drag the when Clock1.Timer do block to the screen.
2. In the My Blocks tab, click My Definitions and drag a set global counter block to the screen.

3. Click the Built-In tab, click Math, and drag the - connector to the empty to slot in the set global counter block.

4. In the My Blocks tab, click My Definitions and drag a global counter block to the first empty slot of the - connector.

5. Click the Built-In tab, click Math, and drag a number block to the second empty slot of the - connector. Change the value of the number block from 123 to 1.

6. Click the My Blocks tab, click TimerRunning, and drag the set TimerRunning.Text block below the set global counter piece.

7. In the My Blocks tab, click My Definitions and drag a global counter block to the empty slot of the set TimerRunning.Text piece.

8. Click the Built-In tab, click Logic, and drag the if test then-do below the set TimerRunning.Text piece.

9. In the Built-In tab, click Math, and drag the = connector to the empty test slot.

10. In the My Blocks tab, click My Definitions and drag a global counter block to the first slot of the = connector.

11. Click the Built-In tab, click Math, and drag a number block to the second slot of the = connector. Change the value of number from 123 to 0.

12. Click My Blocks, click Clock1, and drag the set Clock1.TimerEnabled block to the then-do slot.

13. Click the Built-In tab, click Logic, and drag a false piece to the empty slot of the set Clock1.TimerEnabled block.

14. Click My Blocks tab, click Notifier1, and drag the call Notifier1.ShowAlert notice block below the set Clock1.TimerEnabled piece.

15. Click the Built-In tab, click Text and drag the text piece to the empty slot of the call Notifier1.ShowAlert notice component. Double-click the text piece and change its value to Time is up!.

16. Click My Blocks tab, click ImageSprite1 and drag the set ImageSprite1.Enabled block below the call Notifier1.ShowAlert notice component.

17. Click the Built-In tab, click Logic, and drag a false piece to the empty slot of the set ImageSprite1.Enabled component. This completes the Clock1.Timer block. See Figure 5.17.

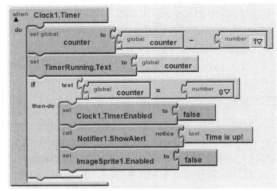

FIGURE 5.17

The `Clock1.Timer` block.

Assemble the `when ImageSprite1.EdgeReached do` **Block**

The next block that you will assemble is the `when ImageSprite1.EdgeReached do` block. This block will enable the ImageSprite1 to reflect off the wall of the canvas whenever it hits the edge of the canvas. Complete the following steps:

1. Click the My Blocks tab, click ImageSprite1, and drag the `when ImageSprite1.EdgeReached do` block to the screen. See Figure 5.18.

FIGURE 5.18

The when ImageSprite1. EdgeReached do block.

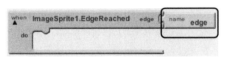

NOTE If you don't see the `name edge` **piece attached to the** `edge` **slot of the** `when ImageSprite1.Edge Reached do` **block, click the My Blocks tab, click My Definitions, and drag the** `name edge` **piece to this slot.**

2. In the My Blocks tab, click ImageSprite1, and drag the `call ImageSprite1.Bounce edge` under this block.
3. In the My Blocks tab, click My Definitions and drag the `value edge` piece to the `edge` slot of the `call ImageSprite1.Bounce edge` component. Your screen should be similar to the one in Figure 5.19.

FIGURE 5.19

The when
ImageSprite1.
Bounce edge
block.

NOTE ImageSprite1.edge checks whether the sprite has hit an edge of the canvas. You can provide a value for the edge as 1 for north, -1 for south, etc. However, if you do not specify a value for the edge, then it is triggered each time the sprite hits any edge of the canvas, which is what you did with this block.

Assemble the when ImageSprite2.EdgeReached do Block

This block ensures that when ImageSprite2 reaches an edge, it bounces back. Follow the instructions for assembling the when ImageSprite1.EdgeReached do block to assemble the when ImageSprite2.EdgeReached do block. See Figure 5.20.

FIGURE 5.20

The when
ImageSprite2.
EdgeReached do
procedure.

Assemble the when ImageSprite1.CollideWith other do block

In this block, you will assemble the set of instructions to increase the score each time the image sprite collides with other sprites or balls on the canvas. Follow these steps:

1. Click the My Blocks tab, click ImageSprite1, and drag the when ImageSprite1.CollideWith other do block to the screen. This will check for a collision of ImageSprite1 with any other sprite or ball on the canvas.

2. In the My Blocks tab, click My Definitions and drag the set global score piece to the do section of the block.

3. In the Built-In tab, click Math, and drag the + connector next to the set global score piece.

4. In the My Blocks tab, click My Definitions and drag the global score piece to the first slot of the + connector.

5. In the Built-In tab, click Math, and drag the number piece to the second slot of the + connector.

6. Change the value of number to 1. This will increase the score each time the image sprite hits another image sprite or ball on the canvas.

7. Click the My Blocks tab, click ShowScore, and drag the set ShowScore.Text block below the set global score block.
8. Click the My Blocks tab, click My definitions, and drag the global score block to the empty slot of the set ShowScore.Text block. This will display the current score every time it is updated. See Figure 5.21.

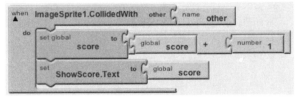

FIGURE 5.21

The when ImageSprite1. CollideWith other do block.

Source: Lakshmi Prayaga. ©2013. All Rights Reserved.

Assemble the Button-Click Events

This is the last section of the blocks assembly. You now have everything set up; all that is required now is to use the various blocks that you set up earlier. You will use the button-click events to trigger the various blocks.

Assemble btnStart

The btnStart click event will call the user-defined ReSet procedure to set all the default values for the user to start the app.

1. Click the My Blocks tab, click btnStart, and drag the when btnStart.Click do block to the center of the screen.
2. In the My Blocks tab, click My Definitions, and drag the call ReSet procedure under the when btnStart.Click do event, as shown in Figure 5.22.

FIGURE 5.22

The btnStart call ReSet procedure.

Source: Lakshmi Prayaga. ©2013. All Rights Reserved.

Assemble btnReset

The btnReset block enables the timer, sets the default values for the score and counter, and enables the image sprites on the screen.

1. Click the My Blocks tab, click btnReset, and drag the when btnRest.Click do block to the center of the screen.

2. In the My Blocks tab, click My Definitions, and drag the `call ReSet` procedure under the `when btnReset.Click do` event. (Note that btnStart and btnReset use the user-defined ReSet procedure.)

Assemble btnLeft

When the btnLeft event is clicked, it changes the image sprite's heading to rotate 90 degrees to the left.

1. Click the My Blocks tab, click btnLeft, and drag the `when btnLeft.Click do` event to the screen.
2. In the My Blocks tab, click ImageSprite1, and drag the `set ImageSprite1.Heading` block under the `when btnLeft.Click do` event.
3. Click the Built-In tab, click Math, and drag the - connector to the empty slot of the `set ImageSprite1.Heading` piece.
4. In the My Blocks tab, click ImageSprite1, and drag the `ImageSprite1.Heading` block to the first slot of the - connector.
5. Click the Built-In tab, click Math, and drag the `number` piece to the second slot of the - connector.
6. Click the `number` piece and change the value to 90. See Figure 5.23.

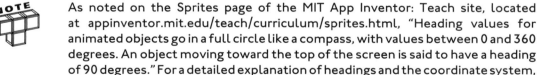

Source: Lakshmi Prayaga. ©2013. All Rights Reserved.

FIGURE 5.23

btnLeft moves car to the left.

As noted on the Sprites page of the MIT App Inventor: Teach site, located at appinventor.mit.edu/teach/curriculum/sprites.html, "Heading values for animated objects go in a full circle like a compass, with values between 0 and 360 degrees. An object moving toward the top of the screen is said to have a heading of 90 degrees." For a detailed explanation of headings and the coordinate system, visit teach.appinventor.mit.edu/curriculum/coordxplore.

Assemble btnRight

When the btnRight event is clicked, it changes the image sprite's heading to rotate by 90 degrees to the right.

1. Click the My Blocks tab, click btnRight, and drag the `when btnRight.Click do` event to the screen.

2. In the My Blocks tab, click ImageSprite1, and drag the set ImageSprite1.Heading block under the when btnRight.Click do event.
3. Click the Built-In tab, click Math, and drag the + connector to the empty slot of the set ImageSprite1.Heading piece.
4. In the My Blocks tab, click ImageSprite1, and drag the ImageSprite1.Heading block to the first slot of the + connector.
5. Click the Built-In tab, click Math, and drag the number piece to the second slot of the + connector.
6. Click the number piece and change the value to 90. This completes the assembly of the button events and the racing-car game.

Optional: Implement Tilt Functionality

This section is optional. It requires that you have a physical device; it will not work on the Emulator, as you cannot tilt the Emulator. The goal of this section is to enable the player to tilt the phone to change the direction of and move the car. You will be using the orientation sensor that you added to the GUI to accomplish this task. So, if you have a device, you can also add this section to your game.

For this section, you will define a new user-defined procedure named moveCar. Follow these steps:

1. Click the Built-In tab, click Definition, and drag the to procedure do block to the screen.
2. Double-click the word procedure and type moveCar.
3. Click the My Blocks tab, click ImageSprite2, and drag the set ImageSprite2.Heading block to the do slot of the moveCar procedure.
4. In the My Blocks tab, click OrientationSensor1, and drag the OrientationSensor1.Angle piece to the to slot of the set ImageSprite2.Heading piece.
5. In the My Blocks tab, click ImageSprite2, and drag the set ImageSprite2.Speed block below the set ImageSprite2.Heading block.
6. Click the Built-In tab, click Math, and drag the * (multiplication) connector to the to slot of the set ImageSprite2.Speed block.
7. Click the My Blocks tab, click OrientationSensor1, and drag the OrientationSensor1. Magnitude piece to the first empty slot of the * (multiplier) connector. The orientation sensor's magnitude returns a number between 0 and 100. Multiplying that number by 100 will determine the speed of the sprite.
8. Click the Built-In tab, click Math, and drag the number block to the second slot of the * connector. Click the 123 and change the number value to 100.
9. Click the My Blocks tab, click Clock1, drag the set Clock1.TimerEnabled block below the set ImageSprite2.Speed block.

10. Click the Built-In tab, click Logic, and drag the true piece to the to slot of the set Clock1Timer.Enabled block.
11. In the My Blocks tab, click ImageSprite2, and drag a set ImageSprite1.Enabled block below the Clock1.Timer.Enabled block.
12. Click the Built-In tab, click Logic, and drag the true piece to the to slot of the set ImageSprite2.Enabled block.
13. Repeat steps 11 and 12 but set the ImageSprite1.Enabled block to false so the other car is disabled. See Figure 5.24.

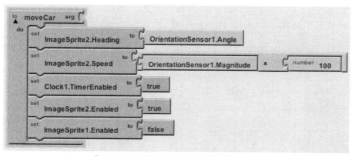

Source: Lakshmi Prayaga. ©2013. All Rights Reserved.

FIGURE 5.24

The user-defined moveCar procedure.

Assemble btnTurnCar

This button will call the moveCar procedure so you can tilt your phone and move the car.

1. In the My Blocks tab, click btnTurnCar, and drag a when btnTurnCar.Click do block to the screen.
2. Click My Definitions and drag the call moveCar block to the when btnTurnCar.Click do block. See Figure 5.25.

Source: Lakshmi Prayaga. ©2013. All Rights Reserved.

FIGURE 5.25

The when btnTurnCar.Click do event.

NOTE

ImageSprite2 has been included in this chapter only to illustrate how the orientation sensor can be used in games, thereby taking advantage of the tilt capabilities of the device. It has not been programmed to keep score, stop after the timer runs out, etc. Those are modifications that you can and should try to make your game more interesting. Have fun with that!

THE TESTING AND DEPLOYMENT PHASE

To test your newly designed app, run it in the Emulator. Note that for this app, you can use the Emulator to test the four buttons—btnStart, btnReset, btnLeft, and btnRight—by clicking them. You should also be testing the timer, the collision detection, the score, and the ReSet procedure.

- When btnStart is clicked, the timerRunning label should start going down from 30 to 0 in intervals of one second.
- When btnLeft is clicked, the car should turn 90 degrees to the left and keep moving.
- When btnRight is clicked, the car should turn 90 degrees to the right and keep moving.
- When btnReSet is clicked, the whole game should start again with the timer set back to 30 seconds and the score set back to 0.

In addition, you should test to see whether the score label is updated and incremented each time your car hits any other object on the screen. These tests will ensure that your app is working accurately.

Note that you cannot test the tilting part of the app unless you install it on a physical device or connect to it via WiFi. After you do that, you can also test the orientation sensor and check whether ImageSprite2 changes direction whenever you tilt the phone left, right, up, or down.

SUMMARY

In this chapter, you learned to use a clock as timer for a car-racing game. You also learned about the collision-detection event built in for image-sprite components, which comes in very handy to design games such as a car-racing game. Finally, you looked at how to use the OrientationSensor component to move the car in the game.

Additional suggestions to improve the car-racing game include allowing the user to choose one of the interfaces at the beginning (control the car via the buttons or control the car via the titling mechanism) and adding the scoring system and timer to the game when the user chooses the tilt mechanism.

CHAPTER 6

TRIVIA QUIZ

CHAPTER OBJECTIVES

- Implement a database using TinyDB
- Use checkboxes as option buttons
- Use multiple screens
- Compare responses to stored values
- Keep track of the score
- Keep track of the number of turns taken

INTRODUCTION

Quizzes are always fun and popular (except in school, of course). Whether it's a TV show, a video game, a survey, or a test in school, quizzes are used everywhere. In this chapter, you will learn how to create a quiz of your own as a mobile application.

THE DESIGN PHASE

Your app will consist of four screens: Screen1, Questions, Answers, and Victory. Their tasks are pretty well described by these names. Screen1 is your first screen. Questions is where the questions will be asked. Answers is where the correct answer will be displayed to the player. Victory is the final screen, telling the player whether he or she was victorious. Remember, any time a screen is mentioned in these instructions, it's referring to an app screen within the builder, not your monitor screen.

Creating the App

To create the app, follow these steps:

1. Create a new project in the App Inventor and name it MyComicsQuiz. If you have created other projects, you may find that the software forwards you to the project screen before you are able to create a new project. If this happens, click My Projects at the top of the window and then create your project. Once your project is created, your screen should look like the one shown in Figure 6.1.

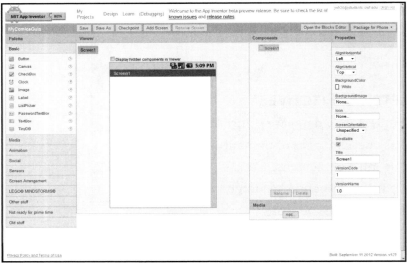

FIGURE 6.1

A blank starting screen.

2. Click the Add Screen button to create a new screen. Name the new screen "Questions." Click OK. The Questions screen will contain the quiz questions followed by checkboxes with the answer choices, much like a multiple-choice test.

3. Click the Add Screen button again to create another new screen. Name this new screen "Answers." Click OK. After the player makes a choice, he or she will advance to the Answers screen, which will indicate whether the answer the player selected was right or wrong.

4. Click the Add Screen button one more time to create a third new screen. Name the new screen "Victory." Click OK. The Victory screen will be used to present the player with his or her final score results and the option to try the quiz again. As shown in Figure 6.2, you now have four screens, with the last one being displayed.

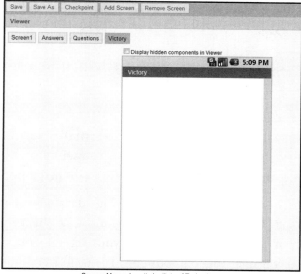

Source: Massachusetts Institute of Technology.

FIGURE 6.2

All four screens
have been created.

5. Click the Screen1 button. This will be your welcome screen. You'll use it to initialize
   components that you need and to present the app's title.
6. Open the Background Color menu in the Properties panel and change the color of the
   background to dark gray. (See Figure 6.3.)

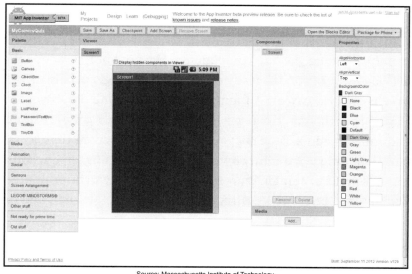

Source: Massachusetts Institute of Technology.

FIGURE 6.3

Change the
background color.

7. Repeat step 6 for the remaining screens.

Adding Components

The next step is to add the necessary components to each screen in your app. Read on for details.

Adding Components to Screen 1

As mentioned, you are going to use the first screen, Screen1, to initialize various components and variables that will be used by all four screens of the app. You will also add some visible components in the form of a title message and a button to advance the game.

The first component to add is a TinyDB component. This is your database. (This is discussed in greater detail later, when you move into using the Blocks Editor for this project.) For now, simply drag the TinyDB icon from the Basic menu over to your screen. Unlike buttons and labels, the TinyDB component is a non-visible component. It is used to create functionality behind the scenes; it does not actually show up on the screen during use. After you've added it you should see it listed just below your app screen, as shown in Figure 6.4.

FIGURE 6.4

Non-visible components appear below the app screen in the builder.

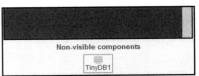

Source: Massachusetts Institute of Technology.

A TinyDB is somewhat unique among the app components. Most of your components exist on one screen only. When you move beyond that screen, they are no longer accessed. A TinyDB exists across all the screens—with a caveat: An app can only have one database. You can create more than one TinyDB, but this can create problems if you use the same tag more than once. The normal procedure is to add a TinyDB component to each screen that accesses it. Even though you seem to be adding a different component to a different screen, you are in fact simply creating an access point to a single shared data source. You will be prompted later to add more TinyDB components, but if you desire, you can go ahead and add one to each screen now.

You will also be creating two variables, one for the score and one to keep track of turns. These will also be non-visible, but unlike the database, they will be code variables without components associated with them. For this reason, they will be discussed when you move into the Blocks Editor.

To finish Screen1, you need to add two visible components: a label to display the title, and a button to enable the player to move to the next screen so he or she can begin to play the game. To add the label, follow these steps:

1. Drag a Label component from the Basic tab in the Palette onto Screen1.
2. Open the Background Color menu in the Properties panel and change the label's background color to blue.
3. Click the FontBold and FontItalic checkboxes to select them.
4. Type 60 in the FontSize field.
5. Open the FontTypeface menu and choose Sans Serif.
6. In the Text field, type Welcome to the Comic Book Quiz!.
7. Click in the TextColor field and choose Yellow from the menu that appears.
8. Under Width, select the Fill Parent option button. (See Figure 6.5.)

Source: Massachusetts Institute of Technology.

FIGURE 6.5

Label l properties.

NOTE   As you can see, the background color appears to cover only the first line of your text. Don't worry. When the app is actually running, the color will cover all of the text.

9. Next, you want to add a button to enable the player to advance to the next screen. Buttons are added to the left side of the screen by default, but you have a couple options for centering it so it is more attractive. One is to make the button the same width as the screen; the other is to change the alignment of the screen itself. You are going to change the screen alignment. To do this, simply change the AlignHorizontal property to Center (see Figure 6.6). This property was only recently added and makes life much easier.

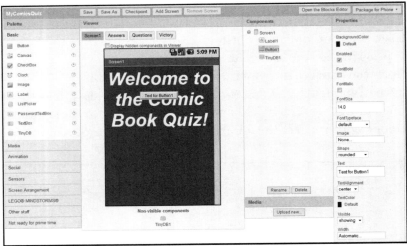

FIGURE 6.6

Your newly added button.

Source: Massachusetts Institute of Technology.

10. Change the Shape property of the button to Rounded.
11. In the Text field, type `Take the Quiz`.

If you want to check the look of this screen live, you can run it in the Emulator. Alternatively, install it on your device to see how the actual appearance differs from what you see in App Inventor.

Adding Components to the Questions Screen

You will add the components that make up the actual game to the Questions screen. Follow these steps:

1. Click the Questions button to change to the Questions screen.
2. Drag a Label from the Basic tab in the Palette onto the screen.
3. Drag three CheckBox components from the Palette onto the screen.
4. For both the Label and the CheckBox components, change the TextColor property to white.

5. On Screen1, you used the AlignHorizontal property of the screen to center the text. This centers all of the text on the screen. For this screen, you want the question and answers to retain their left justification, but you want the button to move to the next screen to be centered. To center an item within the screen without affecting the entire screen, you can use a HorizontalArrangement component. Drag a HorizontalArrangement component from the Screen Arrangement tab in the Palette onto the screen.

6. In the Properties panel, under Width, select the Fill Parent option button.

7. In the Properties panel, open the AlignHorizontal menu and choose Center.

8. Drag a Button component from the Basic tab in the Palette into the HorizontalArrangement component.

9. In the Button component's Text field, type Next.

10. Change the Shape property of the button to Rounded. Don't worry about changing the text of the label and checkboxes; they will be controlled by the database later. Your screen should look similar to the one shown in Figure 6.7.

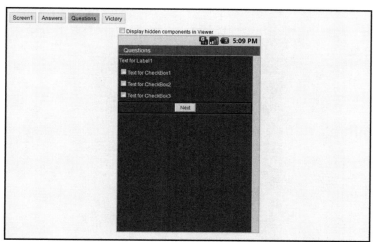

Source: Massachusetts Institute of Technology.

FIGURE 6.7

Multiple-choice question layout for your quiz.

Adding Components to the Answers Screen

The Answers screen will appear when the user clicks the Next button on the Questions screen. If the player answered the question incorrectly, he or she will receive a message to that effect. If the player got the answer right, then he or she will see not only a message saying that the answer was correct, but also trivia related to the correct answer. Both versions of the screen will have a Next button. To show all this, you need four components: two Label components, a Horizontal Arrangement component, and a Button component. To add them, follow these steps:

1. Click the Answers button to view the Answers screen.
2. Drag two Label components from the Basic tab on the Palette onto the screen.
3. For both Label components, set the Width property to Fill Parent and the TextAlignment property to Center.
4. For the first Label component, set the background color to blue, select the FontBold and FontItalic checkboxes to select them, change the font size to 42, and the text color to cyan.
5. For the second Label component, set the text color to white and the font size to 24.
6. Drag a HorizontalArrangement component from the Screen Arrangement tab on the Palette onto the screen.
7. Set the Width and Height properties to Fill Parent and the horizontal and vertical alignment to Center.
8. Drag a Button component from the Basic tab in the Palette into the HorizontalArrangement component. Change the Shape property of the button to Rounded, and type Next in the Text field. Your screen should look like the one shown in Figure 6.8.

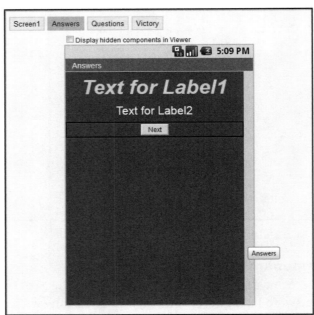

FIGURE 6.8

The layout of the Answers screen.

Source: Massachusetts Institute of Technology.

Adding Components to the Victory Screen

The Victory screen needs only a few components: a label to display a win or lose message, two labels to display the score, and a button to return the player back to the start screen. Follow these steps:

1. Click the Victory button to view the Victory screen.
2. Drag a Label component from the Basic tab on the Palette onto the screen. Set the width to Fill Parent, the font size to 42, the text alignment to Center, and the text color to green.
3. Drag two HorizontalArrangement components from the Screen Arrangement tab on the Palette onto the screen. For both, change the width to Fill Parent and the horizontal alignment to Center.
4. Add two Label components to the first HorizontalArrangement component. Change the text for the first label from Text for Label2 to Score: (making sure to include a couple of spaces). Change the font color of both labels to white.
5. Add a Button component to the second HorizontalArrangement component. Change the Shape property of the button to Rounded, and set the button text to Would you like to try again? See Figure 6.9.

Source: Massachusetts Institute of Technology.

FIGURE 6.9

The layout of the Victory screen.

THE CODE PHASE

Now that you have the visible components laid out, the first thing you need to do to make your app actually work is to create a database. Even if you're not familiar with databases and how they work, you encounter them every day—probably without even realizing it. Every time you search for something on Google or log in to a website, you're interacting with a database.

Databases consist of tables, which contain rows and columns. Each row relates to a different object, or entity, and each column contains an attribute, or characteristic, of those objects. For example, let's say you have a car dealership. You have lots of cars. Each car may be a different color, be a different model, have two or four doors, etc. These cars can be put into a database as in Table 6.1.

TABLE 6.1 CARS			
Name	**Color**	**Model**	**NumberOfDoors**
Nissan I	Red	Pathfinder	4
Chevrolet I	Blue	Corvette	2

 NOTE A normal database would have other characteristics such as keys, which can be used to create relationships between multiple tables, but you don't need to worry about that here.

App Inventor uses a very simple database component called TinyDB. You may recall you added this component at the beginning of the chapter. Each item (row) in this database is limited to two columns. The first is a tag, which is like a nickname or shortcut, and the second is the actual value, which can be either a number or a string. (In programming, a "string" is a series of characters. A sentence is a string. A word is a string. A number can also be a string.)

This quiz is going to consist of three questions, each with three answers. Each question will be on a different screen. When each question is answered, the app will change to a different screen indicating whether the answer was correct. If you did not employ a database, you would need many more screens—a different screen for each question. By utilizing a database, you can reuse the same screen over and over and just change the values that appear each time. (That's where the turn variable will come in, but I'll discuss that later.) The quiz will be structured as follows:

- In what title did Superman first appear?

    1. Action Comics (correct)
    2. Adventure Comics
    3. Superman

- What famous film director almost made a big-budget Spider-Man movie in the 1990s?

    1. Steven Spielberg
    2. Tim Burton
    3. James Cameron (correct)

- Which comic-book writer was honored in 2012 by the Queen of England?

    1. Alan Moore
    2. Grant Morrison (correct)
    3. Warren Ellis

Now it's time to enter each of these questions and answers as components in your database.

Initializing the Database

In this section you will create the necessary block connections to set your database values when the app is opened by the user. Follow these steps:

1. Click the Screen1 button to return to the Welcome screen.
2. Open the Blocks Editor.
3. Click the My Blocks tab in the left column. Then click Screen1. A list of blocks will appear. From that list, drag the `Screen1.Initialize` block onto the workspace.
4. You want the database to be the first thing populated, so you will add values here. To begin, click TinyDB1 in the My Blocks tab; then drag the `TinyDB1.StoreValue` block onto the workspace. Attach it to the `Initialize` block, as shown in Figure 6.10.

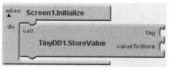

Source: Massachusetts Institute of Technology.

FIGURE 6.10

The
TinyDB1.
StoreValue
block.

5. Click the Built-In tab. Then click the Text menu, drag two text blocks over, and attach them to the StoreValue block. Name the first one question1. In the second, type the actual question (In what title did Superman first appear?), as shown in Figure 6.11.

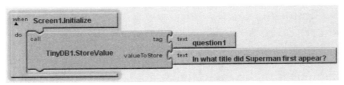

Source: Massachusetts Institute of Technology.

6. Add three more StoreValue blocks; then add tags and values for each answer to the first question. Give them the tags answer1-1, answer1-2, and answer1-3. The workspace should match what's shown in Figure 6.12.

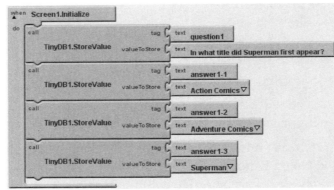

Source: Massachusetts Institute of Technology.

7. Continue adding StoreValue and text blocks, as shown in Figure 6.13, until you have all the questions and answers accounted for. When you're finished, you will have a total of 12 StoreValue blocks.

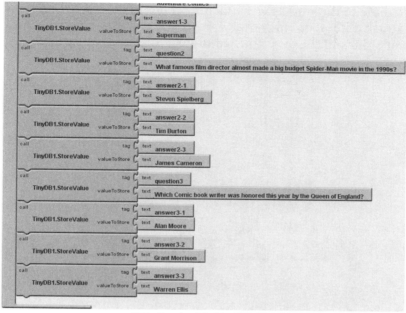

Source: Massachusetts Institute of Technology.

FIGURE 6.13

Tags and values stored for the second and third set of questions and answers.

8. You need a couple of other variables that will act as global variables. There is an option to create global variables by themselves, but that type of variable is accessible only to a single screen. You want your variables to update between screens, so you'll need to add these to the database. To begin, click Definition in the Built-In tab. Then drag a `variable` block to the workspace. Click Math and attach a `number` block to the variable block. Change the name of the variable to `score`, and change the value of the number to 0.

9. Repeat step 8 to create a second variable, called `turn`. You should have two variable blocks, as shown in Figure 6.14.

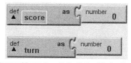

Source: Massachusetts Institute of Technology.

FIGURE 6.14

Defining global variables: `score` and `turn`.

10. Move back to where you added all the `StoreValue` blocks and add two more to the bottom of the list. For now, you won't add anything to them.

11. Click the My Blocks tab and click My Definitions. Notice that there are now new blocks available, including a `set global` block for both `turn` and `score`.

12. Add one of each of these to the workspace, attaching them to the last StoreValue block. To each of these, attach a number block from the Math menu. Change the value of the one attached to score to 0 and the one attached to turn to 1. (See Figure 6.15.)

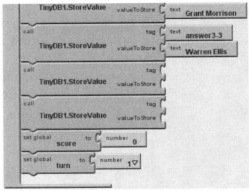

Source: Massachusetts Institute of Technology.

FIGURE 6.15

Setting global variables when the screen is initialized.

13. The last thing you need to do is create tags and values for the empty StoreValue blocks you added in step 10. To begin, add text blocks, naming one score and one turn and place one in each of the empty tag sockets.
14. Connect one global block to the score tag and another to the turn tag by using the valueToStore socket in both cases. Now one StoreValue block should have a turn tag and a global turn variable valueToStore, and the other should have a score tag and a global score valueToStore.
15. The computer processes everything in a linear fashion, which means that things must be done in order. To ensure the questions on the next screen load properly, rearrange the blocks slightly so that the two set global blocks (score and turn) come before the final two TinyDB1.StoreValue blocks, as shown in Figure 6.16.

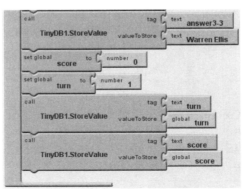

Source: Massachusetts Institute of Technology.

FIGURE 6.16

Adding global variables to the TinyDB.

Activating the Button

The next thing you need to do is create the code to activate the Take the Quiz button so the player can move to the next screen. Follow these steps:

1. In the My Blocks tab, click Button1, and drag a Button1.Click block to the workspace.
2. Click the Built-In tab. Then click Control and scroll down to the open another screen block. Attach it to the Button1.Click block.
3. Click the Text menu, attach a text block to the open another screen block, and change the text to Questions (see Figure 6.17). You are now finished with the first screen.

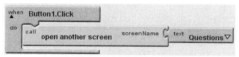

Source: Massachusetts Institute of Technology.

FIGURE 6.17

Creating the function to advance to the next screen by clicking a button.

Updating Components from the Database

The Questions screen is where the bulk of the work is done. Of the tasks you have to work out, the two biggest are updating the questions and answers from the database and working out the function of the checkboxes. You will also need to handle the score and turn variables in this screen. Follow these steps:

1. Click the Questions button in the App Inventor to switch to the Questions screen. When you do that, the Blocks Editor should automatically update to a new workspace. If it doesn't, you will need to close the Blocks Editor and reload it. Also, make sure to save your work every few steps.
2. If you haven't already, drag a TinyDB block onto the Questions screen. Although it may appear you're creating a second database, remember that each App Inventor app has only one database and each TinyDB component will access that shared database. You're just making your existing database accessible to a new screen. As with Screen1, you should have TinyDB1 showing as a non-visible component on the Questions screen.
3. Initialize the visible components. To do so, you are going to call upon the TinyDB for help. If it's not still open, begin by opening the Blocks Editor. Then, in the My Blocks tab, drag a Questions.Initialize block from the Questions menu onto the workspace.
4. Click TinyDB1 in the My Blocks tab and drag four TinyDB1.getValue blocks onto the workspace.
5. Click Label1 and drag a set Label1.Text block onto the workspace. Attach this block to the Questions.Initialize block. Do the same for CheckBox1.Text, CheckBox2.Text, and CheckBox3.Text. (See Figure 6.18.)

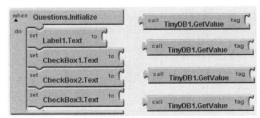

Source: Massachusetts Institute of Technology.

FIGURE 6.18

Initializing the
`Label` and
`CheckBox` text.

6. Take the four `TinyDB1.GetValue` blocks and attach one to each of the label and checkbox text blocks you just attached to the `Initialize` block.

7. In the Built-In tab, click the Text menu, and add four `text` blocks to the workspace. Attach one to each of the `GetValue` blocks. Change the values to `question1`, `answer1-1`, `answer1-2`, and `answer1-3`, as shown in Figure 6.19. (Note that you will be making an adjustment to this cluster of blocks shortly.)

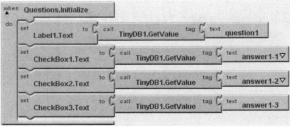

Source: Massachusetts Institute of Technology.

FIGURE 6.19

Setting the text
using the values
stored in the
TinyDB.

8. Recall that you have a `turn` variable that you need to use to track how many questions the player has answered. Why do you need this variable? Because the questions and answers will change based on the turn. (That will be the change you'll make shortly.) From the Button1 menu in the My Blocks tab, drag a `Button1.Click` block to the workspace.

9. From the TinyDB1 menu in the My Blocks tab, drag a `TinyDB1.StoreValue` block to the workspace. Attach this block to the `Button1.Click` block.

10. Drag a `text` block to the workspace and attach it to the `StoreValue` block `tag` socket and change its value to `turn`. This is the purpose of tags: You can use them to tell the database which item you want to change the value of.

11. Click the Math menu and locate the block that has two empty sockets separated by a plus sign (+). Drag it to the workspace.

12. In the first socket, attach a `TinyDB1.GetValue` block. Then attach a `text` block to that (you're still in the first socket; the second socket should still be empty) and change the text to `turn`.
13. Drag a `number` block from the Math menu to the second socket. Change the number to 1.
14. Add that cluster of blocks to the `valueToStore` socket of the `StoreValue` block. (See Figure 6.20.)

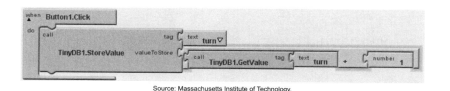

Source: Massachusetts Institute of Technology.

FIGURE 6.20

Using the button to increment the `turn` variable.

The logic of this operation works like this:

- Get the current value of turn (which you set to 1).
- Add 1 to it.
- Store the new value in the old slot.

So every time this button is clicked, the turn will be incremented by 1. Later you will add a similar function for incrementing the score.

Let's go back to the `Questions.Initialize` block. You want the questions and answers to be different based on what turn it is. To do this, you need the app to ask itself some questions. You will do this by using `if` blocks. In other words, you will use `if` statements to check on what turn it is. Follow these steps:

1. In the Built-In tab, click Control, and drag an `if test then-do` block onto the workspace. Notice that the first socket is labeled `test`. This is where your test condition goes.
2. Click the Math menu and locate the block with two empty sockets separated by an equals sign (=). Drag it to the workspace and attach it to the `test` socket.
3. The first half of your test condition will be the value of `turn`, so once again, drag a `TinyDB.GetValue` block over as well as a `text` block with the value changed to `turn`, placing both in the first socket.
4. For the second socket, place a `number` block with the value changed to 1, as shown in Figure 6.21. This test says `if(the value of turn = 1)`.

FIGURE 6.21

Making a decision
based on a
condition.

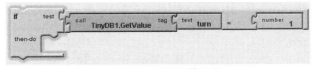

Source: Massachusetts Institute of Technology.

So what do you want to happen if turn is equal to 1? Those text blocks you added earlier in this section, in step 5, which you changed to the first set of question and answers, need to be placed in here. Follow these steps:

1. Click the Label1.Text block that is already on the workspace (refer to Figure 6.19) and move it into the then-do slot of your if block. All the blocks attached to it will move with it.

2. Move the ifelse block back into the Questions.Initialize block. The Questions.Initialize block should now look like Figure 6.22.

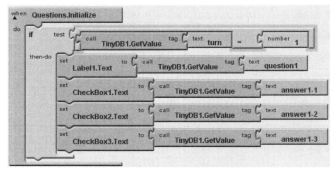

FIGURE 6.22

Completed
decision
statement.

Source: Massachusetts Institute of Technology.

So what if turn doesn't equal 1? You have three questions, so you have three turns. This means you'll need a total of three if blocks. Each block will look like the configuration in Figure 6.22, except the comparisons need to be to 2 and 3, and the label and checkboxes need to be updated as well. Using Figure 6.22 as an example, create if block clusters for the next two turns and attach them to the Questions.Initialize block. You will need to update not just the turn variable for each test, but also the question and answer numbers. When you're finished, your Initialize block should look like the one in Figure 6.23.

TIP You can copy and paste a block or cluster of blocks rather than dragging each individual block from the menus again. To do so, click a block once on the workspace to highlight it, press Ctrl+C, and then press Ctrl+V. The block and all blocks attached to it will be copied to the workspace. Then, you just need to move the newly pasted block cluster to where you need it and change the text values.

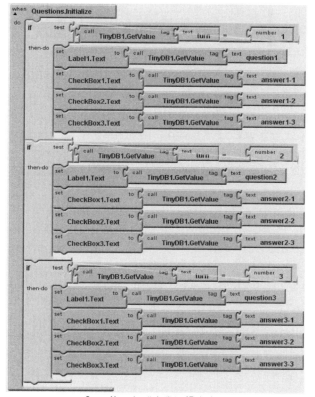

Source: Massachusetts Institute of Technology.

FIGURE 6.23

Multiple decisions to change results based on three different conditions.

Now that you have the text labels taken care of, you need to get the checkboxes to actually work! Here is where the App Inventor hits a little snag. Typically in programming, different types of buttons are used for different things. Aside from the normal buttons, like the one you used to move from Screen1 to Questions, there are radio buttons and checkboxes. In normal programming, radio buttons are used when you want to select one item from a list, such as the type of crust for a pizza (it can't be thin crust *and* deep dish; it has to be one or the other). In contrast, checkboxes are for selecting multiple items, such as the toppings to put on a pizza (see Figure 6.24).

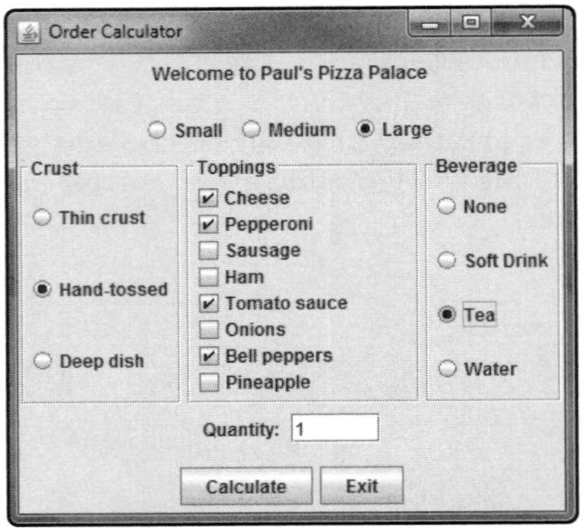

FIGURE 6.24

Radio buttons and
checkboxes used
for selecting pizza
choices.

Unfortunately, App Inventor does not yet have radio buttons, so what you will have to do is
use the checkboxes and code them to behave like radio buttons. This takes some doing, but
isn't too difficult. To get started, follow these steps:

1. In the My Blocks tab, click CheckBox1, and drag a `CheckBox1.Changed` block to the
   workspace. This block will detect whether the checkbox is checked.
2. Next, you'll need a decision block. In the Built-In tab, click the Control menu, and drag
   an `if test then-do` block to the workspace. (Note that this is the same control block you
   used for `Questions.Initialize`.)
3. From the Math menu, drag a block with two empty sockets separated by an equals
   sign—again, the same as was used in `Questions.Initialize`—to the workspace and
   connect it to the `if test then-do` block's test socket.
4. In the first socket of the = block, place a `CheckBox1.Checked` block. (By now, you should
   know which menu to use to get this.) In the second socket, place a `true` block from the
   Logic menu.
5. The test is `if(CheckBox1.Checked = true)`. If it's true, you have to deactivate the other
   two checkboxes to make sure only one can be selected. To achieve this, drag over the
   `set CheckBox2.Enabled` and `CheckBox3.Enabled` blocks from the menus for each of the
   other checkboxes and set them to `false`.
6. You also want the player to be able to change his or her answer. If the buttons are disabled
   how will the player do that? To deal with this, you'll need another `if test then-do` block
   so that players can uncheck the selected checkbox and check another one. The
   second `if test then-do` block will be structured just like the first one, except the true/
   false condition will be reversed. That is, if `CheckBox1.Checked` is false, then the
   `CheckBox2.Enabled` and `CheckBox3.Enabled` are true. Add the blocks to make that happen.
   When you're finished, it should look like Figure 6.25.

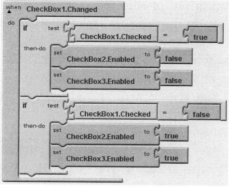

FIGURE 6.25

Using decisions to activate and deactivate checkboxes.

Source: Massachusetts Institute of Technology.

7. Repeat the preceding process for the other two checkboxes. Be careful to pay attention to the numbers; they can get confusing. When you're finished, you should have three block clusters that look like the setup in Figure 6.26.

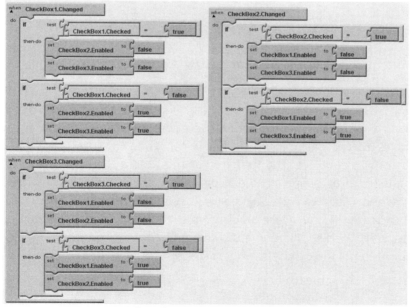

FIGURE 6.26

Applying the activation/ deactivation code to all three checkboxes.

Source: Massachusetts Institute of Technology.

As mentioned earlier, you will need to increment not only turn, but score. But score will be implemented only if the player gets the answer right. To handle this, it's time to revisit the

`Button1.Clicked` block cluster. The condition for this one will be a bit complicated because you have to call upon the database. You know the first correct answer is Action Comics, so you can go ahead and set half of the condition to a text block with the value of `Action Comics`. But what are you going to compare to Action Comics? You set the text of each button to a value from the database, and you know that the first answer, `answer1-1` in the database, is the correct answer. But that answer will be right only if the first checkbox is checked. How can you compare the text of each checkbox to `Action Comics`? Not only that, but depending on which turn it is, the three checkboxes may have completely unrelated values, in which case `Action Comics` may not be the value you want to check against. The easiest way will be to create a variable, similar to how you created `score` and `turn` on the first screen. Follow these steps:

1. Create a definition named `guess` and set the value to `text: none`.
2. From the My Definitions menu, add a `set global guess` block to your `Questions`. `Initialize` block below the last `if test then-do` block. Attach a `global guess` block from the same menu to the `set global` block. (See Figure 6.27.)

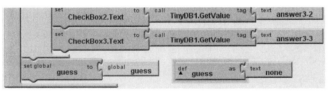

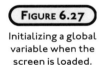

FIGURE 6.27

Initializing a global variable when the screen is loaded.

3. Now that you have a variable that can hold the guess, you need to get the guess from the checkboxes to the variable so that you can then get the guess from the variable to the button. To complete the first step of this, add a series of blocks to each `CheckBox.Changed` cluster already on your workspace. Find the `if test then-do` block for the first checkbox, where `CheckBox1.Checked = true`. Just below the `set CheckBox3.Enabled` to `false` group, place a `set global guess` block from the My Definitions menu. Find the `CheckBox1.Text` block in the `CheckBox1` menu, and add that to the guess block. Your `CheckBox1` block should now look like the one in Figure 6.28.

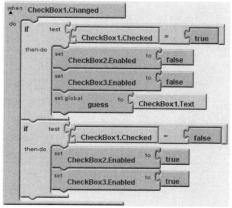

Source: Massachusetts Institute of Technology.

FIGURE 6.28

Updating the global variable when a checkbox is checked.

NOTE You may ask, why do I need a variable? Why can't I just compare the checkboxes directly to the answer when the button is clicked? The answer is twofold. First, the guess must change dynamically when the checkboxes are checked (in case the player changes an answer). Second, when the button is clicked, the app will change to a different screen, so it will be too late.

4. Repeat step 3 for the other two checkboxes. Take care that you use CheckBox2.Text and CheckBox3.Text for each one!

Now that you have the first part of the comparison done, there's another hiccup to deal with. Earlier, you set an if/else block to compare something to Action Comics. The problem is, the correct answer won't always be Action Comics; that's only if turn is set to 1. So you'll need to add if test then-do blocks to your button block to account for which turn it is. Follow these steps:

1. Temporarily drag everything out of the Button1.Click block. Put three if test then-do blocks in it. For each if test then-do block, there needs to be a test comparing the turn value from the TinyDB to 1, 2, or 3. At this point, your button block should look like the one in Figure 6.29.

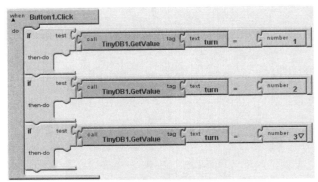

FIGURE 6.29

Checking which turn the player is on.

2. Now you need a second test for each turn. Drag three more if test then-do blocks to the workspace and place one inside each of the existing if test then-do blocks. The test for each of these blocks will be to check the value of guess to each of the correct answers. What you end up with is logic that flows like this (see Figure 6.30):

```
If turn = 1
        Check if guess = Action Comics
If turn = 2
        Check if guess = James Cameron
If turn = 3
        Check if guess = Grant Morrison
```

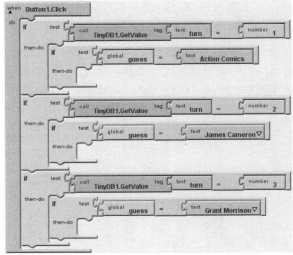

FIGURE 6.30

Nested decisions checking for a correct guess based on turn.

3. To complete this set of tests, you need to determine what will happen based on these decisions. If the answer is correct, you'll want to increment the score. Otherwise, you don't want to do anything. (There are a couple of other actions you want to perform, such as advancing to the next screen, but since these are not dependent on the rightness or wrongness of the answer they can go after the if blocks.) In each then-do socket, place a cluster of blocks to set the score variable in the TinyDB. This series of blocks will look just like the one you dragged out of the Button block, except the text blocks will refer to score instead of turn. When you're finished, your Button1.Click block should look like Figure 6.31 and your logic flow now looks like this. (Remember, you can copy and paste frequently reused blocks to save time.)

```
If turn = 1 and guess = Action Comics
        score = score + 1
If turn = 2 and guess = James Cameron
        score = score + 1
If turn = 3 and guess = Grant Morrison
        score = score + 1
```

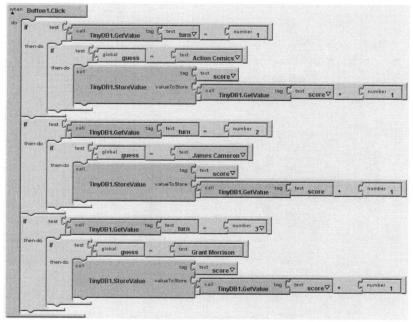

Source: Massachusetts Institute of Technology.

FIGURE 6.31

Updating the score when a correct answer is selected.

4. Now you can take that `StoreValue` block for turn that you dragged out earlier and put it back in the `Button.Click` block, below the very last `if test then-do` block. (The reason you had to take it out to begin with is that things have to be done in order. If you incremented `turn` before doing all those comparisons, they would all turn out wrong.)

5. There's one final step for this screen. When the player moves to the next screen, that screen will vary based on whether the answer was right or wrong. To do that, you need to pass that value when you initialize it. To begin, create one more `global` variable (from the Definition menu) and name it `correct`.

6. Assign the new variable a value of `false` and set it just as you did with `guess`. (Important: Make sure you use a logic `false` block, not a `text` block with the text changed to `false`.) Notice the color is different in Figure 6.32.

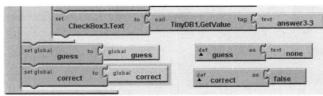

Source: Massachusetts Institute of Technology.

FIGURE 6.32

Creating another global variable.

7. In each of the `if test then-do` blocks in the `Button1.Click` cluster, add a line to set `correct` to `true` using blocks from My Definitions and Logic. (See Figure 6.33.) Now, if the answer is correct, then `correct` is set to `true`. Otherwise, it remains `false`.

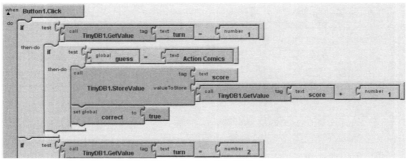

Source: Massachusetts Institute of Technology.

FIGURE 6.33

Adding an update to the correct variable when a correct answer is selected.

8. Add an `open another screen with start value` block from the Control menu. Add it at the bottom of the `Button1.Click` block. The `screenName` needs to be a `text` block with the value set to `Answers`. The `startValue` is the global variable `correct`. You are finished with this screen! See Figure 6.34 for what your `Button1.Click` block should look like.

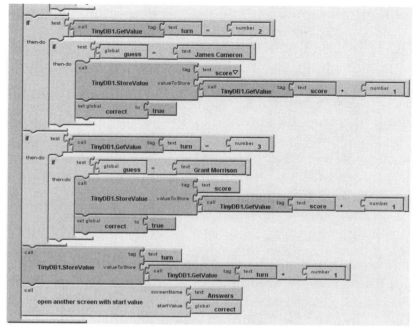

Source: Massachusetts Institute of Technology.

FIGURE 6.34

The rest of the
`Button1.Click`
block cluster
(continued from
Figure 6.33).

Adding Messages to the Answers Screen

Switch to the Answers screen. Compared to the Questions screen, this screen will be pretty basic. It has three simple functions:

- Tell the player whether his or her answer was right or wrong.
- Give the player a bit of trivia about the answer.
- Either return to the Questions screen to provide a new question or to the Victory screen, depending on what turn it is.

Follow these steps:

1. From the Answers menu in the My Blocks tab, drag `Answers.Initialize` to the workspace.
2. In the main browser window, make sure you have a TinyDB component below the screen as a non-visible component.
3. There are two pieces of information you need to set your text. You need the start value you sent forward from the last screen (`correct`) and the turn. The text you use will vary based on those choices. First, you'll need to handle the `turn` variable. You incremented `turn` at the end of the last screen, so `turn` should be 2. Drag three `if` blocks onto the workspace (see Figure 6.35) and the components necessary to make decisions for the following scenarios:

- If turn = 2
- If turn = 3
- If turn = 4

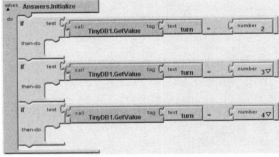

Source: Massachusetts Institute of Technology.

FIGURE 6.35

Determining which turn the player is on.

4. Inside each of the if blocks, you now need an if/else to check for the correct value. To each if/else block, add the = block as used earlier for turn. Then add for the first part of the condition a get start value block. (This can be difficult to find; it is in the Control menu, whereas one might think it should be in the Screen menu.) As you'll recall, you set up correct as a true/false, or Boolean variable, so it needs to be compared to true or false. In this case, compare it to true. (See Figure 6.36.)

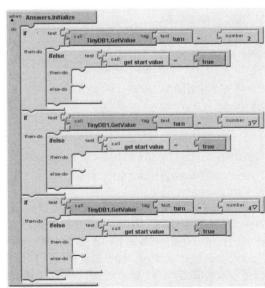

Source: Massachusetts Institute of Technology.

FIGURE 6.36

Checking the start value, which is the same as the "correct" value passed from the previous screen.

5. If the answer was correct, you'll want to set the first label to You're Right! or something similar. Otherwise, set it to WRONG!

6. For the second label, you'll set the text more specifically. If turn = 2 and the answer is correct, set the text to Superman debuted in Action Comics #1 in 1938.

7. If turn is 3 and answer is correct, set it to James Cameron wrote a script and was going to direct and produce Spider-Man.

8. If turn is 4 and the answer is correct, set it to The Queen bestowed the honor of Member of the British Empire to Grant Morrison.

9. If the answers are wrong, set it to Sorry! Try again next time. (See Figure 6.37.)

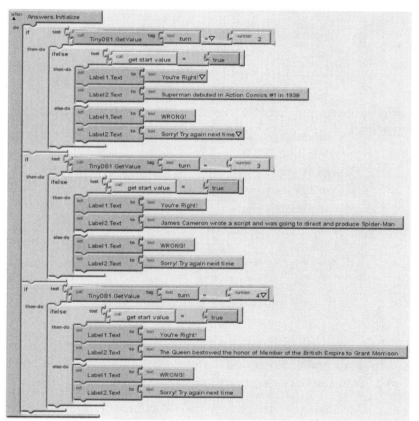

Source: Massachusetts Institute of Technology.

FIGURE 6.37

Completed decision trees for the Answers.Initialize block cluster.

10. The last thing you'll need to incorporate into this screen is what to do when the player clicks the Next button. If the game is over, he or she will move on to the final screen. Otherwise, the player will go back to the Questions screen. For this, add an if/else block inside the Button1.Click block.

11. The decision will be based on what turn it is, so you'll want to use the same `TinyDB1.GetValue(turn)` decision you used with the `if` blocks in the last section—but with one difference. Rather than comparing the equality of `turn` to 4, you'll need to check if `turn` is less than (<) 4. The player will arrive at this screen three times, and two of those times they'll be sent back. Add the blocks corresponding to this decision so that it matches Figure 6.38.

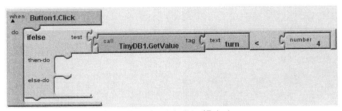

FIGURE 6.38

Checking the `turn` variable.

Source: Massachusetts Institute of Technology.

12. Finally, add the blocks to open a new screen: Questions if `turn` is less than 4, and Victory otherwise. (See Figure 6.39.)

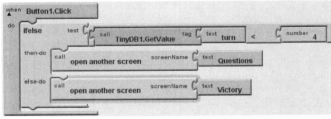

FIGURE 6.39

Opening different screens based on the number of turns.

Source: Massachusetts Institute of Technology.

Finishing the App

Now you have only one screen left: the Victory screen. Change to that screen and reload the Blocks Editor if you need to. Your task for this one is simple: Set the text of two labels and program the button to go back to the first screen. Follow these steps:

1. If there isn't one already, make sure there is a TinyDB component showing up as a non-visible component.
2. Place a `Victory.Initialize` block on the workspace.
3. Add a `set Label1 text` block in it and set that text to something like `Hooray!` or `Congrats!`.
4. Label2 doesn't need to be changed. Label3, however, needs to display the score and some additional text. To do that, you need to concatenate a sentence, meaning you need to

make one string of words out of two smaller strings of words. To do this, add a Label3.Text block and use a join block from the Text menu. In the first socket, put a TinyDB1.GetValue block and get the value for score. In the second socket, put a standard text block and change the text to out of 3. (Notice the space before the word "out." This is so that it prints out as "3 out of 3" rather than "3out of 3".) Your block should resemble the one in Figure 6.40.

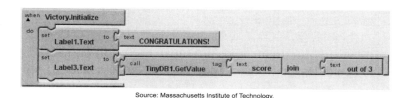

Source: Massachusetts Institute of Technology.

FIGURE 6.40

Setting the victory messages.

5. The very last thing to do now to complete your app is to program the button. Place a Button1.Click block on the workspace. Then add an open another screen block and set it to open Screen1. (See Figure 6.41.) When the app goes back to Screen1, all the values will be reinitialized and the quiz will be restarted.

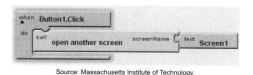

Source: Massachusetts Institute of Technology.

FIGURE 6.41

Setting the behavior of the try again button.

You're finished! All that is left to do is to download the APK file and install it on your phone to test it out.

SUMMARY

There are two important points to take away from this chapter. The first is the power of a database. Many of the most popular websites in the world—Google, Amazon, eBay, and even Facebook—simply would not be possible without massive databases used to store and retrieve information. To be able to use that power on a smaller scale is a convenience to be taken advantage of. To create an app like this one without a database would require a different screen for every set of question and answers. With this app, you could increase the length of the quiz to 10, 20, or even 100 questions and still have only four screens. But if you didn't have access to a database, you would need 10, 20, or 100 screens! That is a lot of work saved!

The other thing to take away from this chapter is that sometimes things won't work quite the way you want them to. In this case, radio buttons would be a much better option for the multiple-choice answers, but you don't have access to them. So you have to find a workaround. Sometimes having to find a workaround for a problem results in better learning than having things go smoothly and easily.

Having completed this chapter, you should be comfortable using databases, checkboxes, and decisions to control the functions of buttons and screens.

THE JIGSAW PUZZLE

CHAPTER OBJECTIVES

- Image sprites
- Collision detection
- Sound effects
- Touch events

MORE FUN WITH IMAGE SPRITES

Who doesn't like jigsaw puzzles? As children, we play with them all the time, whether it be a 20-piece puzzle for a five year old or a 5,000-piece puzzle to challenge us as we're older, millions of people have gotten billions of hours of fun from putting together puzzles. Some folks even put clear epoxy resins on them and frame them like portraits!

As a testament to the popularity of the jigsaw puzzle, there are literally thousands of apps available to play with puzzles on your mobile device. (No exaggeration! Check out play.google.com/store/search?q=jigsaw+puzzle&c=apps.) This chapter will teach you how to implement a jigsaw puzzle–type game.

THE DESIGN PHASE

This app won't take up much real estate, as you won't be tracking a score or marking how many turns have passed. It requires only two screens: a welcome screen, and a screen on which the game will be played.

Create the App

To create the app, follow these steps:

1. Create a new project in the App Inventor and name it MyPuzzle.
2. When the site advances to the first screen (Screen1), change the AlignHorizontal property to Center and the BackgroundColor property to dark gray.
3. Add a second screen and call it Puzzle.
4. When the Puzzle screen loads, change the AlignHorizontal and BackgroundColor settings to the same values as Screen1.

Add Components

With your screens created, it is time to add the components.

Add Screen1 Components

Follow these steps for Screen1:

1. Drag a VerticalArrangement component to the screen. Change the AlignHorizontal property to Center and change the Width and Height settings to Fill Parent.
2. Inside the VerticalArrangement component, add an Image component, and set its Picture property to title.png, uploading the title.png file included with this book.

 You might think it would be easier and look better to set a background image via the BackgroundImage property in the Properties panel, and you'd be right, but this property is buggy at the time of this writing. In addition, using the AlignVertical and/or AlignHorizontal settings can prevent the background image from showing properly on some devices. It appears in line with the other components rather than behind them like a true background.

3. Add a Button component to the VerticalArrangement component, placing it below the title image.
4. In the Button component's Properties panel, change the BackgroundColor setting to orange and the TextColor setting to blue. Select the FontBold checkbox, change the FontSize setting to 30, and change the Shape setting to Rounded.

5. Add a Label component below the Button component. Change the Label component's FontSize setting to 18, its TextColor setting to orange, and its TextAlignment setting to Center. Select the FontBold checkbox, change the BackgroundColor setting to blue, and change the Width setting to 200 pixels. In the Text field, type the instructions: Move the pieces around to form the picture.

6. Add two more Label components. Place the first one between the image and the button, and place the second one between the button and the label containing the instructions. Remove the text from both of these labels. You don't want to actually see these labels; they're just there to act as spacers between the other components. See Figure 7.1.

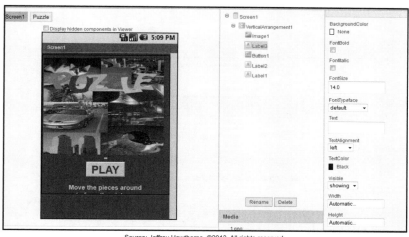

FIGURE 7.1

Screen I with all the components added.

Add Puzzle Screen Components

The layout of components for the Puzzle screen will be very similar to the design of the Whack-a-Mole app you built in Chapter 4, "Whack-a-Mole." In this chapter, you'll revisit canvases, image sprites, and using the Z coordinate to place them in front of one another. Follow these steps:

1. Drag a Canvas component to the Puzzle screen. Change its Width setting to Fill Parent. Change the Height setting to 400 pixels and the BackgroundColor setting to none.

2. In the Palette, click the Animation section, and drag an ImageSprite component to the canvas. Set its Picture property to frame.png (included with this book). Set the X coordinate to 5 and the Y coordinate to 75. (See Figure 7.2.) This frame will show the player where to put the puzzle pieces to complete the puzzle. To avoid confusion later in the development of this app, change the name of ImageSprite1 to ImageSprite13 (see Figure 7.3).

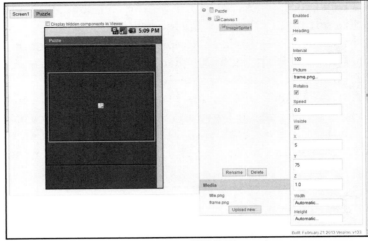

FIGURE 7.2

The Frame image centered within the Canvas component.

FIGURE 7.3

Changing the name of ImageSprite1 to ImageSprite13.

3. Add six more ImageSprite components to the screen. Each of these represents one puzzle piece. For now, place them outside the frame so you don't have any issues selecting them. Set the Z coordinate for each of these ImageSprite components to 2.0. This ensures that each piece will remain above the frame. In the Component panel, renumber these sprites so they read ImageSprite1, ImageSprite2, ImageSprite3, ImageSprite4, ImageSprite5, and ImageSprite6.

4. For ImageSprite components 1–6, attach the correspondingly numbered PNG file included with this chapter via the Picture property. (ImageSprite1 = 1.png, ImageSprite2 = 2.png, and so forth.) Your screen should now look like the one in Figure 7.4. Don't worry about the placement of the images for now; you'll be moving them around shortly, and will use code to move them to their starting positions when the screen is initialized anyway.

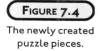

FIGURE 7.4

The newly created
puzzle pieces.

5. Add six more ImageSprite components (7–12). These will be placed at specific coordinates. Change their names to ImageSprite7, ImageSprite8, and so on, through ImageSprite12. Use the following coordinates to set ImageSprite7–ImageSprite12:

- ImageSprite7
  - X = 8
  - Y = 77
  - Z = 3
- ImageSprite8
  - X = 108
  - Y = 77
  - Z = 3
- ImageSprite9
  - X = 208
  - Y = 77
  - Z = 3
- ImageSprite10
  - X = 8
  - Y = 177
  - Z = 3

- ImageSprite11
  - X = 108
  - Y = 177
  - Z = 3
- ImageSprite12
  - X = 208
  - Y = 177
  - Z = 3

6. Place ImageSprite components 1–6 at these positions as well. (Except for the Z coordinates! Don't change those.) You can see how the corners line up, as in Figure 7.5. Make note of these coordinates; you'll be using them again later.

FIGURE 7.5

Image sprites all lined up. The small green squares are the sprites without pictures attached.

7. After you visually confirm that the sprites are where you want them to be, change the Z coordinate of ImageSprite components 7–12 to 1. (Strictly speaking, you don't *have* to do this, but if the empty sprites are on top of the ones with pictures attached, it could make it hard for the player to drag them around when trying to place the pieces.)
8. Place a Button component below the canvas. In the Button component's Text field, type Play Again. Change its BackgroundColor setting to blue, select the FontBold checkbox, change the FontSize setting to 20, change the Shape setting to Rounded, and change the TextColor setting to pink.

9. In the Palette, click the Media section, and drag a Sound component to the screen. This will be a non-visible component, just like the Clock and TinyDB components you used before (see Figure 7.6). Click the Source field in the Sound component's Properties panel and upload the Click.mp3 file included with this book.

FIGURE 7.6

Sound component, listed as a non-visible component.

That's it for the components! Now it's time for you to move to the coding stage.

THE CODE PHASE

The bulk of the coding for this app will revolve around touch events. Touching, dragging, releasing—these are the things that will govern the behavior of the puzzle. But first, you need to code the welcome screen.

Code Screen 1

To code the welcome screen, follow these steps:

1. Switch to Screen1. The only component you need to code on this screen is the button to move to the Puzzle screen.
2. Open the Blocks Editor.
3. Click the My Blocks tab, click Button1, and drag a `when Button1.Click` block to the workspace.
4. Click the Built-In tab, click Control, and drag a `call open another screen` block to the workspace.
5. From the Text menu, drag a `text` block to the workspace. Change the value of the `text` block to `Puzzle`; then assemble the blocks as shown in Figure 7.7. That's all you need for this screen!

Code the Puzzle Screen

This game requires a bit more preparation than some of the others you've done, due to the number of elements you're dealing with. In Chapter 4, you had only one ImageSprite component you had to move around. This time, you have six. Not only that, but those six have to interact with another six. Plus, you want to scatter the pieces when the game loads, so each piece needs to have random numbers attached to the X and Y coordinates.

Scatter the Pieces

To begin coding all this, follow these steps:

1. In App Builder, click the Puzzle button to switch to the Puzzle screen.
2. In the Blocks Editor, click the My Blocks tab, click Puzzle, and drag a `when Puzzle.Initialize` block to the workspace.
3. In the My Blocks tab, click ImageSprite1, and drag a `call ImageSprite1.MoveTo` block to the `when Puzzle.Initialize` block.
4. Click the Built-In tab, click Math, and drag a `call random integer` block to both the `x` socket and the `y` socket of the `call ImageSprite1.MoveTo` block. These should come with `number` blocks already attached. If not, add a `number` block from the Math menu to the `from` and `to` sockets of each `call random integer` block. For the X coordinate, set the range from 1 to 250, and for the Y coordinate, set the range from 1 to 350. Your initialize block should resemble Figure 7.8.

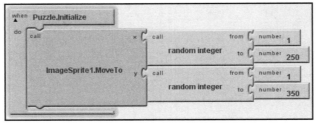

5. Repeat steps 3 and 4 for ImageSprite2 through ImageSprite6. Now you can test your app on a device. When you load the Puzzle screen, the pieces should be scattered around the board.

Code the Pieces' Movement

An important aspect to a puzzle game is the ability to move the pieces. In App Inventor, this is more complex than you might think. Image sprites have a tendency to "stick" to one another. That is to say, if you move a sprite over another sprite, the first sprite will collect the second one so that it appears the second one has vanished. In truth, it is behind the first one. In a puzzle game, this can be a huge problem, as you can end up with only one piece! To prevent this from happening, you can set a variable called `activeSprite` and code your app in such a way that only the `activeSprite` can be moved. This is a necessary step to prevent the sprites from eating each other. Follow these steps:

1. Click the Built-In tab, click Definition, and drag a `def variable` block to the workspace. Rename it `activeSprite`.
2. In the Built-In tab, click Math, and drag a `number` block to the `as` slot of the `def activeSprite` block and change its value to 0. If the value is 0, no sprites are active (see Figure 7.9).

Source: Jeffrey Hawthorne. ©2013. All rights reserved.

FIGURE 7.9

Creating the `activeSprite` `global` variable.

3. Each sprite has three touch events associated with it: `TouchDown`, `TouchUp`, and `Dragged`. `TouchDown` is when the user touches the sprite without letting go. `TouchUp` is when the user releases a sprite, or stops touching it. `Dragged` is exactly what it sounds like. In the My Blocks tab, from the ImageSprite1 menu, drag one of each of these blocks to the editor: `when ImageSprite1.TouchDown`, `when ImageSprite1.TouchUp`, and `when ImageSprite1.Dragged`. Each of these blocks comes with named x and named y blocks attached to them. Leave them as they are. They are used internally to track position and require no adjustment from you.
4. First, let's deal with the `when ImageSprite1.TouchDown` block. Click the My Definitions menu and drag a `set global activeSprite` block to the `when ImageSprite1.TouchDown` block's `do` slot. Then attach a `number` block to the `set global activeSprite` block's `to` socket and change the number to 1. Now, when ImageSprite1 is touched, the `activeSprite` variable is set to 1. See Figure 7.10.

FIGURE 7.10

Setting
ImageSprite 1 to
the active sprite
when touched.

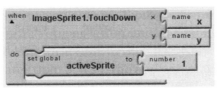

Source: Jeffrey Hawthorne. ©2013. All rights reserved.

5. Set the when ImageSprite1.TouchUp block exactly the same way you did the when ImageSprite1.TouchDown block, only set the activeSprite number to 0. This effectively deactivates the sprite when you let go of it. (See Figure 7.11.)

 FIGURE 7.11

Setting the active
sprite to 0 when
the ImageSprite is
released.

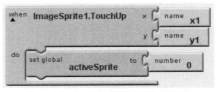

Source: Jeffrey Hawthorne. ©2013. All rights reserved.

6. You'll need a condition to tell the Dragged block that it is the active sprite. Add an if then-do block from the Control menu under the Built-In tab and attach to the test socket an = connector block from the Math menu, where the first socket contains a global activeSprite block (from the My Definitions menu under the My Blocks tab) and the second socket contains a number block from the Math menu back in the Built-In tab set to 1.

7. In the then-do slot, add a call ImageSprite1.MoveTo block. Set the x socket to currentX - 50 and the y socket to currentY - 50 (see Figure 7.12). These blocks (value currentX and value currentY) can be found under My Definitions. They are global variables created when you bring in the parent blocks. Why minus 50? Because the X and Y coordinate represent the upper-left corner of the object. When you touch an image, generally you'll touch it in the middle. Because our images are 100 pixels square, the -50 keeps unwanted movement to a minimum.

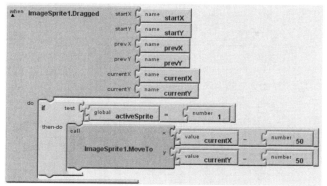

NOTE Regarding the MoveTo blocks: The value currentX and value currentY blocks used *must* match the ones listed in the parent Dragged block. For example, if in the Dragged block it has currentX4 and currentY4, then the connected MoveTo block must also have currentX4 and currentY4.

8. Repeat steps 3–7 for ImageSprite2 through ImageSprite6. See Figure 7.13 through Figure 7.17 for the associated code blocks.

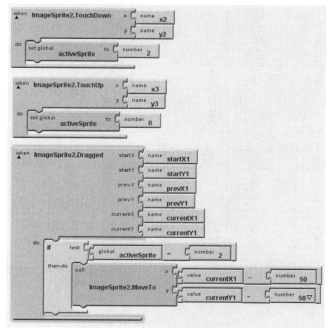

FIGURE 7.12

Making a sprite only moveable when it is the active sprite.

FIGURE 7.13

Touch events for ImageSprite2.

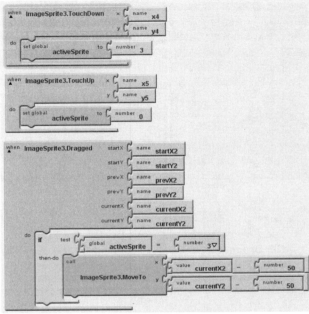

FIGURE 7.14

Touch events for
ImageSprite3.

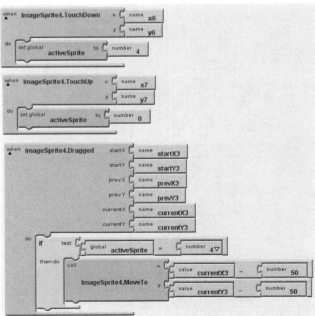

FIGURE 7.15

Touch events for
ImageSprite4.

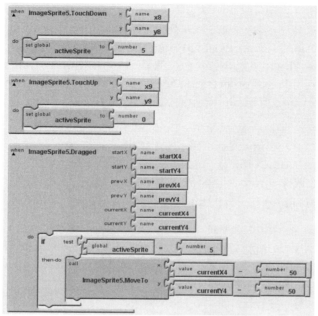

FIGURE 7.16

Touch events for
ImageSprite5.

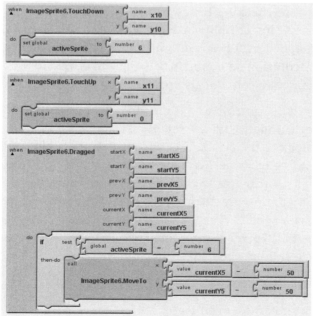

FIGURE 7.17

Touch events for
ImageSprite6.

Code Collision Detection

Now that you have the movement down, you can focus on coding the collision detection. What exactly is collision detection? It sounds obvious: detecting whether two objects collide, like football players on a field. The only problem with that definition is that we're talking about computers. There are no physical objects on the screen to collide, only images. So how do you determine collision between virtual objects? You check the X and Y coordinates.

Remember, computers are essentially very complicated calculators. Everything they do, they do mathematically. Collision detection is no different. Math functions govern the collision status of two objects. Every pixel of an image has an X and Y coordinate. The computer has to keep track of these as the pixel is moved around. If any of these pixels (X_a, Y_a) overlap a pixel of another object or a boundary (X_b, Y_b), then they have collided.

Puzzles work slightly differently. You don't want to prevent the images from overlapping; you want to determine if they overlap precisely—if they are in the same position or close enough to the same position to warrant locking a piece into position. To do that, you need to check only one pixel from each object, not all the pixels. It makes for an elaborate formula, but requires a lot less processing.

You may notice that the ImageSprite components have a number of methods and properties related to collision, such as `CollideWith`. You will not be using these, as they relate to the first version of collision, where you are checking to see if two objects are touching. This would create some awkward actions if the lower-right corner of a piece collided with the associated placeholder sprite and then snapped into position, putting the upper-left corner where the lower-right corner was. Instead, collision detection in this app will be tied to the `TouchUp` event, or when you release control of an image. It will also require a pretty elaborate test condition.

1. Click the Built-In tab, click Control, and drag an `if then-do` block to the `when ImageSprite1.TouchUp` block, underneath the `set global activeSprite` block. Then, click Logic and attach an `and` block to the `test` socket of the `if then-do` block.
2. You'll want to test for a range of values. You already know that you're comparing the ImageSprite1 component's coordinates to the ImageSprite7 component's coordinates, but the chances of them matching exactly are very slim—which would make the game very frustrating. Instead, you need to create a range of values—say, ImageSprite7 X plus or minus 10. That gives you a 20-pixel margin for error. So how do you create a range of values? If a number has to fall between two other numbers, then it has to be greater than the lower number but less than the upper number:
   `Number 1 < ImageSprite1.X < Number 2.`
   To achieve this, click Math and drag a `<` connector to the first `test` socket of the and block. The first half of this condition should be `ImageSprite1.X`. (See Figure 7.18.)

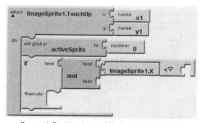

FIGURE 7.18

Beginning of the collision test for ImageSprite1.

3. Drag a + connector from the Math menu to the workspace. In the first socket of the comparison, place an `ImageSprite7.X` block. In the second socket, place a `number` block, and set it to 10. (See Figure 7.19.)

FIGURE 7.19

The first half of a range of values for ImageSprite7, to be used when checking the position of ImageSprite1.

4. Connect that group of blocks to the second socket of the condition from Figure 7.18, so that it now looks like Figure 7.20.

FIGURE 7.20

The comparison for the upper end of the value range.

5. Repeat this process three more times. For the first of these, use the following:
   `ImageSprite1.X > ImageSprite7.X - 10`
   For the next two, repeat the previous two comparisons (you can copy/paste the entire block clusters) but replace `ImageSprite1.X` and `ImageSprite7.X` with `ImageSprite1.Y` and `ImageSprite7.Y`. When all four conditions are complete, your block cluster should look like Figure 7.21.

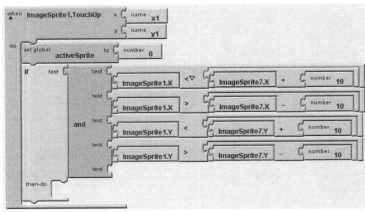

FIGURE 7.21

The completed collision range check for ImageSprite1 and ImageSprite7.

Code the Pieces' Behavior

Now that you have tested whether the puzzle piece is colliding with its placeholder, you can code the behavior of the piece. You want it to snap into position, and you want that snapping to be noticeable to the player. Follow these steps:

1. Drag a `call ImageSprite1.MoveTo` block (this is the same block you used in the `Dragged` blocks) and place it in the `then-do` slot.

2. In the x and y sockets, add `ImageSprite7.X` and `ImageSprite7.Y` blocks from the ImageSprite7 menu under the My Blocks tab. (See Figure 7.22.)

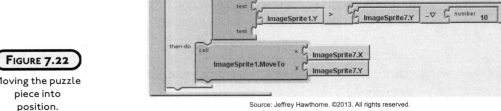

FIGURE 7.22

Moving the puzzle piece into position.

3. Click Sound1 and drag a `call Sound1.Play` block to the `then-do` slot just below the `ImageSprite1.MoveTo` block.

4. Below the `call Sound1.Play` block, add a `set ImageSprite1.Enabled` block, and set it to `false`. That way, if the condition is met, the puzzle piece will move to the fixed location, a click noise will play to confirm for the player that the piece has been placed, and the piece will become disabled, so that it can't accidentally be moved out of position. The complete `when ImageSprite1.TouchUp` cluster should look like Figure 7.23.

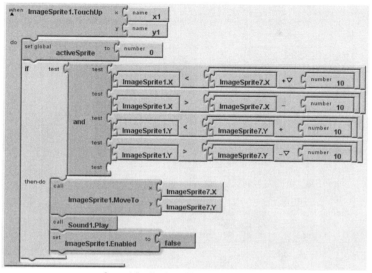

FIGURE 7.23

Locking the ImageSprite into place.

Code the Rest of the Pieces

Follow these steps to code the rest of the pieces:

1. Set up the rest of the TouchUp clusters. For ImageSprite2, match it up to ImageSprite8, as shown in Figure 7.24.

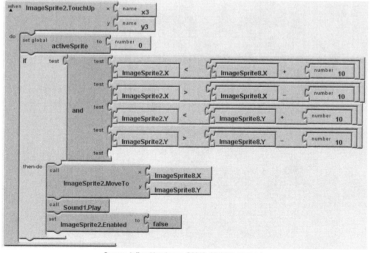

FIGURE 7.24

Collision detection and locking behavior for ImageSprite2.

2. For ImageSprite3, match it up to ImageSprite9, as shown in Figure 7.25.

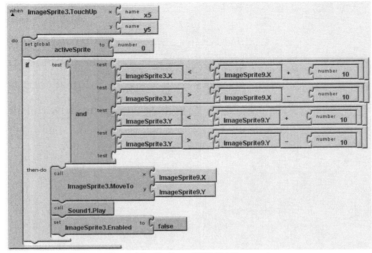

FIGURE 7.25

Collision detection and locking behavior for ImageSprite3.

3. For ImageSprite4, match it up to ImageSprite10, as shown in Figure 7.26.

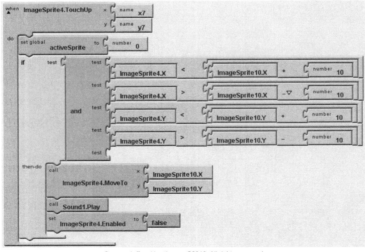

FIGURE 7.26

Collision detection and locking behavior for ImageSprite4.

4. For ImageSprite5, match it up to ImageSprite11, as shown in Figure 7.27.

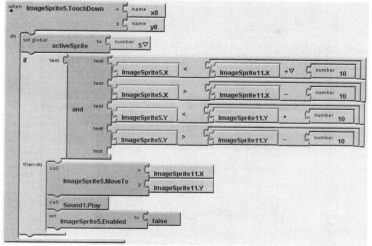

FIGURE 7.27

Collision detection and locking behavior for ImageSprite5.

5. For ImageSprite6, match it up to ImageSprite12, as shown in Figure 7.28.

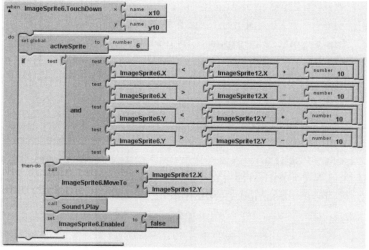

FIGURE 7.28

Collision detection and locking behavior for ImageSprite6.

Now you can test the puzzle if you so desire. (We're almost done, though—just a couple more steps to go.)

Code the Button

All that is left is to code the button. The button code itself is simple; it's just to open another screen. Figure 7.29 shows the code block for it, which is similar to button blocks you've done in other apps, as well as the one for the opening screen in this app.

At this point, however, you're going to do something a little different. You're going to use a procedure. What you'll do is, when the screen is loaded, the button to play the game again will be invisible. Then, when all the pieces have been placed, the button will appear and the player can play again.

So what is a procedure? Over the last few pages, you created a lot of functions that were more or less the same. Unfortunately, you couldn't use a procedure for those because there were significant variations between each cluster of blocks. They were unique for each ImageSprite component, because each ImageSprite component had a different comparison—ImageSprite1 compared to ImageSprite7, ImageSprite2 compared to ImageSprite8, and so on. But sometimes, you have a piece of code that you want to reuse that doesn't require variations. When that is the case, you can use a procedure. A procedure looks like other code block clusters, but when you want to actually *use* the code, you need only call the procedure, not all the bits of code attached to it. This is ideal when you want to use the same code over and over again.

In this app, the code that you want to use over and over again will check for a victory condition, which, in this case, will be if all of the pieces are in the right place. You could do this by checking all the X and Y coordinates again, but an easier way would be to check whether all the pieces have been disabled. Remember, in the TouchUp events, you set ImageSprite.Enabled to false, so this is an easy condition to check for every piece. Follow these steps:

1. Click the Built-In tab, click Definition, and drag a to procedure do block to the screen. (You just need a procedure block here; you don't need a procedureWithResult block, which is what you would use if you wanted to have a returned value. We don't need a returned value, just to do some stuff.) Notice that the to procedure do block has an arg socket, short for arguments. In programming terms, these arguments would be called

parameters. You could import all the `ImageSprite.Enabled` statuses as arguments, but this is unnecessary. It will work fine without it.

2. Change the name of the `to procedure do` block to `makeButton`.

3. Drag an `if then-do` block from the Control menu to the `to makeButton do` block's do slot. Attach an `and` block from the Logic menu to it.

4. Attach an `=` connector to the `and` block's test socket. Inside the first socket of the `=` connector, add an `ImageSprite1.Enabled` block. In the other socket, place a `false` Logic block. Your block cluster should resemble Figure 7.30, and should look a little bit like all those `TouchUp` blocks.

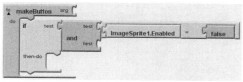

FIGURE 7.30

Creating a procedure.

5. Repeat step 4 for the other five ImageSprite components (2 through 6) so you have six tests, as shown in Figure 7.31.

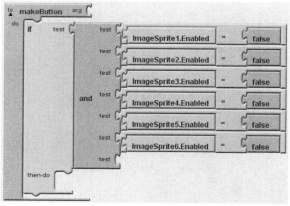

FIGURE 7.31

Checking to see if all of the puzzle pieces have been locked into place.

6. Now that you have the test conditions set, plug in the tasks to be performed. There are two tasks. First, set the `set Button1.Enabled` block to `true`. Second, set the `set Button1.Visible` block to `true` (see Figure 7.32). Both `Button1` blocks are found in the Button1 menu under the My Blocks tab. The `true` blocks can be found in the Logic menu under the Built-In tab.

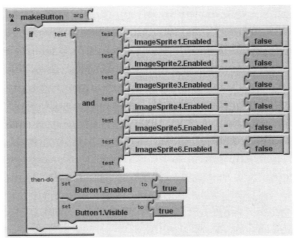

FIGURE 7.32

Enabling the button when the puzzle is complete.

7. Your button is both visible and enabled by default when you create it. That means you need to disable and turn it invisible when you initialize the screen. To do this, copy your `set Button1.Enabled` and `set Button1.Visible` blocks to the `Puzzle.Initialize` block, placing them at the bottom of the list, under all the `call ImageSprite.MoveTo` blocks. Set both of these to `false` (see Figure 7.33).

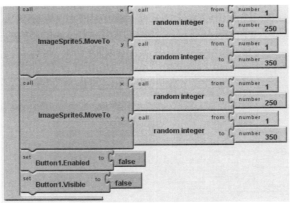

FIGURE 7.33

Disabling the button when the screen is initialized.

8. Now you have to actually *call* the procedure. Right now, it's just kind of floating around in space, doing its own thing, oblivious to the world around it. To connect it to the rest of the world, click My Definitions. There, you'll find a new, purplish block named `call makeButton`. Attach this block to each of your `ImageSprite.TouchUp` blocks, underneath the `set ImageSprite.Enabled to false` blocks (see Figure 7.34).

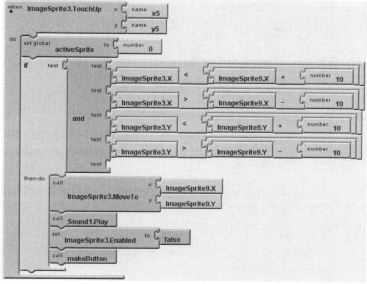

FIGURE 7.34

Calling a procedure.

NOTE It's very important that the procedure be the last thing called in each `TouchUp` block. If you were to call the procedure before the `ImageSprite.Enabled` block is set, then the condition will never be true and your button will stay invisible!

Your puzzle is finished! Procedures can be very useful, especially as your apps become more and more complex. Download your app and test it out on your device.

SUMMARY

In this chapter, you learned not only how to manipulate image sprites, but also how to make sure only one image sprite is manipulated at a time so they don't act as vacuum cleaners when they interact with other sprites. You also learned how to use procedures, which can result in using a lot less duplicated code. This chapter also covered how to create the illusion of two objects colliding, and how to translate that collision into an action such as locking a puzzle piece into place. You know how to tie sound to an action, making it more dynamic and responsive, and how to hide components until they are needed.

PHYSICS-BASED ANIMATION: BRICK BREAKER

CHAPTER OBJECTIVES

- Control object locations using X and Y coordinates
- Control object motion using speed, headings, and intervals
- Program collision behaviors
- Use timers to control app events

INTRODUCTION

With the increase of mobile devices, the gaming industry has made huge shifts to the mobile market from console- and computer-based games. Nowadays, cell-phone and tablet-based games not only compete with console games in terms of complexity, quality, and entertainment, but provide the benefit of being available in the user's pocket at any time. Because of this, games such as *Angry Birds*, *Temple Run*, and *Whale Trail* have gained immense publicity.

What all these games have in common is their interactivity, ease of use, and visual appeal. While the visual appeal depends mostly on the graphics used in the game, much of the games' ease of use and interactivity depend on how the game reacts to the user's inputs—primarily touch-based input. For this reason, much of the quality of a game relies on how realistic and smooth the game effects are—which, for the most part, are physics based. While this book does not delve deep into the physics of game design, this chapter does provide physics formulas to control certain objects' motion. For you to make a visually appealing game, we will provide graphics and content for you to place in the game. If you prefer, you can create your own graphics content.

The game you will be developing is a common game that has been found on mobile devices since the invention of the flip phone: *Brick Breaker*. In *Brick Breaker*, users take control of a paddle that can bounce a ball into the game and break virtual bricks. The angle of the ball's collision with the paddle determines the ball's final trajectory, enabling the player to control where the ball moves. As the game progresses, the ball moves more quickly, making it difficult to control. If the player missed the ball, he or she loses.

APPLICATION DISCUSSION

Brick Breaker has a very basic screen at the component level, consisting of a timer to show the user how much time is left; indicator lights to show how many lives are left; a large canvas, which will contain the actual game play; and buttons to control the game at the bottom.

Within the canvas, there will be three types of objects, represented by image sprites:

- **The bar.** The bar appears along the bottom of the screen. The player can control the bar to bounce the ball in the game area. It hovers at the bottom of the canvas and moves horizontally along the X axis. When the ball hits the bar, the ball is deflected back.

- **The ball.** The ball, represented by a ball animation, is the primary object within the game. The ball will be completely controlled by its interactions with other objects, such as the edge of the screen, the bar, and the bricks. To make the game more challenging, the ball will move more and more quickly with time. Whenever the ball collides with another object, it will be deflected in the opposite direction.

- **The bricks.** The simplest objects in the game, the bricks simply sit at the top of the canvas. If hit by the ball, however, they will break and disappear.

The focus of this application lies in the ball's motion and its reaction to collisions with other objects. For example, when the ball hits the bar, it should bounce back, as it would in real life. The same principal holds true when the ball hits other objects, such as the bricks or the wall. To make these motion changes realistic, you must understand how App Inventor—as well as most programming environments—deals with moving objects: through headings and coordinates.

As with any program, App Inventor apps rely on coordinate points to position objects and render or paint them to the screen for the user to interact with. Together, these coordinates—expressed as an X,Y pair—tell the device where to paint the object on the screen. You can therefore use these coordinates to precisely control how your programmed objects interact within the environment of your app.

App Inventor extends this positioning ability by also giving each object a heading and a speed. In App Inventor, an object's heading refers to its angle or trajectory (in degrees), relative to the screen. For example, an object with a heading of 90 would move to the top of the screen, while and object with a heading of 220 would move toward the bottom-left corner of the screen.

While the heading tells the program the angle of the object's motion, the speed relies on a few other factors—namely the Speed and Interval attributes. The Speed attribute describes how far, in pixels, the object will travel in the designated interval. The interval, therefore, determines how often the screen must re-render the object, therefore updating its location. Note that it is not always best to re-render the object as quickly as possible. Every time you update the object's location, the screen has to refresh—which involves a very long calculation for the device. In addition, there are limitations to how quickly the human eye can see motion. Updating 80 times per second may not look any different to the player from updating 20 times per second, but it will slow down the device's processor and possibly cause your app to crash.

THE DESIGN PHASE

You will begin the creation of the *Brick Breaker* app by uploading the media that you will use and creating the visual components of the app. Follow these steps:

1. Create a new project in the App Inventor Web interface. Name it Brick_Breaker. Note that you will use only a single screen, Screen1, for this app.
2. From the Media tab, upload each of the image files included for this project. They can be obtained from the textbook website at www.cengage.com/download. Your Media tab will look like the one in Figure 8.1.

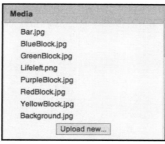

FIGURE 8.1

The Media tab with all uploads.

3. Select Screen1. To create the screen's background, click the BackgroundImage option in the Properties tab and select the Background.jpg file you uploaded. Change the BackgroundColor setting to None.

4. In the Palette, click Basic, and drag a Label component to the top of the screen. In the Label component's Properties tab, change the Width property to Fill Parent and the TextColor property to white. This label will serve as the clock, so rename it clockLabel.

5. In the Palette, click Screen Arrangement, and drag a HorizontalArrangement component to beneath the Label component. In the Properties panel, change the Width property to Fill Parent.

6. In the Palette, click Basic, and drag a Label component into the HorizontalArrangement component. In the Properties panel, change the TextColor setting to white. In the Text field, type `Balls Remaining:`.

7. From the Basic menu in the Palette, drag three Image components into the HorizontalArrangement canvas, to the right of the label. Name them life1, life2, and life3, and set their images to the uploaded LifeLeft.png file.

8. In the Palette, click Basic, and drag a Canvas component underneath the life images. Change the Width setting to Fill Parent, the BackgroundColor setting to None, and the Height setting to 300 pixels.

 The final height may be different depending on your device. Choose a number that fills most of the screen but leaves room for buttons you will place underneath.

9. In the Palette, click Screen Arrangement, and drag another HorizontalArrangement component underneath the Canvas component. Change its Width setting to Fill Parent and its AlignHorizontal setting to Center.

10. In the Palette, click Buttons, and drag three Button components into the HorizontalArrangement component. In the Text field for each button, type `Left`, `Start`, and `Right`, respectively. Rename them leftButton, startButton, and rightButton. Your Screen1 should look like the one in Figure 8.2.

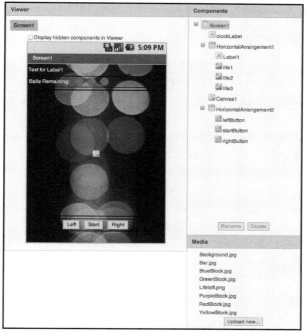

FIGURE 8.2

Adding the Button componenets.

You will now fill the canvas with the bar, bricks, and ball. You will first insert the bricks using image sprites. Unfortunately, you will have to enter them individually. Each brick measures 60 pixels wide by 10 pixels tall. Because you do not want the bricks to touch, you should keep a distance of at least 10 pixels between them. That means for a row of bricks, your X values should be 10, 80, 150, and 220. Your Y values should stay the same for each row, starting at 0 but incrementing by 20 for each new row. Use Figure 8.3 as a guide if you get lost. Follow these steps:

1. In the Palette, click Animation, and drag an ImageSprite component in approximately the correct location of the canvas. Do not worry about changing the name.
2. In the Properties panel, change the ImageSprite component's Picture property to BlueBlock.jpg image.
3. Deselect the Rotates checkbox.
4. Set the X and Y coordinates to 10,0.
5. Repeat steps 1–4 to add three more blue bricks. Set the X and Y coordinates to 80,0, 150,0, and 220,0.
6. Beneath the top row, repeat steps 1–5 to create a new row of bricks. This time, the bricks should be yellow (YellowBlock.jpg). Set the X and Y coordinates to 10,20, 80,20, 150,20, and 220,20.

7. For the third row, you will include a brick that moves from side to side. To do this, repeat steps 1–4, this time using the RedBlock.jpg image and setting the X and Y coordinates to 115,40.

8. Rename this ImageSprite component movingSprite.

9. Beneath the third, repeat steps 1–5 to create a new row of bricks. This time, the bricks should be purple (PurpleBlock.jpg). Set the X and Y coordinates to 10,60, 80,60, 150,60, and 220,60.

10. Drag an ImageSprite component near the bottom of the canvas. Change its Picture setting to Bar.jpg. Set the X and Y coordinates to 100,250. (This number may be different depending on the size of your canvas.) Deselect the Rotates box. Rename this sprite bar.

11. From the Animation menu in the Palette, drag a Ball component into the scene, just above the center of the bar. Change its PaintColor setting to white and its radius to 7. Your screen should look like the one in Figure 8.3.

12. From the Basic palette, drag a Clock component to the screen.

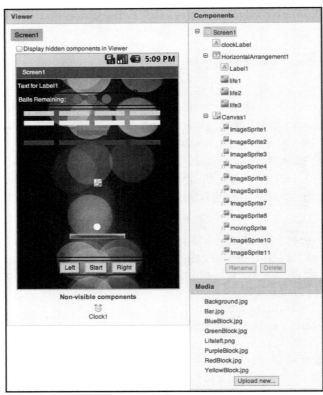

FIGURE 8.3

The completed visual screen.

THE CODE PHASE

You have now completed the screen design of the *Brick Breaker* app. In this section, you'll learn how to program its functionality.

Create Definitions

You have now completed the visual design process and will work in the Blocks Editor. Open it now. You will create two definitions to hold data throughout the game. To do this, follow these steps:

1. Click the Built-In tab, click Definition, and drag three `def variable` blocks to the screen.
2. Click in each `def variable` block and rename them by typing `livesLeft`, `bricksLeft`, and `timeRemaining`, respectively.
3. Click the Built-In tab, click Math, and drag a `Number` block to the `def livesLeft` block's as socket and change its value to 3.
4. Click the Built-In tab, click Math, and drag a `Number` block to the `def bricksLeft` block's as socket and change its value to 13.
5. Click the Built-In tab, click Math, and drag a `Number` block menu to the `def timeRemaining` block's as socket and change its value to 90. These definitions should look like the ones in Figure 8.4.

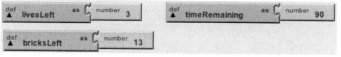

©Alexander Whiteside 2013, All Rights Reserved.

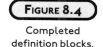

FIGURE 8.4

Completed definition blocks.

Create the Start Procedure

Before programming the app's functionality, you need to create a few helper procedures that you will use in the app—namely, procedures to handle a death, to handle a start, to update the time, and to handle when the ball collides with a brick. To create the procedure to handle a start, follow these steps:

1. Create the first helper function to start a new round. This procedure will be called at the start of every life. To begin, click the Built-In tab, click Definition, and drag a `to procedure do` block to the screen. Click in the block and type `start` to rename it.
2. When the `start` procedure is called, the timer should start. To make this happen, first click My Blocks tab, click Clock1, and drag a `set Clock1.TimerEnabled` block to the `to start do` block's do socket.

3. In the Built-In tab, click Logic, and drag a `true` block to the `to` slot of the `set Clock1.TimerEnabled` block.

4. Next, you must center the ball above the bar and start its motion. To do this, begin by clicking the My Blocks tab, clicking Ball1, and dragging the following blocks to the `do` slot of the `to start do` block: `set Ball1.X`, `set Ball1.Y`, `set Ball1.Speed`, `set Ball1.Interval`, and `set Ball1.Heading`.

5. Return to the App Inventor Web interface to obtain the ball's X and Y values. Then, in the Blocks Editor, attach these values to the `set Ball1.X` and `set Ball1.Y` blocks. To do so, click the Built-In tab, click Math, and drag a `Number` block to the `set Ball1.X` block and a second `Number` block to the `set Ball1.Y` block. Change the value of each `Number` block to match the X and Y values you found in the App Inventor Web interface.

6. Drag another `Number` block to the workspace and attach it to the `set Ball1.Speed` block. Change the `Number` block's value to 5.

7. Drag another `Number` block to the workspace and attach it to the `set Ball1.Interval` block. Change the `Number` block's value to 50.

8. Click the Built-In tab, click Math, and drag a `call random integer` block to the `set Ball1.Heading` block.

9. From the Built-In tab, click Math, and drag a `Number` block to the `from` socket of the `call random integer` block and a second `Number` block to the `to` socket of the `call random integer` block. Change the value of the first `Number` block to 70 and the second `Number` block to 110.

10. Just as you set the ball's X and Y coordinates to their original positions, set the bar back to its original X and Y coordinates. Click the My Blocks tab, click bar, and drag the following blocks to the `do` slot of the `to start do` block: `set bar.X` and `set bar.Y`.

11. Return to the App Inventor Web interface to obtain the bar's X and Y values. Then, in the Blocks Editor, attach these values to the `set bar.X` and `set bar.Y` blocks. To do so, click the Built-In tab, click Math, and drag a `Number` block to the `set bar.X` block and a second `Number` block to the `set bar.Y` block. Change the value of each `Number` block to match the X and Y values you found in the App Inventor Web interface.

12. Remove the start button. To do so, click the My Blocks tab, click startButton, and drag a `set startButton.Enabled` block to the `to start do` block. Then click the Logic menu and drag a `false` block to the `set startButton.Enabled` block. Your `start` procedure should look like the one in Figure 8.5.

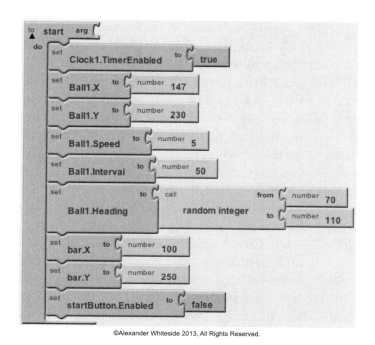

FIGURE 8.5

The completed
start procedure.

Create the Death Procedure

The death procedure will be called whenever the player loses a life. Follow these steps:

1. To create the new procedure, click the Built-In tab, click Definition, and drag a to procedure do block to the screen. Click in the block and type death to rename it.

2. When the death procedure is called, the timer should stop. To make this happen, click the My Blocks tab, click Clock1, and drag a set Clock1.TimerEnabled block to the do socket of the to death do block.

3. In the Built-In tab, click Logic, and drag a false block to the to slot of the set Clock1.TimerEnabled block.

4. You will now decrease the player's life using three if then-do statements. To begin, click the Built-In tab, Control, and drag an if then-do block to the do socket of the to death do block.

5. Click the Built-In tab, click Logic, and drag an = block to the test socket of the if then-do block.

6. Click the My Blocks tab, click My Definitions, and drag a global livesLeft block to the left side of the = block.

7. Repeat steps 4–6 two times to add two more if then-do blocks.

8. Click the Built-In tab, click Math, and drag a `Number` block to the remaining socket of the = block in the top `if then-do` block. Change its value to 1. This compares livesLeft to 1.

9. Click the My Blocks tab, click life1, and drag a `set life1.Visible` block to the `then-do` section of the topmost `if then-do` block. Then click the Logic menu and drag a `false` block to the `to` socket of the `set life1.Visible` block.

10. Because this is the player's last life, you'll need some way of indicating to the player that he or she has lost when the life ends. From the My Blocks tab, click clockLabel, and drag a `set clockLabel.Text` block below the `set life1.Visible` block. Then click the Text menu and drag a `text` block to the `to` socket of the `set clockLabel.Text` block. Change the `text` block's value to `You Lose`.

11. Now it's time to set up the middle `if then-do` block. Click the Built-In tab, click Math, and drag a `Number` block to the remaining socket of the = block in the middle `if then-do` block. Change its value to 2. This compares livesLeft to 2.

12. Click the My Blocks tab, click life2, and drag a `set life2.Visible` block to the `then-do` section of the middle `if then-do` block. Then click the Logic menu and drag a `false` block to the `to` socket of the `set life2.Visible` block.

13. Indicate how many lives are left (in this case, one). To do so, click the My Blocks tab, click My Definitions, and drag a `set global livesLeft` block to the `then-do` section of the middle `if then-do` block. Then click the Built-In tab, click Math, and drag a `Number` block to the `to` socket of the `set global livesLeft` block and change its value to 1.

14. Now it's time to set up the bottom `if then-do` block. Click the Built-In tab, click Math, and drag a `Number` block to the remaining socket of the = block in the bottom `if then-do` block. Change its value to 3. This compares livesLeft to 3.

15. Click the My Blocks tab, click life3, and drag a `set life3.Visible` block to the `then-do` section of the bottom `if then-do` block. Then click the Logic menu and drag a `false` block to the `to` socket of the `set life3.Visible` block.

16. Indicate how many lives are left (in this case, two). To do so, click the My Blocks tab, click My Definitions, and drag a `set global livesLeft` block to the `then-do` section of the bottom `if then-do` block. Then click the Built-In tab, click Math, and drag a `Number` block to the `to` socket of the `set global livesLeft` block and change its value to 2.

17. To re-enable the start button, click the My Blocks tab, click startButton, and drag a `set startButton.Enabled` block to the end of the procedure.

18. In the My Blocks tab, click Logic, and drag a `true` block to the `to` socket of the `set startButton.Enabled` block.

19. To reset the ball's location, click the My Blocks tab, click Ball1, and drag the following blocks to the end of the procedure: `set Ball1.X`, `set Ball1.Y`, and `set Ball1.Speed`.

20. Return to the App Inventor Web interface to obtain the bar's X and Y values. Then, in the Blocks Editor, attach these values to the `set Ball1.X` and `set Ball1.Y` blocks. To do

so, click the Built-In tab, click Math, and drag a Number block to the set Ball1.X block and a second Number block to the set Ball1.Y block. Change the value of each Number block to match the X and Y values you found in the App Inventor Web interface.

21. Click the Built-In tab, click Math and drag a Number block to the set Ball1.Speed block. Change its value to 0. Your procedure should now look like the one in Figure 8.6.

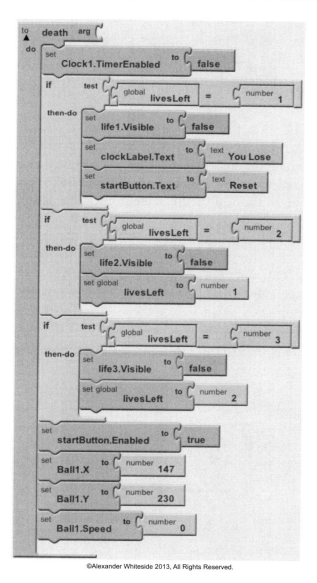

FIGURE 8.6

The completed death procedure.

Update the Time

The next procedure you will create will handle the updating of the time remaining at the top of the screen. This procedure will be called every time the clock timer reaches a new second. Follow these steps:

1. First, define a new procedure. Click the Built-In tab, click Definition, and drag a `to procedure do` block to the screen. Click it and type `updateTime` to rename it.
2. You will first update the `set global timeRemaining` variable by decreasing it by 1. To do this, click the My Blocks tab, click timeRemaining, and drag a `set global timeRemaining` block to the procedure.
3. Click the Built-In tab, click Math, and drag a `-` block to the `to` socket of the `set global timeRemaining` block.
4. Click the My Blocks tab, click My Definitions, and drag a `global timeRemaining` block to the left socket of the `-` block.
5. In the Built-In tab, click Math and drag a `Number` block to the right socket of the `-` block. Change its value to 1.
6. To update the visible timer at the top of the screen, click the My Blocks tab, click clockLabel, and drag a `set clockLabel.Text` block to the bottom of the procedure.
7. Click the Built-In tab, click Text, and drag a `join` block to the `to` socket of the `set clockLabel.Text` block.
8. Click the Built-In tab, click Text, and drag a `text` block to the left side of the `join` block. Click the `text` block and type `Time Remaining:` to rename it. (Be sure to include a space after the colon.)
9. Click the My Blocks tab, click My Definitions, and drag a `global timeRemaining` block to the right side of the `join` block. Your `to updateTime do` procedure should look like the one in Figure 8.7.

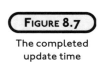

The completed update time procedure.

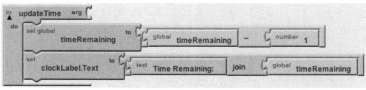

Code the Bricks

The last procedure you will program will be called whenever a brick is destroyed by the ball. It will get the brick as an argument, make it invisible, and then decrease the `bricksLeft` variable. If the number of bricks left is zero, it will signal that the player has won.

1. Click Built-In tab, click Definition, and drag a `to procedure do` block to the screen to create a new procedure. Click it and type `break` to rename it.
2. Click the Built-In tab, click Definition, and drag a `name` block to the `arg` socket of the `to break do` block. Click the `name` block and type `brick` to rename it.
3. Click the Advanced tab, click Any ImageSprite, and drag a `set ImageSprite.Visible` block to the procedure.
4. Click the My Blocks tab, click My Definitions, and drag a `value brick` block to the `component` socket of the `set ImageSprite.Visible` block.
5. Click the Logic menu and drag a `false` block to the `to` socket of the `set ImageSprite.Visible` block.
6. Click the My Blocks tab, click My Definitions, and drag a `set global bricksLeft` block to the procedure.
7. Click the Math menu and drag a `-` block to the `set global bricksLeft` block.
8. From the My Definitions menu of the My Blocks tab, drag a global `bricksLeft` block to the left side of the `-` block.
9. In the Built-In tab, click Math, and drag a `Number` block to the right side of the `-` block. Change its value to 1.
10. To check if that was the last brick, click the Built-In tab, click Control, and drag an `if then-do` block to the end of the procedure.
11. Click the Logic menu and drag an `=` block to the `test` socket of the `if then-do` block.
12. Click the My Blocks tab, click My Definitions, and drag a global `bricksLeft` block to the left side of the `=` block.
13. In the Built-In tab, click Math, and drag a `Number` block to the right side of the `=` block. Change its value to 0.
14. To stop the timer, begin by clicking the My Blocks tab, clicking Clock1, and dragging a `set Clock1.TimerEnabled` block to the `then-do` section of the `if then-do` block.
15. Click the Logic menu and drag a false block to the `set Clock1.TimerEnabled` block.
16. To stop the ball's movement, click the My Blocks tab, click Ball1, and drag a `set Ball1.Speed` block to the `then-do` section of the `if then-do` block.
17. In the Built-In tab, click Math, and drag a `Number` block to the `to` socket of the `set Ball1.Speed` block. Change its value to 0.
18. To tell the user he or she has won, click the My Blocks tab, click clockLabel, and drag a `set clockLabel.Text` block to the `then-do` section of the `if then-do` block.
19. Click the Built-In tab, click Text, and drag a `text` block to the `to` socket of the `set clockLabel.Text` block. Click the `text` block and type `You Won!`. You have completed all of the procedures. Your screen should look like the one in Figure 8.8.

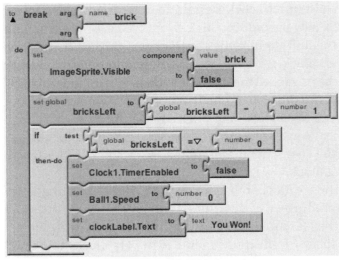

FIGURE 8.8

The completed
break procedure.

You will now define when the procedures are called based on the actions performed in the game. We will begin with the initialization of the app.

Write the Event Handlers

To start the app, a few things have to happen, such as initiating the clock timer and setting up the labels. To set these up, follow these steps:

1. Click the My Blocks tab, click Screen1, and drag a when Screen1.Initialize do block to the screen.
2. Click the My Blocks tab, click clockLabel, and drag a set clockLabel.Text block to the when Screen1.Initialize do block.
3. Click the Built-In tab, click Text, and drag a text block to the set clockLabel.Text block. Click it and type Time Remaining: 90.
4. To ensure the clock has not started, click the My Blocks tab, click Clock1, and drag a set Clock1.TimeEnabled block to the screen. Then click the Logic menu and drag a false block to the set Clock1.Enable block.
5. To animate the moving brick, click the My Blocks tab, click movingSprite, and drag the following blocks to the when Screen1.Initialize do block: set movingSprite.Heading, set movingSprite.Interval, and set movingSprite.Speed.
6. Click the Built-In tab, click Math, and drag a Number block to the set movingSprite.Heading block, a second Number block to the set movingSprite.Interval block, and a third Number block to the set movingSprite.Speed block. Change the value of the Number blocks 0, 50, and 10, respectively. (You can experiment with these values to see what works best for your game.)

7. To make the Brick bounce off the wall, click the My Blocks tab, click movingSprite, and drag a `when movingSprite.Edge Reached do` block to the screen.
8. In the My Blocks tab, click movingSprite, and drag a `call movingSprite.Bounce edge` block to the `when movingSprite.Edge Reached do` block.
9. Click the My Blocks tab, click My Definitions, and drag a name block to the `edge` socket of the `when movingSprite.Edge Reached do` block.
10. Repeat step 9 for the `call movingSprite.Bounce edge` block. At this point, your app is initialized and should look like Figure 8.9.

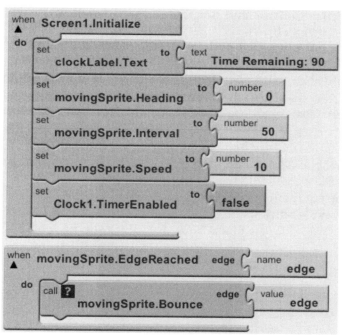

FIGURE 8.9

The completed initialize and edge reached events.

You will now configure the ball's motion and how it reacts to collisions. First, you'll define how the ball collides with another object. Luckily, the ball behaves the same way no matter what object it hits. It always bounces off. To program this behavior, follow these steps:

1. Click the My Blocks tab, click Ball1, and drag a `when Ball1.CollidedWith do` block to the screen.
2. Click the My Blocks tab, click Ball1, and drag a `set Ball1.Heading` block to the `when Ball1.CollidedWith do` block.
3. How the ball bounces off depends on the ball's initial heading. Therefore, you inserted a `set Ball1.Heading` block. However, you do not want the initial heading, but the

opposite heading. To program this, click the Math menu and drag a `call negate` block to the `to` socket of the a `set Ball1.Heading` block. Drag a `Ball1.Heading` block to the `negate` socket.

The next behavior is what happens when the ball collides with an edge. Normally, the ball should just bounce off the wall. However, if the ball hits below the bar, the user should lose a life. Follow these steps:

1. Click the My Blocks tab, click Ball1, and drag a `when Ball1.EdgeReached do` block to the screen.
2. Click the Built-In tab, click Control, and drag an `ifelse then-do else-do` block to the `when Ball1.EdgeReached do` block.
3. Click the Built-In tab, click Math, and drag a `>=` block to the test socket of the `ifelse then-do else-do` block.
4. Click the My Blocks tab, click Ball1, and drag a `Ball1.Y` block to the left side of the `>=` block.
5. In the My Blocks tab, click bar, and drag a `bar.Y` block to the right side of the `>=` block.
6. Click the My Blocks tab, click My Definitions, and drag a `call death` block to the `then-do` section of the `ifelse then-do else-do` block.
7. Click the My Blocks tab, click Ball1, and drag a `call Ball1.Bounce` block to the `else-do` section of the `ifelse then-do else-do` block.
8. Look at the name of the component connected to the `when Ball1.EdgeReached do` block. Find this block in the My Definitions menu of the My Blocks tab and connect it to the `edge` socket of the `call Ball1.Bounce` block. Your procedure should look like the one in Figure 8.10.

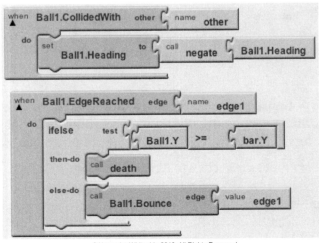

FIGURE 8.10

The completed ball-collision events.

You will now define the actions caused by the buttons at the bottom of the screen and what happens when the user drags the bar. Follow these steps:

1. Click the My Blocks tab, click startButton, and drag a `when startButton.Click do` block to the screen.

2. In the My Blocks tab, click My Definitions, and drag a `call start` block to the `when startButton.Click do` block.

3. In the My Blocks tab, click leftButton, and drag a `when leftButton.Click do` block to the screen.

4. In the My Blocks tab, click bar, and drag a `set bar.X` block to the `do` section of the `when leftButton.Click do` block.

5. Click the Built-In tab, click Math, and drag a `-` block to the `to` socket of the `set bar.X` block.

6. Click the My Blocks tab, click bar, and drag a `bar.X` block to the left side of the `-` block.

7. Click the Built-In tab, click Math, and drag a `Number` block to the right side of the `-` block. Change its value to 10.

8. Click the My Blocks tab, click rightButton, and drag a `when rightButton.Click do` block to the screen.

9. In the My Blocks tab, click bar, and drag a `set bar.X` block to the `when rightButton.Click do` block.

10. Click the Built-In tab, click Math, and drag a `+` block to the `to` socket of the `set bar.X` block.

11. Click the My Blocks tab, click bar, and drag a `bar.X` block to the left side of the `+` block.

12. Click the Built-In tab, click Math, and drag a `Number` block to the right side of the `+` block. Change its value to 10.

13. To implement the drag functionality, click the My Blocks tab, click bar, and drag a `when bar.Dragged do` block to the screen.

14. To update the bar's position, click the My Blocks tab, click bar, and drag a `set bar.X` block to the `do` section of the `when bar.Dragged do` block.

15. Click the My Blocks tab, click My Definitions, and drag a `value currentX` block to the `to` socket of the `set bar.X` block. These procedures are shown in Figure 8.11.

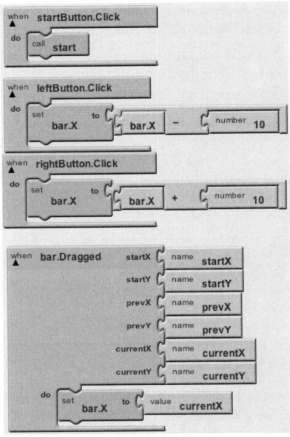

FIGURE 8.11

Completed
events for the
buttons and bar.

You will now update the clock label with the correct time based on the clock timer, and make the player lose when the time has elapsed. Follow these steps:

1. Click the My Blocks tab, click Clock1, and drag a when Clock1.Timer do block to the screen.
2. In the My Blocks tab, click My Definitions, and drag a call updateTime block to the when Clock1.Timer do block.
3. Click the Built-In tab, click Control, and drag an if then-do block to the when Clock1.Timer do block.
4. Click the Built-In tab, click Logic, and drag an = block to the test socket of the when Clock1.Timer do block.
5. Click the My Blocks tab, click My Definitions, and drag a global timeRemaining block to the left side of the = block.

6. Click the Built-In tab, click Math, and drag a Number block to the right side of the = block. Change its value to 0.

7. In the if then-do block, set all the life lights to invisible. To do so, click the My Blocks tab, click life1, and drag a set life1.Visible block to the then-do section of the if then-do block. Then click Logic and drag a false block to the to socket of the set life1.Visible block.

8. Repeat step 7 for life2 and life3.

9. In the My Blocks tab, click My Definitions, and drag a set global livesLeft block to the then-do section of the if then-do block.

10. Click the Built-In tab, click Math, and drag a Number block to the to socket of the set global livesLeft block. Change its value to 1.

11. Click the My Blocks tab, click My Definitions, and drag a call death block to the then-do section of the if then-do block. This event should look like the one in Figure 8.12.

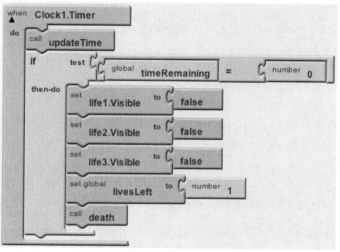

FIGURE 8.12

The completed timer event.

The next thing to do is to call the break procedure each time the ball collides with a brick. Just as when you instantiated them, you must implement their breaking behavior individually. The following outlines the steps for a general brick; then you will program the functionality for each brick. Because each brick reacts in the same way, you do not need to worry about which brick is which. Follow these steps:

1. For a specific brick, click the My Blocks tab, click ImageSpriteX, and drag a when ImageSpriteX.CollidedWith do block to the screen.

2. Click the My Blocks tab, click My Definitions, and drag a `call break` block to the `when ImageSpriteX.CollidedWith do` block.
3. Note the name of the image sprite you selected. Select the same image sprite in the My Blocks tab. Then scroll to the bottom to drag a `component ImageSpriteX` block to the `brick` socket of the `call break` block.
4. Repeat steps 1–3 for each brick image sprite (including the renamed movingSprite). When all the image sprites are completed, your screen should resemble the one in Figure 8.13.

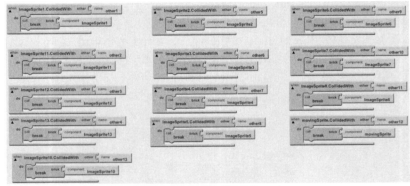

FIGURE 8.13

The completed brick events.

You should now be able to test your *Brick Breaker* app on your Android device! Make sure you can start the app and move the bar, and that bricks indeed disappear when hit.

The last thing to do is to create a reset function for when the player wins or loses, allowing him or her to play again. Essentially, the reset function will restore all the bricks, reset the timer, and reset the player's lives. Follow these steps:

1. To start, let's define a procedure. Click the Built-In tab, click Definitions, and drag a `to procedure do` block to the screen. Click it and type reset to rename it.
2. First, you'll reset the timer. Click the My Blocks tab, click Clock1, and drag a `set Clock1.TimerEnabled` block to the `to reset do` block. Then click the Logic menu and drag a `false` block to the `set Clock1.TimerEnabled` block.
3. To reset the time, click the My Blocks tab, click My Definitions, and drag a `set global timeRemaining` block to the `to reset do` block.
4. Click the Built-In tab, click Math, and drag a `Number` block to the `to` socket of the `set global timeRemaining` block. Change its value to 90.
5. To reset the label, click the My Blocks tab, click clockLabel, and drag a `set clockLabel.Text` block to the `to reset do` block.

6. Click the Built-In tab, click Text, and drag a text block to the set `clockLabel.Text` block. Change its value to `Time Remaining: 90`.

7. To restore the player's lives, click the My Blocks tab, click My Definitions, and drag a set `global livesLeft` block to the `to reset do` block.

8. Click the Built-In tab, click Math, and drag a `Number` block to the `to` socket of the set `global livesLeft` block. Change its value to 3.

9. To make all three life lights visible, first click the My Blocks tab, click life1, and drag a set `life1.Visible` block to the `to reset do` block. Then click the Logic menu and drag a `true` block to the `to` socket of the set `life1.Visible` block.

10. Repeat step 9 for the other two life lights (life2 and life3).

11. To reset the ball's location, click the My Blocks tab, click Ball1, and drag a set `Ball.X` and set `Ball.Y` block to the `to reset do` block. Connect the appropriate X and Y values as before.

12. To restore a specific brick, click the My Blocks tab, click ImageSpriteX, and drag a set `ImageSpriteX.Visible` block to the screen. Then click the Logic menu and drag a false block to the `to` socket of the set `ImageSpriteX.Visible` block.

13. Repeat step 12 for each brick image sprite (including the renamed movingSprite).

14. To ensure that the start button says "Start" and is enabled, click the My Blocks tab, click startButton, and drag a set `startButton.Text` block to the `to reset do` block.

15. Click the Built-In tab, click Text, and drag text block to the set `startButton.Text` block. Change its value to `Start`.

16. To enable the start button, click the My Blocks tab, click startButton, and drag a set `startButton.Enabled` block to the `to reset do` block. Then click the Logic menu and drag a `true` block to the `to` slot of the set `startButton.Enabled` block. The `reset` procedure should look like the one in Figure 8.14.

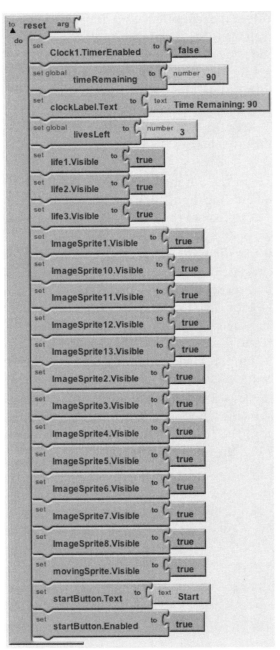

FIGURE 8.14

The completed reset procedure.

To implement the reset procedure you just created, add some blocks to your previous code. Follow these steps:

1. Locate the death procedure and, within it, the first if then-do block, which tests whether the player has lost all his or her lives.
2. Click the My Blocks tab, click startButton, and drag a set startButton.Text block to the end of this if then-do statement (but still inside it). Then click the Built-In tab, click Text, and drag a text block to set startButton.Text block. Change the value of the text block to Reset.
3. Locate the break procedure and, within it, the if then-do block.
4. Click the My Blocks tab, click startButton, and drag a set startButtonText block to the end of this if then-do statement (but still inside it). Then click the Built-In tab, click Text, and drag a text block to the set startButtonText block. Change the value of the text block to Reset.
5. Click the My Blocks tab, click startButton, and drag a set startButton.Enabled block to the end of the if then-do statement (but still inside it). Then click the Logic menu and drag a true block to the to socket of the set startButton.Enabled block.
6. Locate the when startButton.Click do event.
7. Remove the call start block and place it next to the event.
8. Click the Built-In tab, click Control, and drag an ifelse then-do else-do block to the when startButton.Click do block.
9. Click the Built-In tab, click Text, and drag a text= block to the test socket of the ifelse then-do else-do block.
10. Click the My Blocks tab, click startButton, and drag a startButton.Text block to the text1 socket of the text= block.
11. Click the Built-In tab, click Text, and drag a text block to the text2 socket of the text= block. Change its value to Reset.
12. To call the reset procedure, click the My Blocks tab, click My Definitions, and drag a call reset block to the then-do section of the ifelse then-do else-do block.
13. Drag the call start block you moved to the side in step 7 to the else-do section of the ifelse then-do else-do block. These procedures and events should now look like the ones in Figure 8.15.

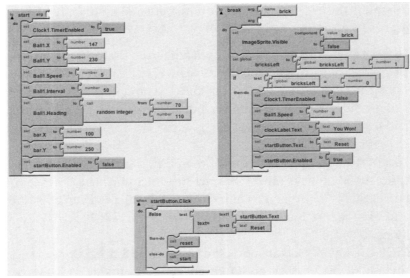

FIGURE 8.15

Updated start, death, and break procedures.

Congratulations! You have completed the *Brick Breaker* app. Download it to your phone and test it out!

OPTIONAL IMPROVEMENTS

While the game is complete, now that you understand the framework, there are many improvements and additions you could write to make the game better. Here are some ideas:

- Create different levels using different screens.
- Make the bricks move differently using rotation and speed commands.
- Enable power-ups, which the player can use to increase the speed, stop the clock, etc.

SUMMARY

Animation and user interaction with graphics have rapidly changed the way we interact with data. Information that used to be text-based is now represented by pictures and moving images, giving a much more realistic interpretation of data. From this new form of visualization, rich graphical interfaces were developed, and video games became prominent for digital devices. Now, even mobile devices such as cell phones can easily be used to run games. With added interaction through touch screens, apps like *Brick Breaker* are only the beginning.

USING PERSISTENT DATABASES: TRACKING YOUR WEIGHT

CHAPTER OBJECTIVES

- Menu-based navigation
- Multiple screens
- Dynamic database functions
- Control-based calculations
- User-interface design
- Need analysis
- Implementation analysis
- Clock-based functions
- Creating and presenting graphs

APP DISCUSSION

Two of the most important functions of computers—particularly mobile computers—are their ability to store data and to perform calculations on the fly. Previously, you learned the basics of using databases to store data, as well as to retrieve the data and use it in other functions. You also learned how to create dynamic, multi-screened apps, which can perform important functions. This chapter brings all these topics together and introduces specialty topics to write an app that tracks one's weight and calculates relevant statistics.

To begin, you will consider exactly what functionality a weight-tracking app should have. Clearly, the basis of the app lies in the capability to add weight data and view previous weight recordings. While these two are the most important core functions, it is also important to display relevant statistics and information relating to one's weight—for instance, general trends and BMI information. To perform these calculations, there must also be the functionality for the user to enter and save pertinent information such as age and gender. Lastly, it is important for the user to be able to easily use the app, so a well-formed menu-based navigation system is necessary.

Now you can determine the best ways to implement these needs and relate them to one another. At the top of the program is the menu system, which must link to the appropriate screens. That means you will have to determine what screens are necessary and link them together using buttons. Because variables are not persistent across screens, you will either have to store data in a database or pass the variables into the new screen. The necessary screens, as determined from the aforementioned needs, are as follows:

- Main Menu
- Add Weight Measurement
- View Weight Measurements
- View Statistics
- Personal Details

The Main Menu screen will have button links to each of the remaining screens, and each screen will have a Back button to return to the Main Menu screen. (Note that this is not strictly necessary, as Android devices provide a Return button on the handset. However, you will include it for completeness.) As well, if the app has never been used before, the app should switch to the Personal Details screen to get initial data.

The rest of the four screens lie below the Main Menu screen and each rely on each other for data. Although the app could rely on passing variables to the different screens as before, because the data must persist after the app is closed or the phone restarted, it is easiest to use a common database that is accessed by all the screens.

Now that you have the navigation and the bottom storage designed, you can move on to the screens themselves. The first screen, Add Weight Measurement, must be able to accept a weight via an input field and store it in the database. Because you want to store an unknown number of weights, you need to use a dynamic naming system for each weight's database tag.

This means you need to keep track of the number of weights that you keep in the database. To do this, you will create a variable named Count and store it in the database. You will then create two lists, named Weights and Times, to store the weights and the date/time each weight was taken, respectively. You will store the current measurements in the Count position of each list so you can match them later. After each measurement, you will increase the Count variable.

The next screen, View Weight Measurements, will display all previously recorded weights, as well as the date measured, in chronological order. However, because graphs display trend data such as weight changes most effectively, you will also create a chart based on the weight and date values and display it on the screen. To retrieve the values to display, you will do the opposite of saving the values: You will start from the counter weight and display each pair, as well as put it into the list to be graphed. You will then query Google charts to generate a graph and embed it in the app.

Both the View Statistics screen as well as the Personal Details screen are very simple compared to the previous screens. View Statistics will simply query the database and calculate various statistics, such as BMI and trends, while Personal Details will allow users to edit their age and gender, which are used to calculate their BMI. Because this is a lot of information to keep in mind while you develop the app, you will use Figure 9.1 as a general guide of the screens and their resources.

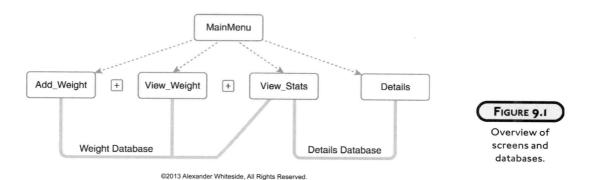

FIGURE 9.1

Overview of screens and databases.

Lastly, it is important to note that you will need an Android device to test and debug your app throughout the development process. This app is structured on database entries as well as different screens that App Inventor, even when connected to the device, does not support. It is recommended that you test sparingly, but do so by downloading the application to your device.

THE DESIGN PHASE

In this section, you will create all the components required for the Weight Tracker app as well as design the screens with which the user will interact. Follow these steps:

1. Create a new project in App Inventor and name it Weight_Tracker.
2. Create the necessary screens: Add_Weight, View_Weight, View_Stats, and Details. These correspond to the aforementioned Add Weight Measurement, View Weight Measurements, View Statistics, and Personal Details screens. The Main Menu screen will be built on Screen1, whose name cannot be changed. After the creation of your screens, your project should look like Figure 9.2.

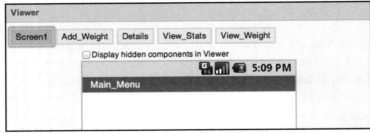

FIGURE 9.2

The screens created for the app.

3. On Screen1, create a table arrangement to organize your buttons. Place a Label component from the Basic palette at the top of the table arrangement. Rename it introduction.
4. Add four Button components to Screen1 to navigate to the other screens. Rename each of them to reflect their function (addWeight, viewWeight, stats, and details), and set their text to show the user their function (Add Weight Measurement, View Weight History, Weight Statistics, and Personal Details). Set each Button component's Width property to Fill Parent.

> **NOTE**
> An important part of app development lies in fully utilizing the screen's space. By using design techniques like full-width buttons, you can make it easier for users without compromising on functionality.

5. To allow communication between screens, add a TinyDB object to the screen. Your screen should look like Figure 9.3.

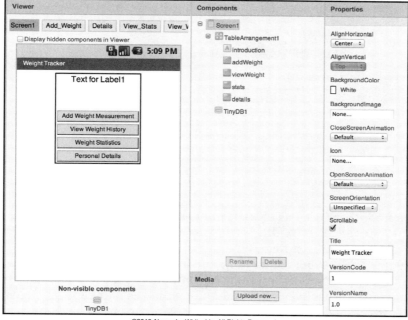

FIGURE 9.3

The completed Screen1.

6. Switch to the Add_Weight screen.

7. Add a label at the top of the screen to provide instructions for the user. Rename it intro and change its Width setting to Fill Parent in the Properties tab.

8. Add a text box under the label for the user to enter his or her weight. Rename it weightEntry and change its Width setting to Fill Parent. In the Properties tab, select the NumbersOnly checkbox.

9. Click Screen Arrangement and drag a TableArrangement component to the screen. Add two checkboxes in the table to provide the option for pounds (lbs) or kilograms (kgs). Rename them lbs and kgs, respectively.

10. Place a submit button and a return button at the bottom of the screen. Rename them submit and return. In the Properties tab's Text field, type Submit Weight for the submit button and Main Menu for the return button. Change both their Width properties to Fill Parent.

11. Add a TinyDB object to the screen.

12. Add a clock to the screen to get the time and dates when weights are submitted.

13. Ensure all components are labeled appropriately, as shown in Figure 9.4.

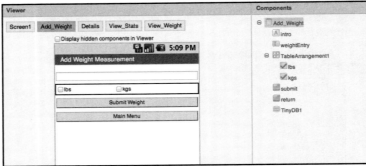

FIGURE 9.4

The completed
Add_Weight
visual.

14. Switch to the Details screen.
15. Add a Label component from the Basic palette to describe the screen. Rename it intro. In the Properties tab, change its Width setting to Fill Parent and its TextAlignment setting to Center. Then, in the Text field, type introduction.
16. From the Basic palette, add a Label component and a TextBox component for the user's name and a second Label component and TextBox component for the user's age. Rename the labels name and age, respectively. Rename the text boxes nameBox and ageBox. In the Properties tab for the ageBox text box, select the NumbersOnly checkbox.
17. Drag a TableArrangement component from the Screen Arrangement palette to the screen. Then, from the Basic palette, drag a Label component and two CheckBox components to the table for the user's gender. Rename the label gender and the checkboxes male and female.
18. From the Basic palette, add buttons for Submit and Main Menu. In the Properties tab, change each of their Width settings to Fill Parent. Rename them submit and mainMenu, respectively.
19. Add a TinyDB object to the screen. Look at Figure 9.5 and make sure all your components are named and labeled correctly.

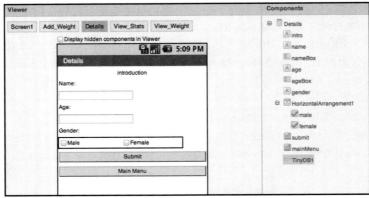

FIGURE 9.5

The completed
Details visual.

20. Switch to the View_Stats screen.
21. Create five labels for the following five statistics. Set their Text properties and rename them as shown in Figure 9.6.

    - Name
    - Age
    - Most Recent Weight
    - Lightest Weight
    - Heaviest Weight

22. Create a Main Menu button at the bottom of the screen. Rename it mainMenu and, in the Properties tab, change its Width setting to Fill Parent.
23. Add a TinyDB object to the screen. (See Figure 9.6.)

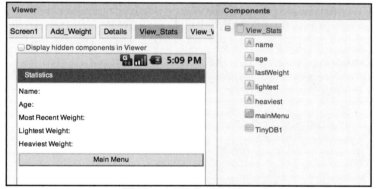

©2013 Alexander Whiteside, All Rights Reserved.

FIGURE 9.6

The completed View_Stats visual.

24. Switch to the View_Weight screen.
25. Insert a Label component at the top of the screen to describe the screen. Rename it intro.
26. Insert an Image component below the label, to be used for a graph of the weight measurements. You do not need to actually select an image or graphic at this time. Rename this component graph.
27. Insert a Label component below the image. Rename it dataList. This will be used to display all the measurements.
28. Ensure all of the components are named appropriately.
29. Insert a clock from the Basic palette.
30. As always, include a TinyDB object and a Main Menu button. Rename the Main Menu Button mainMenu and change its Width setting to Fill Parent in the Properties tab. (See Figure 9.7.)

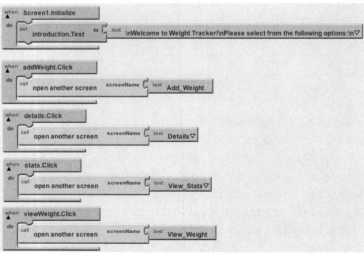

FIGURE 9.7

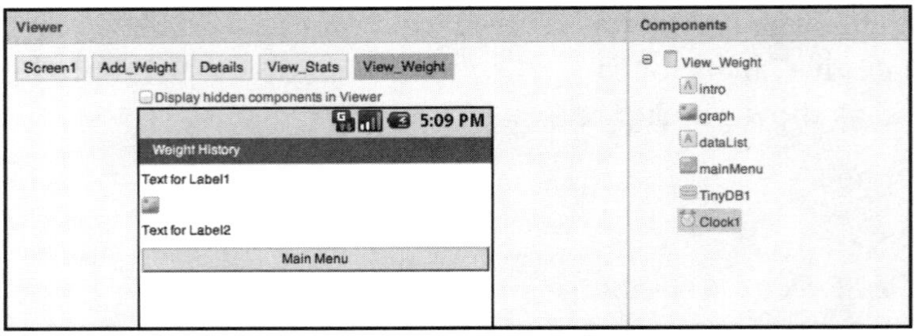

The completed View_Weight visual.

THE CODE PHASE

In this section, you will set up all the navigation links and features in the Main Menu screen. All the steps in this section will occur in the Blocks Editor. To begin, follow these steps:

1. Open the Blocks Editor, making sure that Screen1 is selected in your browser.
2. Begin with the `When Screen1.Initialize do` block, placing a `text` block inside it for the introduction label and filling in the text with a welcome message.
3. Create the navigational links by populating the `Button.Click` blocks with `call open another screen` functions, supplied with the correct screen name. Do this for each button, as shown in Figure 9.8.

FIGURE 9.8

Screen1's completed events.

Ask for Information

As mentioned, if this is the first time the user has opened the app, you should ask for information. To do this, you will now define a tag called isUsed within the TinyDB object to flag whether the app has been opened before and see if it is valid during initialization. Here is how you will test for it during initialization of the app:

1. Add an if statement to the when Screen1.Initialize do block.
2. Within the if then-do block, test whether the tag isUsed is an empty string. To do this, click the Built-In tab, click Text, and drag an is text empty? block to the if then-do block's test socket. To retrieve the value from the database, click the My Blocks tab, click TinyDB1, and drag a call TinyDB1.GetValue block to the text socket of the is text empty? block. Because you are testing the isUsed string, click the Built-In tab, click Text, and drag a text block to the tag socket of the call TinyDB1.GetValue block. Change the value of the text block to isUsed.
3. If it is empty, then set up the app to open the Personal Details screen. To do this, click the Built-In tab, click Control, and drag the call open another screen block to the then-do section of the if block. Then, click Text and drag a text block to the screenName socket. Change the value of the text block to Details. (See Figure 9.9.)

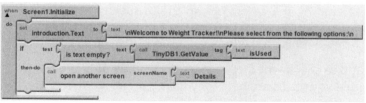

©2013 Alexander Whiteside, All Rights Reserved.

FIGURE 9.9

Screen1's initialize event.

Code the Personal Details Screen

Because so much of your app depends on details about the user, you will construct the Personal Details screen next and integrate it into the app through the database and main menu. To use the database, you will now define the tags that you will use to store the data. Table 9.1 outlines the tags.

TABLE 9.1	DATABASE CONTENT	
Name	**Description**	**Type**
Name	The user's name	String
Age	The user's age	String
isMale	Is the user male?	Boolean
isFemale	Is the user female?	Boolean

Follow these steps:

1. Switch to the Details screen in your browser and Blocks Editor.
2. Set in place the screen's `Initialize` block and use it to populate the introduction label. To do this, click the My Blocks tab, click intro, and drag a `set intro.Text` block to the `when Details.Initialize do` block. Then click the Built-In tab, click Text, and drag a `text` block to the to socket. Change the value to `\nPlease enter your information\nbelow to customize \nyour app.\n`.
3. Either in the browser or in the Blocks Editor, set the text box's hints to show the appropriate text. To do it in the Blocks Editor, click the My Blocks tab, click nameBox, and drag a `set nameBox.Hint` block beneath the `set intro.Text` block. Then click the Built-In tab, click Text, and drag a `text` block to the to socket of the `set nameBox.Hint` block. Change the value of the `text` block to `Enter your name`.
4. Repeat step 3 to add a `set ageBox.Hint` block with the value `Enter your age`.

Next you must set up the app to check whether any data is already populated in the database. Because you have determined your tag names, if they have not been created, they will return an empty string. If there is already information in the database, you should display it and allow the user to edit it. You will create various `if` statements, such as the one shown in Figure 9.10, to accomplish this and place them in the `when Details.Initialize` block. Specific instructions are shown here.

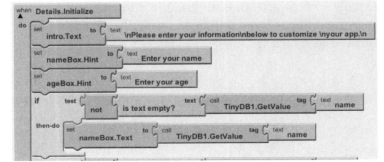

FIGURE 9.10

The first completed `if` `then-do` statement.

1. Click the Built-In tab, click Control, and drag an `if then-do` block to the workspace. Then, click Logic and drag a `not` block to the `test` socket of the `if then-do` block. Next, click Text, and drag an `is text empty?` block to the `open` socket of the `not` block. Lastly, in the My Blocks tab, click TinyDB1, and drag a `call TinyDB1.GetValue` block to the `text` socket of the `is text empty?` block. Finally, click the Built-In tab, select Text, and drag a `text` block to the `tag` socket of the `call TinyDB1.GetValue` block. Change the value of the `text` block to `name`.

2. Click the My Blocks tab, click nameBox, and drag a `set nameBox.Text` block to the `then-do` section of the `if then-do` block. Then click TinyDB1 and drag a `call TinyDB.GetValue` block to the `to` socket of the `set nameBox.Text` block. Next, click the Built-In tab, click Text, and drag a `text` block to the `tag` socket of the `call TinyDB.GetValue` block. Change its value to `name`. Finally, drag this entire block to the `when Details.Initialize do` block.

3. Repeat steps 1 and 2. This time, however, add a `set ageBox.Text` block instead of a `set nameBox.Text` block to the `then-do` section of the `if then-do` block, and change the value of each `name` block to `age`.

4. Repeat steps 1 and 2. This time, however, add a `set male.Checked` block instead of a `set nameBox.Text` block to the `then-do` section of the `if then-do` block, and change the value of each `name` block to `isMale`.

5. Repeat steps 1 and 2. This time, however, add a `set female.Checked` block instead of a `set nameBox.Text` block to the `then-do` section of the `if then-do` block, and change the value of each `name` block to `isFemale`.

6. Ensure all four if blocks are within the `Initialize` block, forcing them to execute when the screen is loaded as shown in Figure 9.11.

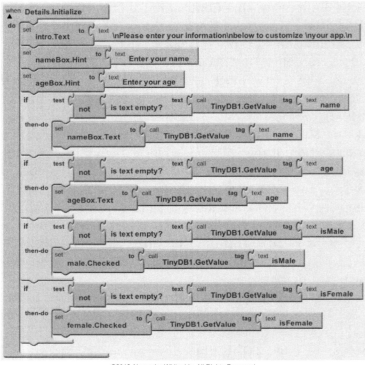

FIGURE 9.11

The completed
when Details.
Initialize do
block.

You must define what happens when the user enters information into the form and clicks the Submit button. At this time, you will also put a value in the isUsed tag so that the user isn't always prompted to update his or her information. Follow these steps:

1. Click the My Blocks tab, click submit, and drag a when submit.Click do block to the workspace.

2. Click the My Blocks tab, click TinyDB1, and drag a call TinyDB1.StoreValue block to the do section of the when submit.Click do block. Then click the Built-In tab, click Text, drag a text block to the tag socket of the when submit.Click do block, and change its value to name. Finally, click the My Blocks tab, click nameBlock, and drag a nameBox.Text block to the valueToStore socket of the when submit.Click do block.

3. Repeat step 2, this time changing the value of the text box to age and dragging an ageBox.Text block to the valueToStore socket of the when submit.Click do block.

4. Repeat step 2, this time changing the value of the text box to isMale and dragging a male.Checked block to the valueToStore socket of the when submit.Click do block.

5. Repeat step 2, this time changing the value of the text box to isFemale and dragging a female.Checked block to the valueToStore socket of the when submit.Click do block.

6. Click the My Blocks tab, click TinyDB1, and drag a call TinyDB1.StoreValue block to the do section of the when submit.Click do block. Then click the Built-In tab, click Text, and drag one text block to the tag socket of the when submit.Click do block and a second text block to the valueToStore socket. Change the first text block's value to isUsed and the second text block's value to true.

7. Add a call close screen block to the end of the when submit.Click do event function.

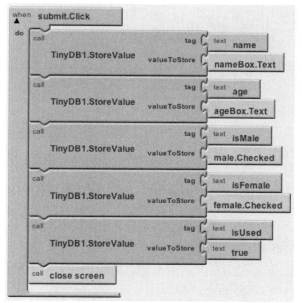

FIGURE 9.12

The completed when submit.Click do event.

8. Set the Main Menu button to return to the main menu. To do so, click the My Blocks tab, click mainMenu, and drag a when mainMenu.Clicked do block to the screen. Then click the Built-In tab, click Control, and drag a call open another screen block to the when mainMenu.Clicked do block. Finally, click Text, drag a text block to the screenName socket, and change its value to Screen1.

Code the Add Weight Screen

Next you will create the code required for the user to enter his or her weight and store it in the app to review later. Follow these steps:

1. Switch to the Add_Weight screen in your browser and Blocks Editor.
2. Drag the `when Add_Weight.Initialize do` block to the workspace for editing.
3. Set the text of the intro text field and weight entry hint using the applicable text setters, as shown in Figure 9.13.

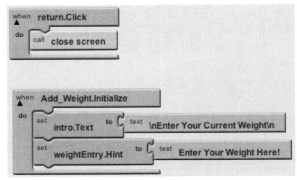

FIGURE 9.13

The `when Add_Weight.Initialize do` and `when return.Click do` events.

4. Set the Main Menu button to return to Screen1.
5. Add the `when submit.Click do` block to the screen.

Inside the `when submit.Click do` block, you will save the user's submitted weight and the date that it was submitted as discussed at the beginning of the chapter. Simply put, you will store a counter variable in the database to keep track of the most current weight entry. That means there are two possible cases that you will have to program for:

- There is a number in the counter, so you save both the weight and the time based on that number and increase the counter.
- There is no counter, so you must create one, set the number to 0, and then retest for a counter (after which your program will follow the previously stated case).

The counter variable you will use is a TinyDB tag named `count`. You will first program the case if the `count` tag has not been created. Follow these steps:

1. Place an `if then-do` statement in the `when submit.Click do` block.
2. Check whether the TinyDB `count` tag is empty. If it is empty, save `count` to the database with value number 1 as shown in Figure 9.14.

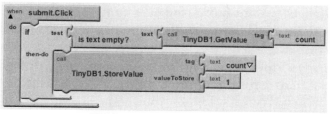

FIGURE 9.14

The completed
when
submit.Click
do block.

Once you know that the count tag exists and has the current count, you must create/retrieve the list of both the weights and the times. To do this, you will first define two variables, weightList and timeList. You will then check whether they exist in the database. If so, you will retrieve them and continue using them. If none have been saved, you will create new ones. From there, once the user enters data, you will save it to the list and update the database with the new list. Follow these steps:

1. To define the two variables, click the Built-In tab, click Definition, and drag two def variable blocks to the workspace. Then click Lists and connect a call make a list block to each def variable block. Leave the item sockets empty. (See Figure 9.15.)

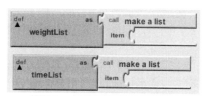

FIGURE 9.15

Two list
definitions.

2. In the Built-In tab, click Control, and drag two if then-do blocks to the when Add_Weight Initialize do block.

3. Your test will be to see whether the stored values of the lists are lists. Therefore, you will retrieve each list from the database using a call TinyDB1.GetValue block. You will then connect the result to a call is a list? block (available from the Lists menu in the Built-In tab), which is connected to the test socket of the if then-do statement. If these cases are true, you will assign the retrieved value to the variables you defined earlier, replacing the empty lists. To do this, click the Built-In menu, click Lists, and drag a call is a list? block to each test connector. Then click the My Blocks tab, click TinyDB1, and connect a call TinyDB1.GetValue block to each call is a list? block. For both tests, click the Built-In tab, click Text, and drag a text block in the tag socket of the call TinyDB.GetValue block. Change the value of the first text block to weightList and the second to timeList.

4. Click the My Blocks tab, click My Definitions, and drag a `set global weightList` block to the `then-do` section of the first `if then-do` block. Then drag a `set global timeList to` block to the `then-do` section of the second `if then-do` block.

5. Click the My Blocks tab, click TinyDB1, and drag one `call TinyDB.GetValue` block to the `to` socket of the `set global weightList` block and a second `call TinyDB.GetValue` block to the `to` socket of the `set global timeList` block. Then add a `text` block to the `tag` socket of each `call TinyDB.GetValue` block and change their values as shown in Figure 9.16.

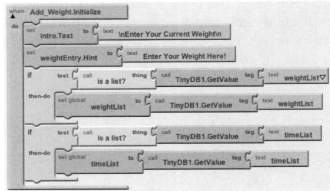

©2013 Alexander Whiteside, All Rights Reserved.

FIGURE 9.16

The completed when Add_Weight. Initialize do event.

6. In the `when submit.Click do` block, add an `ifelse then-do else-do` statement to test whether the kgs checkbox is checked.

7. If it is checked (`then-do`), multiply the entered value by 2.2 to turn it into lbs; then add the multiplied value into the `weightList`. To do so, click List in the Built-In tab and drag a `call insert list item` block to the workspace. Put the multiplied value in the `item` space. (Look ahead to Figure 9.17 for guidance.)

8. In the `index` space, use a `call TinyDB.GetValue` block to use the `count` variable as the index.

9. Set the `list` space to the `global weightList` block (available from the My Definitions menu in the My Blocks tab).

10. In the `else-do` section, save the value as before; however, do not multiply it by 2.2.

11. Insert another `call insert list item` block below the `ifelse then-do else-do` block.

12. Set the `list` to be the `global timeList` block (available from the My Definitions menu in the My Blocks tab).

13. Set the `index` to be `call TinyDB.GetValue` of `count`.

14. Set the `item` to be `call Clock1.FormatDate` (available from the Clock1 menu in the My Blocks tab); then connect a `call Clock1.Now` block (also available from the Clock1 menu in the My Blocks tab).

15. Add one to the count by retrieving it and adding 1 by using a plus statement.
16. Save this to the TinyDB object as the new count.
17. Store both the `weightList` and the `timeList` in the TinyDB object with the respective tags.
18. Close the screen. Your `when submit.Click do` block should look like Figure 9.17.

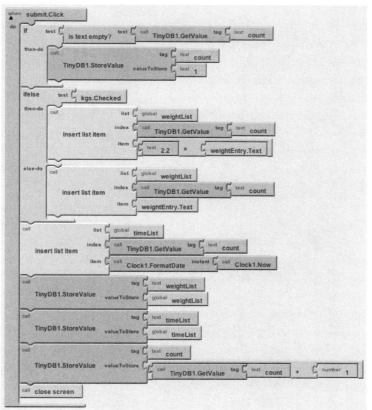

FIGURE 9.17

The completed
when
`submit.Click`
`do` event.

Code the View Weight Screen

You will now create the logic to retrieve and display the measured weights, as well as create a graph using Google's API.

1. Switch to the View_Weight screen in App Inventor.
2. Under My Blocks, select the `View_Weight.Initialize` block and drag it to the screen.
3. Create two variables, called `weightList` and `timeList`.
4. Set each variable to a new `make a list` block from the Built-In tab's List menu, as you did in the Add_Weight section.

5. Create a variable called `index` and set it to the number 1.
6. Create a variable called `param` and set it to a blank `text` block.
7. Create a variable called `param2` and set it to a blank `text` block.
8. Inside the `Initialize` block, add an `ifelse then-do else-do` statement.
9. For the test, check whether the TinyDB value for `weightList` is a list, as you did for Add_Weight.
10. In the `then-do` section, set `weightList` and `timeList` to the values in the TinyDB, as you did on the Add_Weight screen.
11. Drag the `intro.Text` block into the `then-do` space.
12. Add text to display to the user, such as `Below you can see the data you previously recorded`.
13. In the `else-do` space, drag the `intro.Text` block and set it to say `Sorry, there is no data`. (See Figure 9.18.)

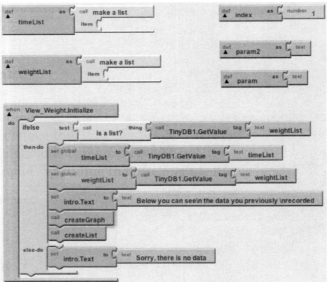

FIGURE 9.18

The completed when View_Weight. Initialize do event with definitions.

You now have two ways to display the data: by graph and by list. To make this simpler to code, you can create two different procedures to contain the code that gets, organizes, and displays the data. You can then simply call these procedures from your `Initialize` block. First, create the graph procedure using the Google API for image charts. This enables you to put your data into a string URL; Google will then generate an image, which you can display in your graph image.

TIP I will not go into detail about how to interact with the Google API, so you may not completely understand many parts of this procedure. Do not worry. This is just an example of how you interact with different programs, such as Google Charts. If you are interested in seeing how Google Charts works and can be used in your Android apps, check out their Getting Started page at https://developers.google.com/chart/image/docs/making_charts.

Follow these steps:

1. Click the Built-In tab, choose Definition, and drag a procedure block to the workspace.
2. Name the procedure block createGraph.
3. Place an if statement inside the procedure block.
4. Set the test to a greater-than (>) block (available from the Math menu in the Built-In tab).
5. Set the left greater-than test to weightList (in the Built-In tab, click Lists, and then length of list).
6. Set the right greater-than test to number 0.
7. In the then-do space, add a set global param block (available from the My Definitions menu in the My Blocks tab).
8. Set the param block to make text (available from the Text menu in the Built-In tab). The first text should be a text box containing chd=t: and the second text should be a number 1.
9. Beneath the if then-do statement, place a set global index (My Definitions) block and set it to number 2.
10. Next, add a while do block (available from the Control menu in the Built-In tab).
11. Set the test to a less-than-or-equal-to (<=) block (available from the Math menu in the Built-In tab).
12. Set the left argument to the index variable.
13. Set the right argument to a length of list block (available from the Math menu in the Built-In tab) connected to the timeList variable. See Figure 9.19.

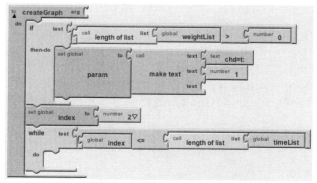

FIGURE 9.19

The current to createGraph do procedure.

14. In the do space, place a set global param block just as you did in the then-do space.
15. Connect a make text block (available from the Text menu in the Built-In tab) to the set global param block.
16. Connect the param variable to the text connector.
17. Set the second text space to a new text block with a comma (,) inside.
18. Set the third text space to a multiply block (available from the Math menu in the Built-In tab).
19. Within the multiply block, set the number 5 and the index variable within the arguments.
20. Beneath the set global param block, place a set global index block.
21. Connect a math addition (+) block to the set global index block. The arguments should be the index variable and the number 1. This way, you will cycle through the number of entries you have in the timeList. See Figure 9.20.

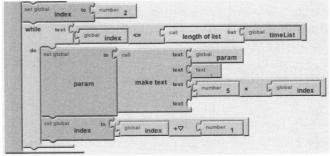

FIGURE 9.20

The finished to createGraph do procedure.

What you have done is created the X axis for your graph based on the length of your timeList. Because you know you have the same number of Y values on the weightList, you can be more efficient and create the Y parameter list while you create the X list. This is why you created the param2 variable. To continue, follow these steps:

1. Begin the list by setting up the param2 string pursuant to Google's API. Place a set global param2 block in the first then-do space, where you set param to chd=t:.
2. As with param, place a make text block in the to slot.
3. Connect a new text block containing a pipe (|) to the text connector.
4. Connect a select list item block (available from the Lists menu in the Built-In tab) to the next text connector.
5. Set the list space to the weightList variable.
6. Set the index to number 1.
7. Scroll down to the while loop.
8. Just before the set global param block, place a set global param2 block.

9. Set `param2` to a new `make text` block (available from the Text menu).
10. Connect `param2` from My Definitions to the `text` connector.
11. Connect a new `text` block containing a comma (,) to the second `text` space.
12. Connect a `select list item` block (available from the Lists menu) to the third `text` connector.
13. Connect the `weightList` variable from My Definitions to the `list` connector.
14. Set the `index` space to the `index` variable.

You have now created two string lists, which you will combine with a specific URL string to request a graph from Google. Follow these steps:

1. Under the `while` loop, place a `set graph.Picture` block (available from the Graph menu in the My Blocks tab).
2. Connect a `make text` block (available from the Text menu in the Built-In tab) to the `graph.Picture` block.
3. Create a new `text` block and connect it to the `text` connector.
4. Set the `text` block to the following: `https://chart.googleapis.com/chart?chxr=0,0,200|1,0,100&chxt=y,x&cht=lxy&chs=200x125&chco=3072F3,ff0000&chls=2,4&chm=s,000000,0,-1,5&chdlp=t&`.
5. Set the next `text` space to the `param` variable.
6. Set the third `test` space to the `param2` variable. Your `createGraph` procedure block should now be complete and look like Figure 9.21.

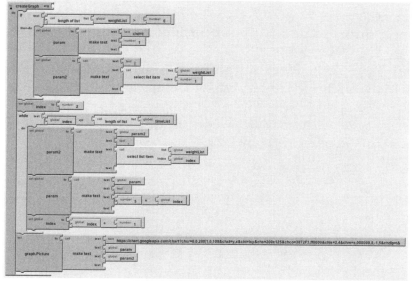

FIGURE 9.21

The completed to createGraph do procedure.

You will now create the list function to display the dates and weights below the graph. Follow these steps:

1. Create a new `procedure` block (available from the Definition menu in the Built-In tab). Name it `createList`.
2. Place a `set global index` block (available from the My Definitions menu in the My Blocks tab) inside `createList`.
3. Set the `index` to number 1.
4. Insert a `set global param` block (available from the My Definitions menu in the My Blocks tab) and connect it to a blank `text` block.
5. Insert a `while` loop (available from the Control menu in the Built-In tab) and set the test to a less-than-or-equal-to (`<=`) block (available from the Math menu).
6. Set the left side of the test to the `index` variable and the right side to the length of the `weightList`, just as in the `createGraph` procedure block.
7. In the `do` space, place a `set global param` block (available from the My Definitions menu in the My Blocks tab).
8. Connect a `make text` block (available from the Text menu in the Built-In tab).
9. Connect the first `text` space to the `param` variable.
10. Connect to the second `text` space to a `select list item` block (available from the List menu in the Built-In tab). Configure it to select from `timeList` and to select the current index.
11. Connect the third `text` space to a new `text` block containing a colon (:).
12. Connect the fourth `text` space to another `select list item` block. Configure it to select the index from `weightList`.
13. Connect the last `text` space to a new `text` block containing \n\n to add space between entries.
14. After the `set global param` block, place a `set global index` block (available from the My Definitions menu in the My Blocks tab) and use it to set the index to the current index plus 1.
15. After the `while` loop, place a `set Text` (available from the dataList menu in the My Blocks tab) to display the `param` variable. See Figure 9.22.

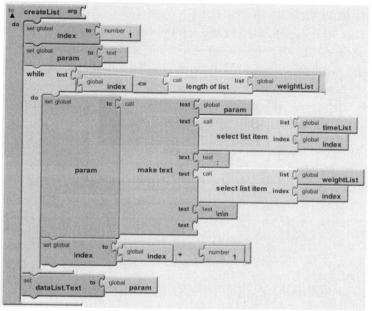

FIGURE 9.22

The to createList do procedure.

16. Call the two functions by placing the `call` blocks found under My Definitions in the My Blocks tab at the end of the `then-do` block within the `Initialize` block, as shown in Figure 9.23.

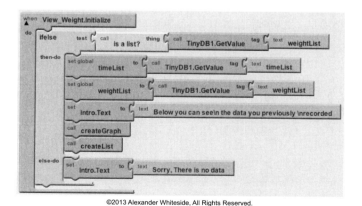

FIGURE 9.23

The updated when View_Weight. Initialize do event.

17. Set the Main Menu button to return to the main menu.

Code the Statistics Screen

Your last step is to code the Statistics screen. This screen is meant to show the user some important information about their weight measurements at a glance. Some of the data can be displayed in one line and will just be coded in the Initialize block, while others will be coded using procedures to make the code cleaner and more understandable. You should become accustomed to writing most of your code in procedures (also called functions and methods in other languages), and only calling these within your main section.

1. Place the View_Stats.Initialize block on the screen.
2. Display the user's name by placing the set Text block (available from the Name menu in the My Blocks tab) in the Initialize block.
3. Retrieve the name by using the TinyDB.GetValue block to get the tag name.
4. Combine this retrieved name with the current name component by using the join block (available from the Text menu in the Built-In tab). Connect this joined text to the name.Text block.
5. Repeat this process to display the user's age.
6. Set the Main Menu button to return to the main menu.

The rest of the Statistic screen requires weight data to already exist, so you will check whether the timeList exists and if it is indeed a list. Follow these steps:

1. Place an ifelse block (available from the Control menu in the Built-In tab) at the bottom of the Initialize block.
2. Set the test to an is a list block (available from the List menu in the Built-In tab). Connect to this a TinyDB.GetValue block and retrieve the timeList tag.
3. In the else portion of the ifelse block, set the lastWeight, lightest, and heaviest labels to read No data available. As before, you will need to use join statements to combine the current text data with the new error.
4. Create two new variables named low and high and set them to the number 1.
5. Create a new procedure block named calculateWeights and a new variable called index, which should be set to 1.
6. In the then-do section of the ifelse block, call the calculateWeights procedure block. (See Figure 9.24.)

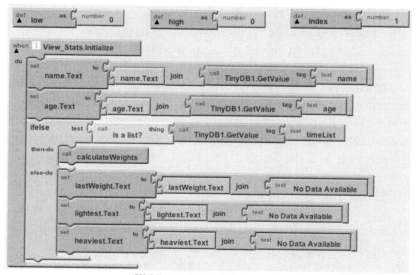

FIGURE 9.24

The completed
when View_Stats.
Initialize do
event.

7. Place the lastWeight.Text block in the calculateWeights procedure. Connect a join block from the Text menu to the lastWeight.Text block.

8. Prepare the join block with the current lastWeight.Text and connect it to lastWeight. Text.

9. Begin the second argument of the join block with a select list item block (available from the List menu).

10. Connect the list with the timeList, which you should retrieve using TinyDB.

11. Connect the index with the length of list block (available from the List menu). This will connect to the timeList, which you should retrieve using TinyDB.

You will now loop through all the weights to find the lightest and heaviest weight, then display them. The way you are going to find the highest and lowest values is to initially set the low and high variables to the first value in the list. You will then go through the entire list and compare each value to the stored high and low values. Then, if the current value is higher than the high variable or lower than the low variable, you will replace the high/low variable with the current index. When you are through with the list, you will have the highest and lowest values.

1. Place a while block (available from the Control menu in the Built-In tab) in the new procedure.

2. Connect a less-than-or-equal-to (<=) block (available from the Math menu) to the while loop.

3. The `comparison` block tests whether the index is less than or equal to the length of `weightList`. Set it up to accomplish this as you have done in previous examples.

4. Place two `if` blocks (available from the Control menu in the Built-In tab) inside the `while` block.

5. For the first `if` statement, place a less-than (<) block (available from the Math menu). For the second if statement, place a greater-than (>) block (available from the Math menu).

6. Set the left argument of each comparison to be the current weight value. This can be found with a select list item (available from the List menu), where the list is a `TinyDB`. `GetValue` with tag `weightList` and the index is the `global index` variable.

7. Set the right argument of each comparison to be another `select list` block connected to the `weightList` retrieved from the database.

8. In the less-than comparison, set the remaining index to the `global low` variable.

9. In the greater-than comparison, set the remaining index to the `global high` variable.

10. In the `then-do` space of the low tester, set the `low` variable to the current index.

11. In the `then-do` space of the high tester, set the `high` variable to the current index.

12. After the second `if` statement, but inside the `while` loop, increase the index by 1 to cycle through all the list weights.

13. After the `while` loop, display the lightest and heaviest weights and dates recorded by placing `lightest.Text` and `heaviest.Text` in the procedure.

14. Connect each of the text setters to a `make text` block.

15. Connect the first text arguments to the appropriate current text (`lightest.Text` or `heaviest.Text`).

16. Connect the second text arguments to a `select list item` block (available from the Lists menu).

17. Set the `list` connector of each `select` block to a `TinyDB.GetValue` with the tag `timeList`.

18. Set the `index` of each block to the correct variable (`high` for heaviest, `low` for lightest).

19. Set each third `text` argument to a new `text` block containing a colon (:).

21. Set each fourth `text` argument to another `select list item` block (available from the List menu).

22. Set the lists to the `weightList` via the database.

23. Set the indexes to the respective index (`high` or `low` variable). (See Figure 9.25.)

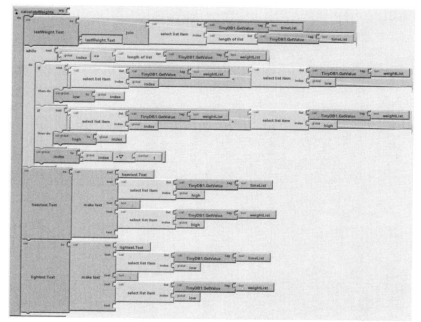

FIGURE 9.25

The completed to
calculateWeights
do procedure.

THE TESTING PHASE

Due to the nature of this app, it has been very difficult to test and debug within the emulator or through App Inventor. Now that it is complete, however, you should be able to download it to your device through the interface or share it with others.

Although this application is now functional, there are numerous improvements you could apply to make it more user friendly and better looking. Here are a few suggestions. Good luck and happy coding!

- Add color scheme and custom images.
- Improve the graph quality by using Google visualizations.
- Calculate more statistics such as BMI or average weight.

SUMMARY

Now that you have successfully created this application, you can see how simple ideas can turn into huge applications due to the sheer number of components. Although almost everything you implemented was very simple on its own, getting all the pieces to work together can be very challenging. In fact, it is typically the integration of components that causes the most errors when programming. However, as you saw, as long as you pay attention to your code, it can develop into a great tool!

THE QUIZZLER

IN THIS CHAPTER

- Image sprites
- Checkboxes
- Procedures
- The TinyDB component
- Random numbers
- Persistence of data between screens
- Tracking variables
- Comparing responses to stored values
- Lists

INTRODUCTION

In Chapter 4, "Whack-A-Mole," and Chapter 7, "The Jigsaw Puzzle," you learned how to manipulate image sprites to play *Whack-a-Mole* and to put together a jigsaw puzzle. In Chapter 6, "Trivia Quiz," you learned how to create a quiz using checkboxes in place of option buttons, and where the questions and answers were stored in a TinyDB database. You've also learned how to use procedures to cut down on redundancy in your coding. In this chapter, you will use those skills to create an application in which a puzzle is slowly revealed when the player correctly answers questions. The main differences between this and what you've done before is that this has much more code. (You'll be handling nine questions, 27 answers, and nine image sprites.) In addition, rather than using touch events to manipulate the images, you'll be tying them to the quiz answers.

The Design Phase

This app will be composed of three screens: The standard welcome screen, containing the title and instructions; the Game screen, where the questions will be asked and answered; and the Victory screen, which will, if the answers were all correct, show the completely revealed picture.

Create the App

To begin building the app, follow these steps:

1. Create a new project in the App Inventor and name it QuizReveal.
2. When App Inventor advances to the first screen (Screen1), change the AlignHorizontal setting in the Properties dialog box to Center and the BackgroundColor property to dark gray.
3. Add a second screen and call it Game. When this screen loads, change the BackgroundColor and AlignHorizontal settings to the same values as in Screen1.
4. Add a third screen and call it Victory. When this screen loads, change the BackgroundColor setting to black and the AlignHorizontal setting to the same value as Screen1 and Game. With that set, go back to Screen1.

Add Components

With the screen properties set, it's time to add the components to the screens that you'll need to make them work.

Add Screen I Components

To add the necessary Screen1 components, follow these steps:

1. Drag six Label components to Screen1. Make sure they are lined up vertically. The first two Label components will hold the title.
2. Click Label1. In the Properties panel, select both the FontBold and FontItalic checkboxes, change the FontSize setting to 20, change the FontTypeface setting to Sans Serif, and type The in the Text field. Finally, change the TextAlignment setting to Center and the TextColor setting to white.

3. Click Label2. In the Properties panel, select both the FontBold and FontItalic checkboxes, change the FontSize setting to 60 (yes, this line will be a bit bigger), change the FontTypeface setting to Sans Serif, and type QUIZZLER in the Text field. Finally, change the TextAlignment setting to Center and the TextColor setting to white.

4. Click Label3. In the Properties panel, select both the FontBold and FontItalic checkboxes, change the FontTypeface setting to Sans Serif, and type Guess the correct answers to questions about video games to reveal a screenshot from a classic online game in the Text field. Then, change the TextAlignment setting to Center and the TextColor setting to yellow. Finally, for this one, change the Width setting to 200 pixels. That will keep it from filling up the entire width of the screen.

5. Labels 4, 5, and 6 are going to act as spacers, so the button doesn't butt up against the text. In each of these, delete Text for Label? from the Text field so that the field is empty.

6. Drag a Button component to Screen1. In the Properties panel, change the BackgroundColor setting to green. Make sure both the Enabled and FontBold checkboxes are selected. Change the FontSize setting to 30, the FontTypeface setting to Sans Serif, and the Shape property to Rounded. In the Text field, type Play. Finally, change the TextAlignment setting to Center and the TextColor setting to blue.

7. Add a TinyDB component to the screen. Make sure it shows up as a non-visible component (see Figure 10.1). These are all of the components you'll need for the first screen.

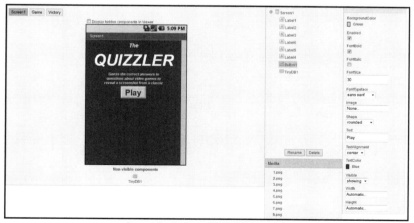

FIGURE 10.1

Screen 1 with all of the added components.

Add Game Components

This screen will start out very much like the puzzle game you created in Chapter 7. Follow these steps:

1. Click the Game button at the top of the App Builder screen to advance to the next screen.
2. Add a Canvas component to the screen. In the Properties panel, change the BackgroundColor setting to none, the Width setting to Fill Parent, and the Height setting to 300 pixels.
3. Add nine ImageSprite components to the Canvas component. Place the ImageSprite components at the following coordinates:

- ImageSprite1
  - X = 1
  - Y = 1
- ImageSprite2
  - X = 100
  - Y = 1
- ImageSprite3
  - X = 200
  - Y = 1
- ImageSprite4
  - X = 1
  - Y = 100
- ImageSprite5
  - X = 100
  - Y = 100
- ImageSprite6
  - X = 200
  - Y = 100
- ImageSprite7
  - X = 1
  - Y = 200

- ImageSprite8
  - X = 100
  - Y = 200
- ImageSprite9
  - X = 200
  - Y = 200

4. For each ImageSprite component, upload the associated PNG file included with this book. (ImageSprite1 = 1.png, ImageSprite2 = 2.png, etc.)

5. Add a Label component directly below the Canvas component. Make sure it appears centered within the space horizontally. In the Properties panel, change the FontSize setting to 12, the FontTypeface setting to Sans Serif and the TextColor setting to white.

6. In the Palette, click Screen Arrangement, and drag a TableArrangement component below the Label component. Set it for the three columns and three rows and change the Width setting to Fill Parent.

7. Inside the TableArrangement component, add three CheckBox components. Place one in each row, all in the left column (see Figure 10.2). For all three CheckBox components, change the FontSize setting to 12 and the TextColor setting to white.

8. For CheckBox2, change the Width setting to 200 pixels.

9. Drag a Label component to the TableArrangement component and place it in the middle cell (column 2, row 2), just to the right of CheckBox2. Change the Width setting for the Label component to 40 and clear the Text field. This label is going to be used as a spacer, just like Label4–Label6 on the first screen. The width for CheckBox2 and Label2 are set to a predetermined amount so the button you are about to install doesn't move back and forth when the length of the answer changes.

10. In the last cell of the middle row, just right of the empty label you just added, add a Button component. In the Properties panel, change the BackgroundColor setting to green, make sure the Enabled and FontBold checkboxes are selected, and change the FontTypeface setting to Sans Serif. Finally, change the Shape to Rounded and type Go! in the Text field, and make sure the TextAlignment setting is set to Center.

11. The last component you need for this screen is another TinyDB component. As you'll recall, you need the database to store and save values from one screen to another. There's only one database per app, but you have to put the component on each screen from which you want to access the values. As with Screen1, the database should be listed as a non-visible component. Your screen should now look like the one in Figure 10.2.

FIGURE 10.2

Game screen with all of the added components.

Add Victory Screen Components

For this screen, click the Victory button at the top of the App Builder screen to advance to the next screen. Then repeat steps 2–4 in the preceding section, "Add Game Components." This time, however, uncheck the Visible checkbox for each of the nine sprites. You should now have a list of nine sprites under Canvas1, but on the actual screen, you should see only the icon for the Canvas itself (see Figure 10.3).

With that done, follow these steps:

1. Under the Canvas component, add one Label component. Change the FontSize setting to 20, the FontTypeface setting to Sans Serif, the TextAlignment setting to Center, and the TextColor setting to white.
2. Drag over a Button component. In the Properties panel, change the BackgroundColor setting to blue, make sure the Enabled and FontBold checkboxes are selected, change the FontSize setting to 20, change the FontTypeface setting to Sans Serif, and change the Shape setting to Rounded. In the Text field, type `Play Again`. Finally, change the TextAlignment setting to Center and the TextColor setting to orange. See Figure 10.3.

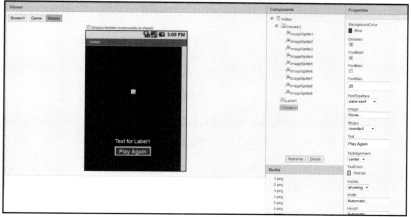

FIGURE 10.3

Victory screen with all of the added components and the sprites set to not visible.

THE CODE PHASE

In App Builder, return to Screen1. There are two tasks to perform on this screen. The first task is to code the button to move to the next screen. This should be old hat by now. Just open the Blocks Editor and match up your screen to the one in Figure 10.4. The second task will be to set up the questions and answers.

FIGURE 10.4

Coding the button to advance to the Game screen.

Set Up the Question and Answer Bank

To set up your question and answer bank, follow these steps:

1. Drag a `when Screen1.Initialize do` block to the workspace.
2. Drag a `call TinyDB1.StoreValue` block from the TinyDB1 menu under the My Blocks tab to the `when Screen1.Initialize do` block. Then drag over two `text` blocks from the Text menu under the Built-In tab, placing one in each socket of the `call TinyDB1.StoreValue` block. Change the text for the `text` block attached to the `tag` socket to `question1` and the text for the `text` block attached to the `valueToStore` socket to `This game holds the record for the longest development time ever`. See Figure 10.5.

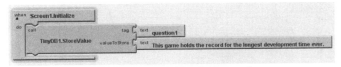

FIGURE 10.5

Storing the first question to the database when Screen1 is initialized.

3. Repeat step 2 for all of the questions and answers listed in Table 10.1. Number your tags question1 through question9 and answer1 through answer27, as shown in Figure 10.6.

NOTE Table 10.2, shown later in this chapter, contains the answer key. You'll need this later to check for correct answers. There will be three checkboxes for each question, as there were in Chapter 6. The Position column in Table 10.2 indicates which checkbox is associated with which answer.

TABLE 10.1 QUESTION AND ANSWER BANK

Tag	ValueToStore
question1	This game holds the record for the longest development time ever.
answer1	Team Fortress 2
answer2	Duke Nukem Forever
answer3	Starcraft II
question2	This Sci-Fi channel series was going to be an MMORPG until the developer went bankrupt.
answer4	Stargate SG-1
answer5	Farscape
answer6	Warehouse 13
question3	This MMORPG still has more subscribers than any other in history.
answer7	Everquest
answer8	World of Warcraft
answer9	Star Wars: The Old Republic
question4	The concept of "zerging" your enemy stems from what game?
answer10	Minecraft
answer11	Warcraft
answer12	Starcraft
question5	Angelina Jolie played this video game heroine in two movies.
answer13	Joanna Dark

answer14	Samas Aran
answer15	Lara Croft
question6	What game tells you that it's sorry, but the princess is in another castle?
answer16	Super Mario Brothers
answer17	Legend of Zelda
answer18	Final Fantasy
question7	What was the first commercially successful video game?
answer19	Asteroids
answer20	Pong
answer21	Pac Man
question8	This game is considered the first MMORPG.
answer22	World of Warcraft
answer23	Ultima Online
answer24	Everquest
question9	Which MMORPG is the above screenshot taken from?
answer25	Asheron's Call
answer26	Everquest
answer27	Dark Age of Camelot

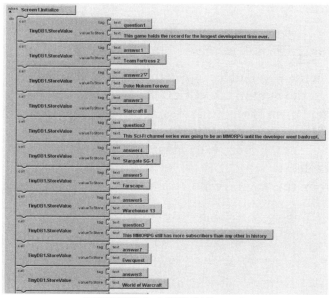

FIGURE 10.6

Adding more questions and answers to the database.

If you find you're running out of room at the bottom of the work area, right-click the work area and choose Resize Workspace from the menu that appears. (See Figure 10.7.) This adjusts the work area so that everything will fit. You may need to do this more than once as you add code to your app.

FIGURE 10.7

Right-click the workspace and use this to resize it to accommodate more block clusters.

Source: Jeffrey Hawthorne. ©2013. All rights reserved.

After you have entered all 36 values into the database, you're finished with this screen.

Code the Game Screen

On the Game screen, you need to set up four variables. The first is a random number that will be used to govern which question will be asked. The second is a variable to enumerate that question, similarly to how the active sprite was controlled in Chapter 7. Next is a counter used to track how many questions have been asked, and finally a variable to pass on to the last screen telling it whether or not the game was won.

Define the Variables

To define the variables for this screen, follow these steps:

1. Click the Game button in the App Builder screen to switch to that screen.
2. In the Blocks Editor, click the Built-In tab, click Definition, and drag four `def variable` blocks to the screen. Name them `random`, `question`, `turn`, and `isWin`.
3. Drag out three `number` blocks from the Math menu, connecting them to the `random`, `turn`, and `question` blocks. Set the `random` and `question` blocks to the number 0 and set the `turn` block to the number 1.
4. Drag a `false` block from the Logic menu, connecting it to the `isWin` block. See Figure 10.8.

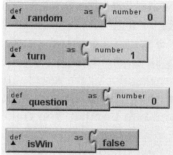

FIGURE 10.8

Defining the four global variables for the Game screen.

Now it's time to define some procedures. As you'll recall, a procedure is a code cluster that can be reused over and over again. This app relies heavily on procedures. You'll use procedures to get and set the variables, to check for correct answers, and to reveal the picture.

Define the Procedures

To define the procedures, follow these steps:

1. In the Built-In tab, click Definition, and drag a `to procedure do` block to the workspace.
2. Rename the `to procedure do` block `setRandom`.
3. Click the My Blocks tab, click My Definitions, and drag a `set global random` block to the workspace and attach it to the `do` slot of the `to setRandom do` block.
4. Click the Built-In tab, click Math, and drag a `call random integer block` to the `to` socket of the `set global random` block.
5. There should be two `number` blocks already attached to the `from` and `to` sockets of the `call random integer` block. If there aren't, drag two `number` blocks from the Math menu to the workspace, connecting them to the `call random integer` block's `from` and `to` sockets. Change the value of the first number block to 1 and the second number block to 9. (See Figure 10.9.) Now, whenever this procedure is called, it will reset your `global random` variable to a new random number.

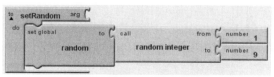

FIGURE 10.9

The completed `setRandom` procedure.

6. Drag another `to procedure do` block to the workspace and name it `setQuestion`.

7. In the My Blocks tab, click My Definitions, and locate the `call setRandom` block. This block calls the `setRandom` procedure you created a moment ago. Drag this `call setRandom` block to the `toset Question do` block. Now you have a procedure that calls another procedure.

8. Below this call, add a `set global question` block. Set it to your `global random` variable, as shown in Figure 10.10. (Both of these blocks are also found in the My Definitions menu.) Now this procedure sets the `global random` variable to a new random number, and then sets the question to that random number. You could code this procedure in such a way that you set the question to a random number directly and just get rid of the `setRandom` procedure, but there will be a small change at the end of the chapter that should make it apparent why that's not a good idea.

FIGURE 10.10

A procedure calling another procedure.

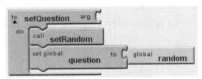

9. Those procedures were small and simple. The next ones will be substantially bigger. You'll use the next one to set the question and answer labels. To begin, drag another `to procedure do` block from the Definition menu under the Built-In tab to the workspace. Name it `getQuestion`.

10. Place an `if then-do` block from the Control menu inside it. In the `test` socket of the `if then-do` block, attach an equals (=) connector block from the Math menu. Click the My Blocks tab and drag a `global question` block from the My Definitions menu to the first socket of the = connector and a `number` block from the Math menu to the second socket. Change the value of the `number` block to 1. (See Figure 10.11.)

FIGURE 10.11

Creating a test condition for setting the question and answer text.

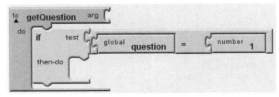

11. Drag the following blocks to the workspace: set Label1.Text (from the Label1 menu), set CheckBox1.Text (from the CheckBox1 menu), set CheckBox2.Text (from the CheckBox2 menu), and set CheckBox3.Text (from the CheckBox3 menu). Place them all in the then-do slot.

12. In the My Blocks tab, click the TinyDB1 menu, and drag four call TinyDB1.GetValue blocks to the workspace, placing one in each to socket of the Label and CheckBox blocks.

13. Click the Built-In tab, click Text, and drag a text block to each tag socket. Set the text of the one connected to set Label1.Text to question1; the one connected to set CheckBox1.Text to answer1; the one connected to set CheckBox2.Text to answer2; and the one connected to set CheckBox3.Text to answer3. Now when this procedure is called, if the question has been set to 1, the text on the screen will be set to the first question and the first three answers. (See Figure 10.12.)

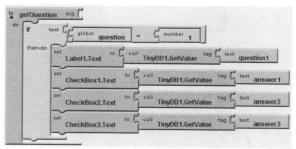

FIGURE 10.12

If the question variable equals 1, then assign question1, answer1, answer2, and answer 3 from the TinyDB to the label and checkboxes.

14. Repeat steps 10–13, dragging the new if then-do block below the last one. This time, however, change the value in the number block in the equals (=) connector block to 2, set the Label1.Text value to question2, set the CheckBox1.Text value to answer4, set the CheckBox2.Text value to answer5, and set the CheckBox3.Text value to answer6. (See Figure 10.13.)

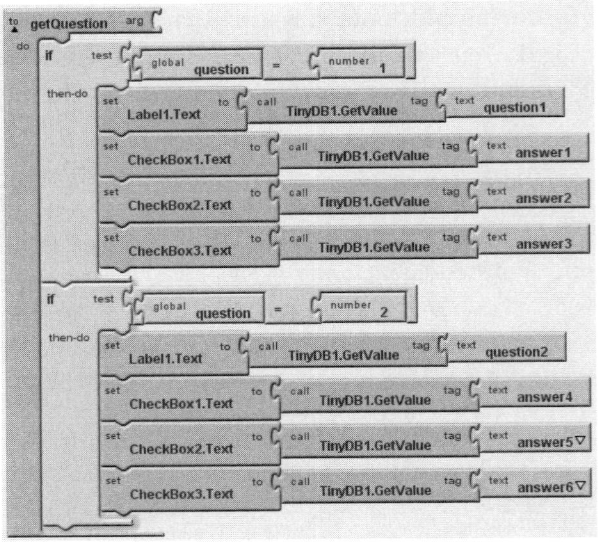

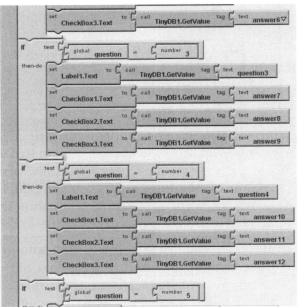

FIGURE 10.13

A new decision added for question2.

15. Repeat step 14 until you have all nine questions and 27 answers accounted for. (See Figures 10.14 through 10.17.)

FIGURE 10.14

Decisions for questions 3 and 4.

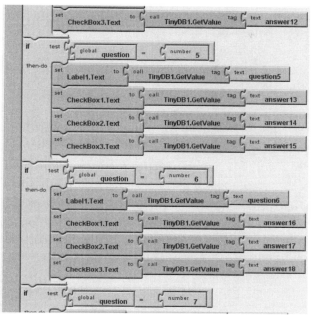

FIGURE 10.15

Decisions for questions 5 and 6.

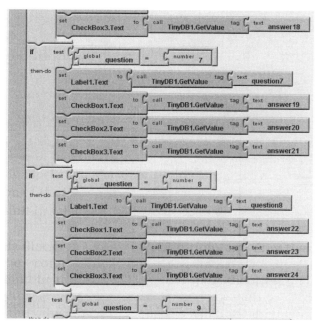

FIGURE 10.16

Decisions for questions 7 and 8.

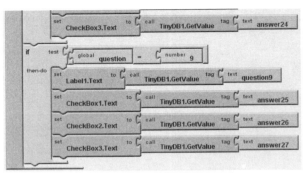

FIGURE 10.17

Decision for question9.

16. You're not quite finished with this procedure! If you'll recall from Chapter 6, there's a lot of enabling/disabling involved with checkboxes to get them to behave like option buttons, so that needs to be handled between turns. In Chapter 6, this was done off screen, as you changed screen with every guess. This time, the screen won't change; only what is displayed on it will. That means the re-enabling and unchecking must be handled onscreen. To begin, drag a set `Enabled` block and a set `Checked` block for each of the three CheckBox components (set `CheckBox1.Enabled`, set `CheckBox1.Checked`, etc.). Set all the `Enabled` blocks to `true` and all of the `Checked` blocks to `false` using `true` and `false` blocks from the Logic menu under the Built-In tab. Add your assembled block clusters to the bottom of your to `getQuestion` procedure. (See Figure 10.18.)

FIGURE 10.18

The checkboxes must be reset every turn.

17. Next you have two linked procedures. Not linked in a formal sense; there is no linkage block you need to deal with, just two closely related procedures that will interact by one calling the other. When a question is answered, you need to check if that answer is correct. If that answer is correct, then you need to reveal one of the pieces of the picture. Because the procedure that reveals the picture is called when the answer is checked, you need to code this one first. To begin, drag over a new to `procedure do` block from the Definitions menu under the Built-In tab to the workspace and name it `revealPic`.

18. Add an `if then-do` block from the Control menu to it. In the `test` socket, attach an equals (=) connector block from the Math menu. Drag a `global turn` block from the My Definitions menu under the My Blocks tab to the first socket of the = connector block and a `number` block from the Math menu under the Built-In tab to the second socket. Change the value of the `number` block to 1.

19. You want the images to appear to be revealed somewhat randomly, so pick a random `set ImageSprite` component. (This example uses ImageSprite7.) In the `then-do` slot, use the necessary blocks to set `ImageSprite7.Visible` to `true`. (See Figure 10.19.)

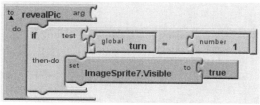

FIGURE 10.19

Revealing an image sprite based on the turn variable.

20. Repeat steps 18 and 19 until you have enough `if test then-do` blocks for nine turns. Increment the number side of the comparison each time. Place a different `set ImageSprite.Visible` block in each one. This book has them in the following order: ImageSprite7 (already accounted for), ImageSprite5, ImageSprite3, ImageSprite2, ImageSprite9, ImageSprite6, ImageSprite1, ImageSprite8, and ImageSprite4. See Figures 10.20 through 10.22.

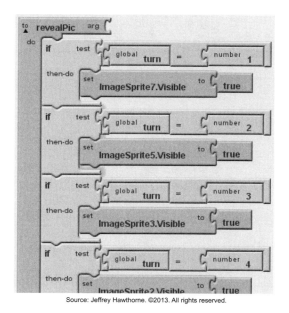

FIGURE 10.20

Revealing ImageSprites 2 through 4.

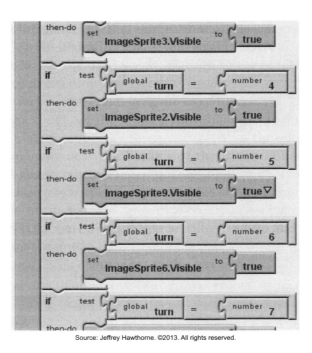

FIGURE 10.21

Revealing
ImageSprites 5
through 7.

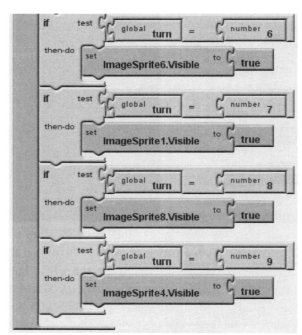

FIGURE 10.22

Revealing
ImageSprites 8
and 9.

21. Drag a new to procedure do block to the screen and name it checkAnswer.
22. Add two if then-do blocks from the Control menu under the Built-In tab, placing one inside the other. (This is known as a "nested" if, with one decision nested within another decision.) In the outer if then-do block, set the condition to the global random variable equaling 1. For the inner if then-do block, set the condition to test whether or not CheckBox2.Checked equals true. Why CheckBox2? Look at Table 10.2. It lists the position of the correct answers. For question1, the position is 2. In the then-do slot, place a call to your revealPic procedure. (See Figure 10.23.)

TABLE 10.2   ANSWER KEY

Question	Answer	Position
question1	answer2	2
question2	answer4	1
question3	answer8	2
question4	answer12	3
question5	answer15	3
question6	answer16	1
question7	answer20	2
question8	answer23	2
question9	answer27	3

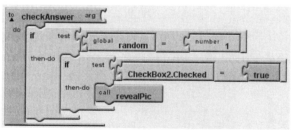

FIGURE 10.23

A nested decision, checking the value of random, followed by checking the checked status of the correct answer.

23. Repeat step 22, for each turn, until you have nine nested block clusters. In the outer if block of each cluster, increment the number part of the condition. In the inner if block, match the CheckBox.Checked block to the correct position from Table 10.2. See to Figures 10.24 through 10.26.

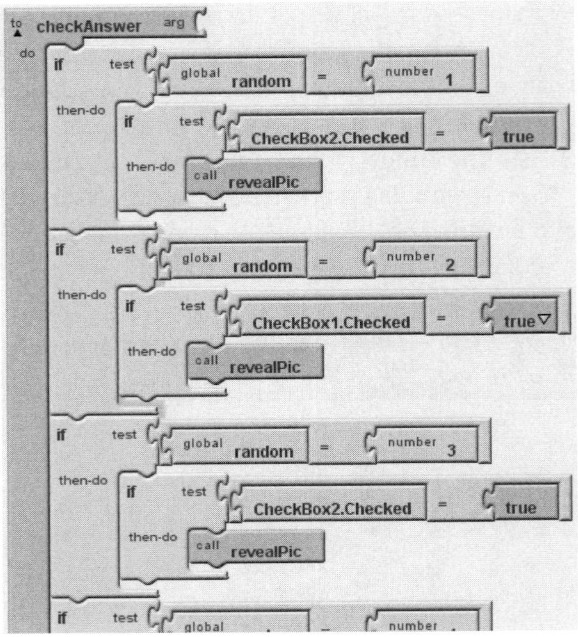

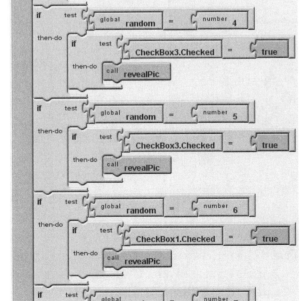

FIGURE 10.24

Nested decision for random numbers 2 and 3.

FIGURE 10.25

Nested decision for random numbers 4, 5, and 6.

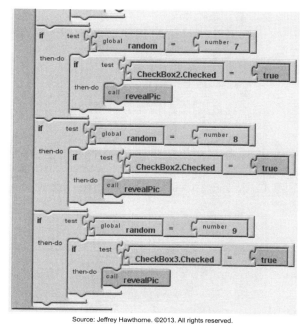

FIGURE 10.26

Nested decision for random numbers 7, 8, and 9.

24. Drag one last `to procedure do` block from the Definition menu under the Built-In tab to the workspace, bringing your total to six procedures. Name this one `checkIfPicComplete`.

25. You'll have one button on this screen, which will be used to advance the turn. The player will answer a question and then press the button, at which point the next question will be asked. (That is, unless nine turns have gone by, in which case the button press will advance the player to the next screen, which will indicate whether the player won or lost.) To make this work, drag another `if then-do` block from the Control menu to the workspace, placing it in the `to checkIfPicComplete do` block.

26. In the `test` socket, place an `and` block from the Logic menu. (You need the `and` block because there are 10 conditions to check. Nine conditions are used to determine victory: Are all nine images visible?)

27. Place a comparison in the `and` block to determine whether `ImageSprite1.Visible` equals `true`. (See Figure 10.27.)

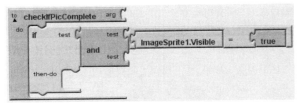

FIGURE 10.27

Using and to test multiple conditions at the same time.

28. When you added the condition, another socket was added to the and block. Add another comparison to it for `ImageSprite2.Visible`. Keep adding comparisons for each image sprite until you have enough to determine whether all nine images are visible. (See Figure 10.28.)

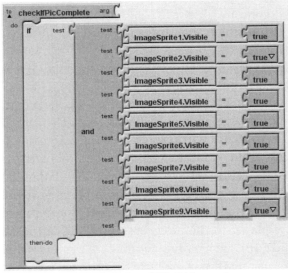

FIGURE 10.28

Testing the visibility of all nine image sprites with an and block.

 TIP

When you have a decision that requires many things to be true (such as the 10 decisions required in this procedure), an and block can save you vast amounts of time and space. The alternative would be to have 10 if then-do blocks nested within each other, which would result in a difficult-to-read mess!

29. There is also the 10th condition to add: Have nine turns been played? Add one more condition to check this equality (`global turn = 9`). In the `then-do` slot of this block, set your `global isWin` variable to `true`. (See Figure 10.29.)

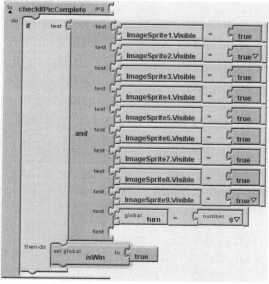

FIGURE 10.29

Completed
decision block
used to assign the
victory condition.

30. Add another `if then-do` block below the current one. Don't nest it; place it below the first one. In the `test` condition of this block, compare your `global turn` variable to 9, but instead of using an = block, use a >= block (greater than or equal to). Now if something happens and the app isn't advanced to the next screen as it should be when the turn hits nine, it will correct itself.

31. In the `then-do` slot of this block, place a `call open another screen with start value` block from the Control menu. In the `screenName` socket, place a `text` block from the Text menu and rename it `Victory`. In the `startValue` socket, place a `global isWin` block from the My Definitions menu under the My Blocks tab. When the screen is advanced, the `global isWin` variable will be passed to it. If the value was set to `true` by the previous `if` block, then `true` will be passed. If the value was not set to `true`, then `false` will be passed. (See Figure 10.30.)

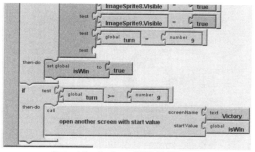

FIGURE 10.30

Completed
decision to pass
the `global`
`isWin` variable to
the next screen
once nine turns
have been played.

You may wonder: Why use two `if` blocks here rather than an `if-else` block? The reason is that you want the screen to advance regardless. You could use an `else` statement to set `isWin` to `false`, but because `isWin` was set to `false` when you initialized it, that is an unnecessary step.

Code the Components' Functionality

With the procedures defined, you can now code the functionality of the screen components. Follow these steps:

1. The first component that needs functioning is the screen itself, so drag a `Game.Initialize` block from the Game menu under the My Blocks tab to the workspace.
2. Inside the `when Game.Initialize do` block, place a `set ImageSprite.Visible` block for each ImageSprite component (`set ImageSprite1.Visible`, `set ImageSprite2.Visible`, etc.) and set all of them to `false`.
3. Below the `set ImageSprite.Visible` blocks, call two of your procedures: `setQuestion`, which will assign the random number to the question variable, and `getQuestion`, which will take that question variable and set the labels and checkboxes to the appropriate values based on the question variable. (See Figure 10.31.)

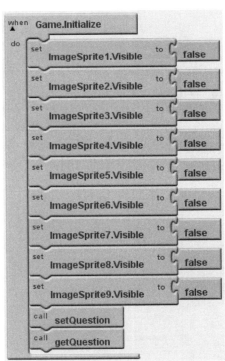

FIGURE 10.31

Using the screen initialization to turn off image sprites and call procedures.

4. Now you need to set the functionality of the checkboxes. As discussed in Chapter 6, you need the checkboxes to behave like option buttons, meaning only one can be selected at a time. To begin, drag a `when CheckBox1.Changed do` block from the CheckBox1 menu to the workspace.

5. Drag two `if then-do` blocks to the workspace and place them inside the `CheckBox1.Changed` block, one below the other.

6. In the Built-In tab, click Math, and drag an = block to the `test` socket of each `if then-do` block. In the first half of the = condition, place a `CheckBox1.Checked` block. In the second half, place a `true` block. So the test is, `if(CheckBox1.Checked = true)`. If it's true, you have to deactivate the other two checkboxes.

7. From the menus for each of the other checkboxes, drag over the `set CheckBox2.Enabled` and `set CheckBox3.Enabled` blocks. Set both to `false`.

8. Remember, you also want the player to be able to change his or her answer. To allow that, you'll need the other `if then-do` block, so that the player can uncheck a checkbox and select another one. Structure the second `if then-do` block just like the first one, except for the true/false condition, which you need to reverse. The test condition will be `if (CheckBox1.Checked = false)`, and the action will be to set `CheckBox2.Enabled = true` and `CheckBox3.Enabled = true`. Add the blocks to make that happen. When you're finished, it should look like Figure 10.32.

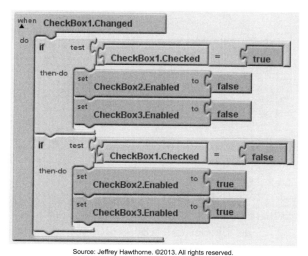

FIGURE 10.32

CheckBox1.
Changed block
cluster.

9. Repeat steps 4–8 for the other two checkboxes. Pay attention to the numbers. When you're finished, you should have two more block clusters arranged as in Figure 10.33 and Figure 10.34.

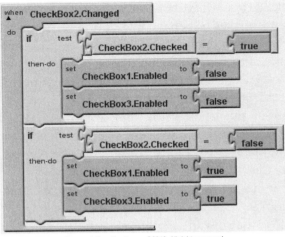

FIGURE 10.33

CheckBox2.
Changed block
cluster.

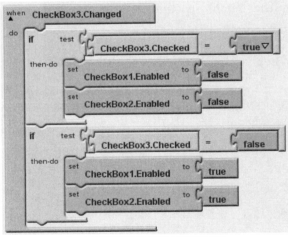

FIGURE 10.34

CheckBox3.
Changed block
cluster.

10. Drag a `when Button1.Click do` block to the workspace. The player will click this button after each guess to advance to the next question.

11. Inside the `when Button1.Click do` block, call the following procedures, in order: `checkAnswer`, `CheckIfPicComplete`, `setQuestion`, and `getQuestion`. Note that if the picture is complete, the `setQuestion` and `getQuestion` calls will be ignored, because the player will have moved on to the next screen. Assuming it is called, `getQuestion` will change the question and answers, provided nine turns haven't been played.

12. Add a set global turn variable. Add to it a plus (+) connector block from the Math menu under the Built-In tab. In the first socket of the + connector, add a global turn block. In the second socket, add a number block, and set its value to 1. (See Figure 10.35.)

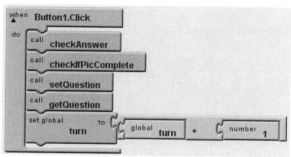

Source: Jeffrey Hawthorne. ©2013. All rights reserved.

FIGURE 10.35

Calling procedures when the button is clicked.

Finish the Game Screen

Your app works now, but with one major shortcoming: Because random numbers are, by their very nature, random, the same question may (and probably will) be asked more than once. You could end up playing a game where the same question is asked four or five times, sometimes all in a row. It would be great if you could code the game in such a way that once a question is asked, it doesn't get asked again. Fortunately there is a pretty easy way to do this. You'll need three things to make this happen: a new variable, a new procedure, and a modification to an existing procedure.

The new variable will be a list. A list is like a TinyDB in that it can hold multiple values. It differs from a database in that the values do not persist. After you change screens, the list and all its values go away. It is also much easier to manipulate when it comes to adding and removing values.

If you are familiar with Java programming, it has a Lists class. It is also similar to arrays in other languages. If you are unfamiliar with programming, your list will work like this: Imagine you have nine eggs, each with a number written on it from one to nine. The list is an empty egg carton. Your new procedure will select a random number, and then look inside the egg carton. Let's say the random number is three. Is there a three in the egg carton? Not yet, it's empty. In this case, then, you'll set the question to three and put the egg with a three written on it inside the carton. Now it's the next turn. You pick a new random number, which happens to be a three again. You look inside the egg carton. Yep, there's an egg with a three on it, so you can't use that number. Better go back and pick a new number. You continue to check the egg carton whenever a new number is picked to make sure it's not in there.

To create your list variable, follow these steps:

1. Drag a `def variable` block from the Definition menu under the Built-In tab to the workspace. Name it `listOfQuestions`.
2. Click the Lists menu and drag a `call make a list` block to the `as` socket of the `def listOfQuestions` block to define your variable. That's all you need to do with this; the list itself can be empty. (See Figure 10.36.)

FIGURE 10.36

Creating a list.

The `setQuestion` procedure is set up so that the random number is set, and then the question is set. Here, you will add an intervening step in the form of a new procedure: `checkList`. This procedure will check the list to see if the random number selected already exists in the list. If the number does exist, then the procedure will roll a new random number. It will continue to do this until it finds a number that is not in the list. To enable this, follow these steps:

1. Drag a `to procedure do` block from the Definition menu to the workspace and name it `checkList`.
2. Because you need to check the list more than once, you'll want a loop. A while loop is best for this situation because there will be two test conditions: is the item in the list, and is the turn less than 9? The second condition is extremely important, as you'll see shortly. Place a `while do` block from the Control menu inside the `to checkList do` block in the do slot.
3. Place an `and` block from the Logic menu in the `test` socket, then place a `call is in list?` block (found in the Lists menu) in the `test` socket of the `and` block. Finally, in the `thing` socket, place a `global random` block from the My Definitions menu under the My Blocks tab, and in the `list` socket, place a `global listOfQuestions` block, also found in the My Definitions menu. (See Figure 10.37.)

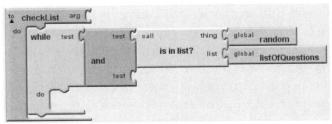

FIGURE 10.37

Setting the test condition to check for numbers in a list.

4. In the do slot of the `while-do` block, add a `call setRandom` block. While the `global random` variable is equivalent to any number listed in the list, it will call the `setRandom` procedure over and over again until it finds one number that isn't.

5. This list needs to grow so that the questions are never repeated, so below the `while do` block, place a `call add items to list` block from the Lists menu under the Built-In tab. In the `list` socket, again add the `global listOfQuestions` block, and in the `item` socket, place another `global random` block. Now, after the loop has ended, the procedure will place the new number in the list, so next time the procedure is called it will have a slightly bigger list to choose from.

6. Below the `call add items to list` block, add a `set global question` block, and set it to `global random` (see Figure 10.38). As you can see, it would have been a bad idea to set the question to a random number directly earlier in this chapter. If you had done that, it would have changed the question many times during the loop, resulting in a lot more processing. It may even have created some graphical glitches.

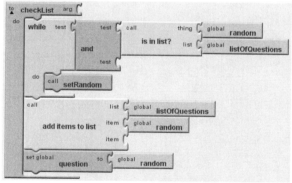

FIGURE 10.38

The completed checklist procedure.

7. Move over to the `setQuestion` procedure you created earlier. You no longer need to set the global question to random; that is being handled inside the `checkList` procedure now. Instead, pull those two blocks out of the `setQuestion` block and throw them in the trash. In their place, add a `call checkList` block (see Figure 10.39). Now this will set the random variable, check the list to see if that variable exists within the list, and when it gets to one that isn't, sets the question to the `random` variable.

FIGURE 10.39

The reconfigured setQuestion procedure.

Now you've fixed the problem with repeating the same question, but not so fast! There's a new problem, and it's even bigger. After all the pieces have been placed, all the numbers 1 through 9 will be in the list. Your setRandom procedure sets the random variable to a number between 1 and 9. That means the number will *always* be in the list at this point. And *that* means the loop checking the list will go on forever! This is known as an *infinite loop*, and your device will not appreciate that. This is where the second condition that I mentioned earlier comes into play. In the second test socket of the and block in the checkList procedure, place a less-than (<) connector block from the Math menu under the Built-In tab. In the first socket of the connector, place your global turn variable. In the second socket place a number block, and change its value to 9. Now the loop will fire only if the turn is less than 9. You're safely out of the infinite loop zone (see Figure 10.40).

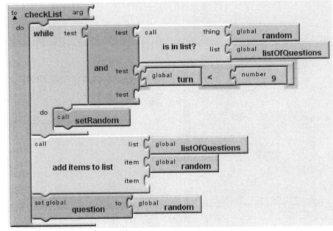

FIGURE 10.40

A second condition (turn < 9) has been added to the checklist procedure.

Set Up the Victory Screen

Now you can move on to the last screen, the Victory screen. The first cluster of blocks for the Victory screen revolves primarily around the ImageSprite components. Follow these steps:

1. Drag a when Victory.Initialize do block from the Victory menu under the My Blocks tab to the workspace.
2. Place an ifelse then-do else-do block inside the when Victory.Initialize do block. For the test condition, add an = connector from the Math menu under the Built-In tab. In the first socket of the = connector, add a call get start value block (found in the Control menu). In the second slot, add a true block (from the Logic menu).

3. If `call get start value` is true, add a `set Label1.Text` block from the Label1 menu under the My Blocks tab; then add a `text` block to the `to` socket and change its text to `Congratulations! You got them all right!`.

4. Set the `ImageSprite.Visible` property to `true` for all the ImageSprite components. The blocks for steps 3 and 4 should all be added to the `then-do` slot, not the `else-do` slot. (See Figure 10.41.)

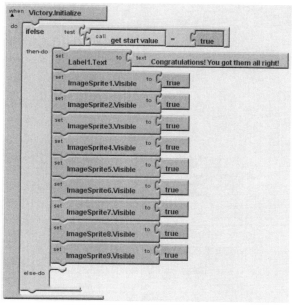

FIGURE 10.41

Rendering the complete picture visible upon victory.

5. In the `else-do` slot, add a `set Label1.Text` block; then add a `text` block and change its text to `Sorry! Maybe next time..`.

6. Set the `ImageSprite.Visible` property to `false` for all of the ImageSprite components. (See Figure 10.42.)

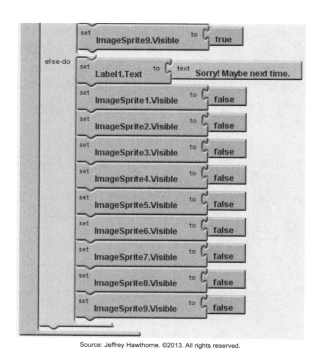

FIGURE 10.42

Rendering the complete picture invisible upon loss.

7. Drag a `when Button1.Click do` block to the workspace.
8. Add a `call open another screen` block from the Control menu under the Built-In tab to the `Button1.Click` block. Set the `screenName` to Screen1. (See Figure 10.43.)

FIGURE 10.43

Adding functionality to the Play Again? button.

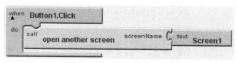

Done!

One of the key points of object-oriented programming discussed in earlier chapters is breaking tasks down to smaller and smaller pieces. The development of this app is a demonstration of that principle. Chapters 4, 6, and 7 all had something to contribute to the design of this app. So if you decide to design your own app, consider your design, ask yourself what the individual tasks are that you need to perform, and then, as part of your development, build a smaller app that focuses on just one of those tasks. Once you have one task complete, you can move on to another task, knowing that if you accidentally "break" the first part, you have something you can go back to for reference. This can help speed up development considerably.

SUMMARY

Most of this chapter reviews skills you developed in earlier chapters. You've learned how to take small simple programs and combine them into a larger, more robust program. You could make this app even more complex while utilizing already-learned concepts by adding more layers of interaction. For example, instead of the picture being revealed randomly, the player could click one of the squares, which would then reveal a question and answer. You could add a *Hangman* aspect by having a word or name associated with the images or guessing what it is a picture of. You have the skills; now use your imagination!

CONTROLLING NXT ROBOTS

CHAPTER OBJECTIVES

- Connect to NXT-based robots
- Learn about physical sensors and connections
- Program logic to control real-life sensors
- Remotely control robots from your Android device

INTRODUCTION

In recent years, robots have become popular in nearly every market. Businesses use robots to automate tasks and build products. Hospitals use robots to perform procedures and count pills. Even the general public has begun using robots for both productivity and entertainment. Within this surge of robotics, many people have begun programming their own robots, which can be purchased through suppliers like Lego or VEX.

For information about personal robot components, including the Lego NXT robots used in this chapter, check out VEX Robotics (www.vexrobotics.com) and Lego (mindstorms.lego.com).

Often, programming robots requires working knowledge of a programming language, such as C or Java. The innovators at these consumer robot companies, however, have created tools that enable anyone to create programs for these robots, no code required! App Inventor has also implemented this functionality, but goes a step further, enabling your Android device to connect to an NXT robot via Bluetooth, send commands, and receive data!

Some Background on Lego Mindstorm NXT Robots

Lego Mindstorm NXT 2.0 robots come as a kit from Lego and enable anyone to easily build, program, and use a small robot. Designed to be built with Lego simplicity, each set comes with various motors, sensors, and components that allow movement and the intake of information about the robot's environment. Controlling all these components is a micro-controller known as an NXT Brick. The Brick serves as the "brains" of the robot and can run user-created programs, connect to other Bluetooth-enabled devices, send commands to motors, and process information from sensors connected to the Brick.

Motors give the robot mobility, and give you, the programmer, complete control over robot motion. In addition, motors can be used with claws, pulleys, and other devices for movement. Push sensors enable the robot to determine when it has hit something in its environment. These sensors send a signal to the Brick when they are activated. The microphone monitors sound levels around the robot and reports the noise level to the Brick. Using these three sensors, you can move and monitor your robot. And with App Inventor, you can do it from your phone.

Setup and Construction

While the exact configuration of your device and robot are flexible, this chapter will demonstrate a standard NXT robot configuration called the tri-bot. The instructions to construct a tri-bot are found on the Lego website (mindstorms.lego.com/en-us/support/buildinginstructions/8527-/Tribot.aspx) and can also be found on the resources site for this book (www.cengage.com/downloads).

After your robot is constructed, you will need to pair your Android device to the NXT Brick. Follow these steps:

1. In the Brick's menu, select Bluetooth.
2. Ensure that the Brick's Bluetooth settings are turned on and discoverable.
3. On your Android device, open the Settings menu, choose Wireless, choose Bluetooth, and ensure that the Bluetooth setting is turned on.

4. You should see a list of available devices, one of which says NXT. Select this device and pair it to your phone.

5. You may be asked to enter a passcode, which can be found in the Bluetooth settings on the NXT Brick.

App Discussion

In this chapter, you will create an Android app to control an NXT Robot via Bluetooth and monitor its surroundings through the use of sensors and motors. You will begin by connecting to the robot through a simple selection of the paired robot. Once connected, you will provide an interface that enables the user to move the robot forward and backward, as well as alert the user if the robot hits an obstacle via the touch sensor or if the noise level in the room is high. You will alert the user through the use of labels on the screen. You will also provide the functionality to autonomously stop the robot if the robot touches something—say, it hits a wall. You will also enable the user to play a noise through the robot.

Throughout previous app, as well as in this one, you use procedures that occur whenever the user or event does something—for example, the click procedure for buttons or an event caused by the shaking of the phone. These procedures have a unique position in modern programming; as such, they have interesting mechanisms. The Java language, which is commonly used for these types of projects, refers to these events handlers as "action listeners."

How action listeners work is beyond the scope of this text, but it is important for you to have a general overview. Each object—whether a button or, as you will see, a robot sensor—has certain parameters, such as pressed, which will trigger hooks. You can create action listeners and attach them to a hook. When this hook occurs, a message indicating this is propagated throughout the program. When the paired action listener hears this message, it activates and performs the programmed function.

As you can imagine, this is an incredibly important ability of a user interface and is a paradigm shift from traditional sequential programming to event-driven programming. This type of programming is typically used for user interfaces and other event-driven environments, as the method of alerting listeners is (relatively) lengthy. It is too slow for many applications, but much faster than we as humans can react, making it perfect for user interfaces like this one.

The Design Phase

The user interface for this app is pretty simple: just a few buttons and labels. However, the enabled buttons will depend on whether a robot is connected. Therefore, a lot of interface setup will be done in the Blocks Editor instead of the main App Inventor screen. Follow these steps:

1. Create a new project and name it NXTapp.
2. Drag a ListPicker component to the top of the screen. In the Properties panel, in the Text field, type Connect. Then change the Width setting to Fill Parent. This will enable the user to select the robot to which he or she will connect. Name the ListPicker component Connect. Ensure that the TextAlignment Property is set to Center.
3. Drag a Button component beneath the ListPicker component. In the Properties panel, in the Text field, type Move Forward. Then change the Width setting to Fill Parent. Name the button Forward. This button will be used to move the robot forward. Ensure that the TextAlignment Property is set to Center.
4. Drag a Label component beneath the Button component. In the Properties panel, change the Width setting to Fill Parent. Rename the label touchLabel. Ensure that the TextAlignment Property is set to Center. You will use this label to alert the user if the robot's touch sensor registers an object.
5. Drag a Button component beneath the Label component. In the Properties panel, in the Text field, type Play Noise. Then change its Width setting to Fill Parent. Name the button Noise. Ensure that the TextAlignment Property is set to Center. This will be used to tell the robot to beep.
6. Drag another Button component beneath the last one. In the Properties panel, in the Text field, type Stop. Then change its Width setting to Fill Parent. Name the button Stop. Ensure that the TextAlignment Property is set to Center. You will use this button to stop the robot.
7. Drag a Label component beneath the Stop button. In the Properties panel, change its Width setting to Fill Parent. Rename it microphoneLabel. Ensure that the TextAlignment Property is set to Center. You will use this button to alert the user about the noise level in the room.
8. Drag a Button component beneath the microphoneLabel component. Name it Reverse. In the Properties panel, in the Text field, type Move Backwards. Then change its Width setting to Fill Parent. Ensure that the TextAlignment Property is set to Center. You will use this button to tell the robot to reverse. That's all there is to the visual portion of the user interface. Yours should look like the one in Figure 11.1.

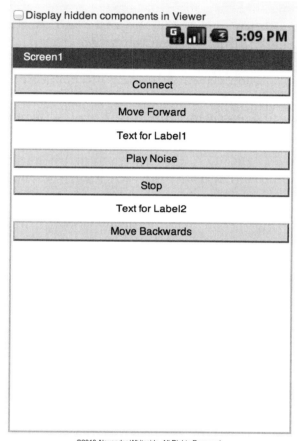

☐ Display hidden components in Viewer

🔋📶📧 5:09 PM

Screen1

Connect

Move Forward

Text for Label1

Play Noise

Stop

Text for Label2

Move Backwards

FIGURE 11.1

Screen 1 with
completed visual
components.

Before you turn to the Blocks Editor, let's add the necessary hidden components. Follow these steps:

1. In the Palette, click Other Stuff, and drag a BluetoothClient component to the screen.
2. In the Palette, click LEGO MINDSTORMS, and drag a NxtDirectCommands component to the screen.
3. Change the BluetoothClient setting for the NXTDirectCommands component to BluetoothClient1.
4. From the LEGOMINDSTORMS section of the Palette, drag a NxtTouchSensor component to the screen.
5. In the Properties tab, select BluetoothClient1 from the BluetoothClient selection box.

6. In the Properties panel, change the SensorPort setting to the port on your robot to which you have connected your touch sensor (for example, AB for ports A and B). Then click the PressedEventEnabled checkbox to select it. The ReleasedEvenEnabled checkbox should also be checked.

7. From the LEGOMINDSTORMS section of the Palette, drag a NxtSoundSensor component to the screen.

8. In the Properties tab, select BluetoothClient1 from the BluetoothClient selection box.

9. In the Properties panel, change the SensorPort setting to the port on your robot to which you have connected your microphone. Then click the AboveRangeEventEnabled checkbox to select it.

10. From the LEGOMINDSTORMS section of the Palette, drag a NxtDrive component to the screen.

11. In the Properties tab, select BluetoothClient1 from the BluetoothClient selection box.

12. In the Properties panel, change the DriveMotors setting to the ports on your robot to which you have connected your motors. For example, if you plugged your motors into ports A and B, type AB. Once these are added, you are ready to start coding. See Figure 11.2.

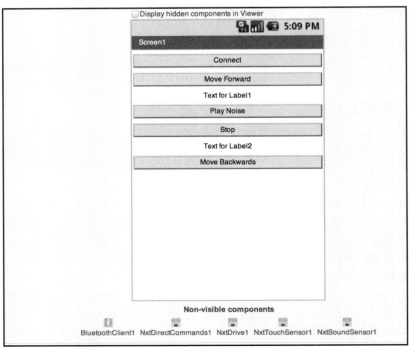

FIGURE 11.2

A complete Screen1 containing hidden components.

THE CODE PHASE

You will now create the logic to power the buttons and labels you placed in the previous section. You will begin with the initialization of the screen and the Connect button at the top of the screen and work your way down.

Initializing the Screen and the Connect Button

When you are initializing, you need to disable all the buttons and labels other than Connect. Follow these steps:

1. Open the Blocks Editor.
2. Click the My Blocks tab, click Screen1, and drag a `when Screen1.Initialize do` procedure to the screen.
3. Next, you'll disable all the buttons and labels individually. To begin, in the My Blocks tab, click Forward, and drag a `set Forward.Enabled to` block to the `when Screen1.Initialize do` block.
4. Click the Built-In tab, click Logic, and drag a `false` block to the `set Forward.Enabled to` block.
5. Click the My Blocks tab, click microphoneLabel, and drag a `set microphoneLabel.Visible to` block to the `when Screen1.Initialize do` block.
6. Click the Built-In tab, click Logic, and drag a `false` block to the `set microphoneLabel.Visible to` block.
7. Click the My Blocks tab, click Noise, and drag a `set Noise.Enabled to` block to the `when Screen1.Initialize do` block.
8. Click the Built-In tab, click Logic, and drag a `false` block to the `set Noise.Enabled to` block.
9. Click the My Blocks tab, click Reverse, and drag a `set Reverse.Enabled to` block to the `when Screen1.Initialize do` block.
10. Click the Built-In tab, click Logic, and drag a `false` block to the `set Reverse.Enabled to` block.
11. Click the My Blocks tab, click Stop, and drag a `set Stop.Enabled to` block to the `when Screen1.Initialize do` block.
12. Click the Built-In tab, click Logic, and drag a `false` block to the `set Stop.Enabled to` block.
13. Click the My Blocks tab, click touchLabel, and drag a `set touchLabel.Visible to` block to the `when Screen1.Initialize do` block.
14. Click the Built-In tab, click Logic, and drag a `false` block to the `set touchLabel.Visible to` block. Your initialization procedure should look like the one shown in Figure 11.3.

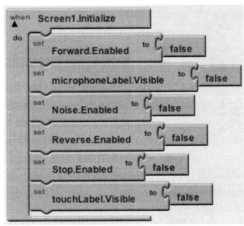

FIGURE 11.3

The completed initialization procedure.

The Connect button should list available connections and allow the user to select a robot connection to control. You will therefore have two states: a Before Picking state, in which you will get all the available connections and set the initial buttons to disabled, and an After Picking state, in which you will connect to the selected robot and, upon connection, enable the buttons. Follow these steps:

1. In the Blocks Editor, click the My Blocks tab, click Connect, and drag a when Connect. BeforePicking do block to the screen.
2. From the Connect section of the My Blocks tab, drag a set Connect.Elements to block to the when Connect.BeforePicking do block.
3. In the My Blocks tab, click BluetoothClient1, and drag a BluetoothClient1. AddressesAndNames block to the set Connect.Elements to block. This will display all the connected devices for the user to select. Your when Connect.BeforePicking do block should now look like the one in Figure 11.4.

FIGURE 11.4

The completed when Connect. BeforePicking do event.

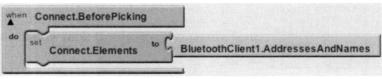

You will now create the After Picking procedure. Follow these steps:

1. In the Blocks Editor, click the My Blocks tab, click Connect, and drag a `when Connect. AfterPicking do` block to the screen.
2. Click the Built-In tab, click Control, and drag an `if test then-do` block to the `when Connect.AfterPicking do` block.
3. Click the My Blocks tab, click BluetoothClient1, and drag a `call BluetoothClient1. Connect address` block to the `test` socket of the `if test then-do` block.
4. In the My Blocks tab, click Connect, and drag a `Connect.Selection` block to the `address` socket of the `call BluetoothClient1.Connect address` block.
5. In the `then-do` section of the `if test then-do` block, you want to enable all the buttons and labels. To begin, click the My Blocks tab, click Forward, and drag a `set Forward. Enabled to` block to the `when Connect.AfterPicking do` block.
6. Click the Built-In tab, click Logic, and drag a `true` block to the `set Forward.Enabled to` block.
7. Click the My Blocks tab, click Noise and drag a `set Noise.Enabled to` block to the `when Connect.AfterPicking do` block.
8. Click the Built-In tab, click Logic, and drag a `true` block to the `set Noise.Enabled to` block.
9. Click the My Blocks tab, click Reverse, and drag a `set Reverse.Enabled to` block to the `when Connect.AfterPicking do` block.
10. Click the Built-In tab, click Logic, and drag a `true` block to the `set Reverse.Enabled to` block.
11. Click the My Blocks tab, click Stop, and drag a `set Stop.Enabled` to block to the `when Connect.AfterPicking do` block.
12. Click the Built-In tab, click Logic, and drag a `true` block to the `set Stop.Enabled to` block.
13. Click the My Blocks tab, click touchLabel, and drag a `set touchLabel.Visible to` block to the `when Connect.AfterPicking do` block.
14. Click the Built-In tab, click Logic, and drag a `true` block to the `set touchLabel.Visible to` block.
15. Click the My Blocks tab, click microphoneLabel, and drag a `set microphoneLabel.Visible to` block to the `when Connect.AfterPicking do` block.
16. Click the Built-In tab, click Logic, and drag a `true` block to the `set microphoneLabel. Visible to` block.
17. Next, you'll change the text of the labels to indicate that everything is normal. You will do so individually. To begin, click the My Blocks tab, click microphoneLevel, and drag a `set microphoneLabel.Text to` block to the `then-do` section of the `if test then-do` block.
18. Click the Built-In tab, click Text, and drag a `text` block to the `to` socket of the `set microphoneLabel.Text to` block. In the `text` block, type `Microphone Level: Normal`.

19. Click the My Blocks tab, click touchLabel, and drag a set touchLabel.Text to block to the then-do section of the if test then-do block.

20. Click the Built-In tab, click Text, and drag a text block to the to socket of the set touchLabel.Text to block. In the text block, type Touch Sensor: Not Pressed. Your when Connect.AfterPicking do block should look like the one in Figure 11.5.

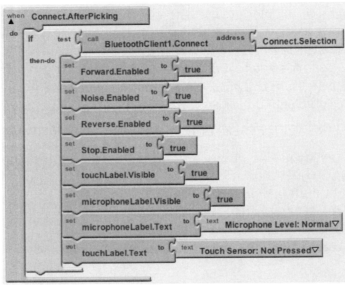

FIGURE 11.5

The completed when Connect. AfterPicking do event.

Coding the Buttons

You will now write the logic for each of the buttons. As stated at the beginning of the chapter, the Forward, Backward, and Stop Buttons control the motion of the robot, and therefore affect the motors. The microphone label will be used when the microphone detects sound above a certain level, while the touch label will be used whenever the robot hits something, registered by the touch sensor.

Coding the Motion

You will begin with the robot's motion. Follow these steps:

1. In the Blocks Editor, click the My Blocks tab, click Forward, and drag a when Forward.Click do block to the screen. This will make the robot move forward.

2. In the My Blocks tab, click NxtDrive1, and drag a call NxtDrive1.MoveForwardIndefinitely power block to the when Forward.Click do block.

3. Click the Built-In tab, click Math, and drag a `number` (123) block to the `call NxtDrive1.MoveForwardIndefinitely power` block. In the `number` block, type 100.

4. Click the My Blocks tab, click Reverse, and drag a `when Reverse.Click do` block to the screen. You will make the robot move backward when this is clicked.

5. In the My Blocks tab, click NxtDrive1, and drag a `call NxtDrive1.MoveBackwardIndefinitely power` block to the `when Reverse.Click do` block.

6. Click the Built-In tab, click Math and drag a `number` (123) block to the `call NxtDrive1.MoveBackwardIndefinitely power` block. In the `number` block, type 100.

7. Click the My Blocks tab, click Stop, and drag a `when Stop.Click do` block to the screen.

8. In the My Blocks tab, click NxtDrive1, and drag a `call NxtDrive1.Stop` block to the `when Stop.Click do` block to stop the wheels when the Stop button is clicked. The movement commands are now finished. They should look like the ones in Figure 11.6.

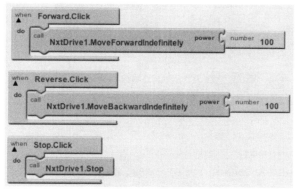

FIGURE 11.6

The completed forward, reverse, and stop commands.

©2013 Alexander Whiteside. All Rights Reserved.

Creating the Listeners

You will now create the listeners to handle the microphone and touch sensor. Follow these steps:

1. In the Blocks Editor, click the My Blocks tab, click NxtTouchSensor1, and drag a `when NxtTouchSensor1.Pressed do` block to the screen. This procedure is called whenever the sensor is pressed.

2. In this procedure, you will alert the user by setting the text of the touch label. To begin, in the My Blocks tab, click touchLabel, and drag a `set touchLabel.Text to` block to the `when NxtTouchSensor1.Pressed do` block.

3. Click the Built-In tab, click Text, and drag a `text` block to the `to` socket of the `set touchLabel.Text to` block. In the `text` block, type Touch Sensor Activated.

4. To make the robot stop hitting the object, click the My Blocks tab, click NxtDrive1, and drag a `call NxtDrive1.Stop` block to the `when NxtTouchSensor1.Pressed do` block.

5. To keep the status of the touch label accurate, you need to revert it to normal when the sensor is released. To do this, in the My Blocks tab, click NxtTouchSensor1, and drag a `when NxtTouchSensor1.Released do` block to the screen.

6. To update the touch label text, in the My Blocks tab, click touchLabel, and drag a `set touchLabel.Text to` block to the `when NxtTouchSensor1.Released do` block.

7. Click the Built-In tab, click Text, and drag a `text` block to the `set touchLabel.Text to` block. In the `text` block, type `Touch Sensor Value: Not Pressed`. Your finished touch sensor listener should look like the one in Figure 11.7.

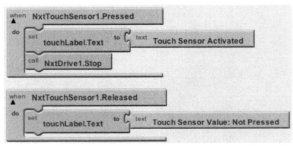

FIGURE 11.7

Touch sensor events.

Handling the Microphone Sensor

You will now handle the microphone sensor. Follow these steps:

1. In the Blocks Editor, click the My Blocks tab, click NxtSoundSensor1, and drag a `when NxtSoundSensor1.AboveRange do` block to the screen.

2. In this procedure, you will alert the user by setting the text of the microphone label. To begin, in the My Blocks tab, click microphoneLabel, and drag a `set microphoneLabel.Text to` block to the `when NxtSoundSensor1.AboveRange do` block.

3. Click the Built-In tab, click Text, and drag a `text` block to the `set microphoneLabel.Text to` block. In the `text` block, type `Microphone Level: High`.

4. To return the alert to normal, click the My Blocks tab, click NxtSoundSensor1, and drag a `when NxtSoundSensor1.WithinRange do` block to the screen.

5. Click the My Blocks tab, click microphoneLabel, and drag a `set microphoneLabel.Text to` block to the `when NxtSoundSensor1.WithinRange do` block.

6. Click the Built-In tab, click Text, and drag a `text` block to the `set microphoneLabel.Text to` block. In the `text` block, type `Microphone Level: Normal`. Your completed sound sensor handler should look like the one in Figure 11.8.

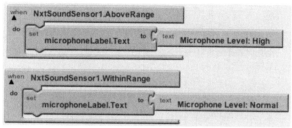

©2013 Alexander Whiteside. All Rights Reserved.

Microphone
sensor events.

Implementing the Play Noise Button

Lastly, you will implement the Play Noise button, which will make the robot beep. Follow these steps:

1. Click the My Blocks tab, click Noise, and drag the `when Noise.Click do` block to the screen.
2. In the My Blocks tab, click NxtDirectCommands1, and drag a `call NxtDirectCommands1. PlayTone frequencyHz durationMs` block to the `when Noise.Click do` block.
3. Click the Built-In tab, click Number, and drag a `number` block to the `frequencyHz` socket of the `call NxtDirectCommands1.PlayTone frequencyHz durationMs` block.
4. Change the value of the `number` block to 450.
5. Click the Built-In tab, click Number, and drag a `number` block to the `durationMs` socket of the `call NxtDirectCommands1.PlayTone frequencyHz durationMs` block.
4. Change the value of the `number` block to 250.

Congratulations! You have successfully implemented all the activity requirements in the Blocks Editor. Your finished screen should look like the one in Figure 11.9.

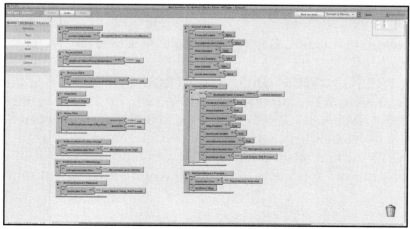

©2013 Alexander Whiteside. All Rights Reserved.

FIGURE 11.9

The complete
application.

The Testing Phase

Unlike previous apps, this one cannot be tested in the Emulator. It must be used on your actual device and constructed robot. To test the commands and run your app, follow these steps:

1. Download the app to your phone and turn on your robot.
2. Ensure that your devices are configured as discussed in the introduction, and pair the phone with your robot.
3. When you start the app, click the Connect button. As you programmed, the button should be replaced with a list of available connections, one being the robot.
4. Select the robot connection. You should now be faced with the rest of your buttons.
5. Test all the functionality by moving forward, backward, and stopping.
6. Clap or make a loud noise and watch the microphone alert change.
7. Drive the robot into a wall and watch the touch sensor activate and the robot automatically stop. You should see the reflected functions happen instantly from the press of the buttons on your mobile device.

On-Your-Own Improvements

While the app provides comprehensive control of the robot, there are some features that would be nice to have. Using skills gained from this lesson and previous chapters, attempt the following modifications:

- Allow the user to enter the speed of the robot by changing the number attached to the `call NxtDrive1.MoveForwardIndefinitely power` and `call NxtDrive1.MoveBackwardIndefinitely power` blocks.
- Make the alerts for touch and microphone sensors more obvious by making them larger or turn red when triggered.
- Allow the user to select what tone to play by changing the `frequencyHz` argument.

Applications of the Remote Robot Control

While many robots are autonomous or controlled by wired remotes, the ability to send robots commands over the air has great implications for robots who simply cannot be tethered. Such robots may have hazardous jobs, such as nuclear-waste removal, or could be as simple as needing mobility, such as a vacuum robot. No matter the reason, wireless communication provides numerous opportunities for robots to provide even more services in our ever-evolving world.

Summary

You have successfully created an Android application to connect to Lego NXT robots over Bluetooth, to send and receive commands from the robot, and to display sensor information on the screen. While these tools and skills apply specifically to Lego NXT robots, the concepts apply to any external system. In fact, the types of commands you used are the same used to control Bluetooth speaker phones, car-navigation systems, and many other hardware-based devices. By understanding these connections, you can take your programming to the next level and interact with other devices!

VIRTUAL REALITY: USING QR CODES

CHAPTER OBJECTIVES

- Explore QR codes and how they work
- Use external apps to read QR codes
- Use the QR protocol to differentiate codes
- See different data types stored in QR codes

INTRODUCTION

Cell phones and other mobile devices have gone beyond communication within the digital realm by interfacing with the world around us through cameras, sensors, and data entry. One of the most common methods used to interact with the real world is the use of QR codes. A QR code, short for quick response code, is a square matrix barcode composed of black and white squares representing bits of information. No doubt, you have seen QR codes used in advertising, such as the business card in Figure 12.1.

FIGURE 12.1

QR codes used in
business cards.

QR codes allow URLs, phone numbers, or any digital information to be embedded within a printed space. Devices with cameras can then take a picture of the QR code, decode it, and use the information embedded within. These codes are gaining widespread popularity as they do not require any special equipment to print and no special hardware to scan.

How Do They Work?

QR codes begin with the selection of data to be encoded within the QR code. Due to many variables such as size and QR type, only a limited number of bytes of data can be encoded. This is due to the way QR codes encode data. To understand this further, see the QR code in Figure 12.2. There are three large squares in three corners and one smaller square near the fourth corner (1). These squares, called finder patterns, allow the scanner to normalize or resize the code to ensure readability from any location or angle. The lines around these squares are separators (2). They separate the finder patterns from the data. Near these strips are the timing patterns (3) and format information (4), which tell the scanner details about the QR code such as pixel width, version ID, and what kind of data is stored within the code. The majority of the rest of the code is devoted to the data (5), which is stored bit by bit, where white represents a zero and black represents a one. The larger the code, the more rows and columns possible, the more data can be encoded. The last section (6) is for error correction. It contains parity information about the data section, ensuring a correct read.

FIGURE 12.2

The anatomy of a
QR code.

After the data is encoded into this format and the code is generated, it can be resized and printed on any medium. Devices can then scan this code. As previously stated, the code is normalized using the finder patterns and then decoded. The resulting stream of bits is then passed to the application to use, whether to add a contact, open a website, or display a message. This application is what you will be creating in this chapter.

APPLICATION DISCUSSION

Writing a program to take a picture of a QR code, normalize it, and then decode the black and white blocks would require extensive programming knowledge and skill. That said, the other half of the program—reading a QR code and using the byte stream—is simple, as well as integral to a QR reader application. Luckily, App Inventor takes care of the code-scanning for you so you can focus on using the QR data. Therefore, in this chapter, you will create a program to launch a QR code reader; wait for the result; determine whether the QR code contains a phone number, Internet URL, or message; and, depending on the data type, call the number, open the Web page, or display the message.

To make this app as user-friendly as possible, we will minimize the number of buttons the user has to press and focus on automation as much as possible. Therefore, we will build the app such that when the user opens it, the app will begin scanning for QR codes immediately by launching the QR reader function. It is important to note that in order for the QR reader to work, a QR reader app must be installed on the device. Some devices come with one preloaded; others will have to download a free app from the Play Store.

After the scanner returns the data, the app will have to analyze it to determine whether the data contains a phone number, a message, or a URL. Luckily, encoded within the QR code is an identifier for the type of data within the code. The three data types for which you will be programming are found in Table 12.1.

TABLE 12.1	QR CODE PREFIXES
Data Type	**Prefix**
Phone number	TEL:
URL	http://
Message	none

After the app determines which type of data the QR code contains, it will execute the appropriate action. For phone numbers, it will parse the number, and then tell the device to call that number. If the QR code contains a URL, it will open a Web browser and direct it to the Web address contained in the QR code. If neither of these two conditions are met, it will simply display the QR code string for the user to read.

To make the application easy to understand, you will create three procedures: one to display the string, one to make a phone call, and the last to display in a Web browser. After creating these functions, you will program the logic to determine the correct function. Last, you will test the application on various types of QR codes.

THE DESIGN PHASE

In this section, you will create the application and instantiate all the needed components. Follow these steps:

1. Create a new project in App Inventor. Name it QR_Reader.
2. In the Palette, click Basic, and drag a Label component to Screen 1 and name it message.
3. In the Properties panel, change the message label's Width setting to Fill Parent and the TextAlignment Property to Center.
4. From the Basic section of the Palette, drag a Button component to Screen1 and name it rescan.
5. In the Properties panel, change the rescan button's Width setting to Fill Parent. Change the TextAlignment Property to Center.
6. From the Basic section of the Palette, drag another Button component to Screen1 and name it close.
7. In the Properties panel, change the close button's Width setting to Fill Parent. Change the TextAlignment Property to Center.
8. In the Palette, click Social, and drag a PhoneCall component to Screen1.
9. In the Palette, click Other Stuff, and drag an ActivityStarter component to Screen1.

10. From the Other Stuff section of the Palette, drag a BarcodeScanner component to Screen1. Your completed Screen1 should look like the one in Figure 12.3.

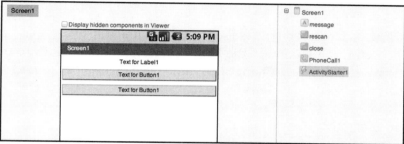

FIGURE 12.3

The completed visual interface.

THE CODE PHASE

Now that you have designed the interface, you will program the three helper functions to display the message, open the webpage, and place the phone call.

Display the Message

To program the helper function to display the message, follow these steps:

1. Open the Blocks Editor.
2. Click the Built-In tab, click Definition, and drag a `to procedure` block to the screen.
3. Click the `to procedure do` block and type `displayMessage` to rename it.
4. From the Definition section of the Built-In tab, drag a `name` block to the `arg` socket of the `to displayMessage do` block. Change the name of the `name` block to `result`.
5. Click the My Blocks tab, click Message, and drag a `set message.Text` block to the `do` portion of the `to displayMessage do` procedure.
6. Click the My Blocks tab, click My Definitions, and drag a `value` block to the `set message.Text` block. Your function should look like the one in Figure 12.4.

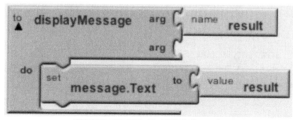

FIGURE 12.4

The completed display message procedure.

Open the Web Browser

You will now create a procedure to open the webpage specified by the QR code:

1. In the Blocks Editor, click the Built-In tab, click Definition, and drag a `to procedure do` block to the screen.
2. Click the `to procedure do` block and type `displayURL` to rename it.
3. As before, from the Definition section of the Built-In tab, drag a `name` block to the `arg` socket of the `to displayURL do` block. Change the name of the `name` block to `result1`.
4. Click the My Blocks tab, click ActivityStarter1, and drag a `set ActivityStarter1.Action` block to the `do` portion of the `to displayURL do` block.
5. Click the Built-In tab, click Text, and drag a `text` block to the `to` socket of the `set ActivityStarter1.Action` block. Change the value of the `text` block to `android.intent.action.VIEW`. (Activity starters interface with the low-level operating system software, which explains the more consolidated and cryptic value. For more information, take a look at the note at the end of this section.)
6. Click the My Blocks tab, click ActivityStarter1, and drag a `set ActivityStarter1.DataUri` block below the `set ActivityStarter1.Action` block.
7. In the My Blocks tab, click My Definitions, and drag a `value` block to the `to` socket of the `set ActivityStarter1.DataUri` block. Change the name of the `value` block to `result1`.
8. In the My Blocks tab, click ActivityStarter1, and drag a `call ActivityStarter1.StartActivity` block to the end of the procedure. Your completed procedure should look like the one in Figure 12.5.

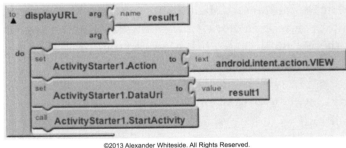

FIGURE 12.5

A completed display URL method.

TIP Activity starters enable your app to start other apps (either created by you or installed on the device) from within your app. To see how to interface with other apps, check out http://beta.appinventor.mit.edu/learn/reference/other/activitystarter.html.

Place a Phone Call

You will now create a procedure to place a phone call. Follow these steps:

1. In the Blocks Editor, click the Built-In tab, click Definition, and drag a `to procedure do` block to the screen.
2. Click the `to procedure do` block and type `callNumber` to rename it.
3. As before, from the Definition section of the Built-In tab, drag a `name` block to the `arg` socket of the `to callNumber do` block. Change the name of the `name` block to `result2`.
4. Unlike the message and URL procedures, the form of the phone number that the QR reader returns is not directly callable. You will first have to parse it and remove the "TEL:" text. To start, click the Built-In tab, click Text, and drag a `call segment` block to the screen.
5. Click the My Blocks tab, click My Definitions, and drag a `value result2` block to the text socket of the `call segment` block.
6. Click the Built-In tab, click Math, and drag a `number` block to the `start` socket of the `call segment` block.
7. Repeat step 6, this time connecting a `number` block to the `length` socket of the `call segment` block.
8. QR code readers return phone numbers in the following form: TEL:555-555-5555. The `call segment` block takes the text argument, ignores the first [number specified in `start`] characters, and returns a new text block containing the next [number specified in `length`] characters. In this case, you want to start at position 4 and continue for 11 characters. To start, change the value of the `number` block attached to the `start` socket to 4.
9. Change the value of the `number` block attached to the `length` socket to 11.
10. Click the My Blocks tab, click PhoneCall1, and drag a `set PhoneCall1.PhoneNumber` block to the `do` section of the `to callNumber do` procedure.
11. Connect the `call segment` block to the `to` socket of the `set PhoneCall1.PhoneNumber` block.
12. In the My Blocks tab, click PhoneCall1, and drag a `call PhoneCall1.MakePhoneCall` block to the end of the `to callNumber do` block. Your callNumber procedure should now look like the one in Figure 12.6.

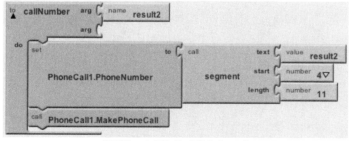

FIGURE 12.6

The completed call number procedure.

Your three procedures to handle QR data have now been created. Now you will create the logic to decide which procedure to handle the data.

Code the Remaining Functionality

In this section, you will program the brains of this application, including scanning the code and deciding which procedure to call to handle the returned data. As well, you will program the menu buttons, etc. To make the app more user-friendly, you will program it to begin scanning for QR codes on startup. Follow these steps:

1. In the Blocks Editor, click the My Blocks tab, click Screen1, and drag a `when Screen1. Initialize do` block to the screen.
2. In the My Blocks tab, click Close, and drag a `set close.Text` block to the `do` section of the `when Screen1.Initialize do` block.
3. Click the Built-In tab, click Text, and drag a `text` block to the `to` socket of the `set close.Text` block. Change the value of the `text` block to `Close App`.
4. Click the My Blocks tab, click Rescan, and drag `set rescan.Text` block to the `when Screen1.Initialize do` block.
5. Click the Built-In tab, click Text, and drag a `text` block to the `to` socket of the `set rescan.Text` block. Change the value of the `text` block to `Scan Again`.
6. Click the My Blocks tab, click Message, and drag a `set message.Text` block to the `when Screen1.Initialize do` block.
7. Click the Built-In tab, click Text, and drag a `text` block to the `to` socket of the `set message.Text` block. Change the value of the `text` block to `Scan Completed`.
8. Click the My Blocks tab, click BarcodeScanner1, and drag a `call BarcodeScanner1.DoScan` block in the `when Screen1.Initialize do` block. Your `when Screen1.Initialize do` block is now complete and should look like the one in Figure 12.7.

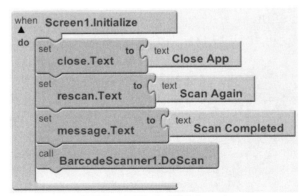

FIGURE 12.7

The completed initialization procedure.

You will now define the functions for the close and rescan buttons.

1. In the Blocks Editor, click the My Blocks tab, click Close, and drag a `when close.Click do` block to the screen.
2. Click the Built-In tab, click Control, and drag a `call close application` block to the `when close.Click do` block.
3. Click the My Blocks tab, click Rescan, and drag a `when rescan.Click do` block to the screen.
4. In the My Blocks tab, click BarcodeScanner1, and drag a `call BarcodeScanner1.DoScan` block to the `when rescan.Click do` block. These blocks should now look like the ones in Figure 12.8.

©2013 Alexander Whiteside. All Rights Reserved.

The completed close and rescan procedures.

You will now create the actual logic that will determine which procedure gets called. To determine which procedure to call, you will extract the first four characters of the data and compare them to your three scenarios. If the first four characters equal TEL:, you will call the `call callNumber` procedure. If the first four characters are http, you will call the `call displayURL` procedure. Otherwise, you will call the `call displayMessage` procedure. Follow these steps:

1. Click the My Blocks tab, click BarcodeScanner1, and drag a `when BarcodeScanner1.AfterScan` block to the screen.
2. If a `name` block is not already attached to the `result` socket, click the Built-In tab, click Definition, and drag a `name` block to the `result` socket of the `when BarcodeScanner1.AfterScan` block.
3. Click the `name` block and type `result3` to rename it.
4. Click the Built-In tab, click Control, and drag an `ifelse then-do else-do` block to the `when BarcodeScanner1.AfterScan` block. This will check if the data is a URL or a Phone Number.
5. From the Control section of the Built-In tab, drag an `ifelse then-do else-do` block to the `else-do` portion of the existing `ifelse then-do else-do` block. This will check if the data is a URL.
6. In the Built-In tab, click Text, and drag a `text=` block to the `test` socket of each `ifelse then-do else-do` block.

7. Click the Built-In tab, click Text, and drag a `call segment` block to the `text1` socket of each `text=` block.
8. Click the My Blocks tab, click My Definitions, and drag a `value result3` block to the `text` socket of each `call segment` block.
9. Click the Built-In tab, click Math, and drag a `number` block to each `start` and `length` socket of each `call segment` block.
10. Click the `number` block in the first `start` socket and type 1 to change its value. Repeat for the `number` block in the second `start` socket.
11. Click the `number` block in the first `length` socket and type 4. Repeat for the `number` block in the second `length` socket.
12. In the Built-In tab, click Text, and drag a `text` block to the `text2` socket of each `text=` block.
13. Click the first `text` block and type `TEL:`.
14. Click the My Blocks tab, click My Definitions, and drag a `call callNumber` block to the `then-do` section of the first `ifelse then-do else-do` block.
15. In the My Blocks tab, click My Definitions, and drag a `value result3` block to the `result2` socket of the `call callNumber` block.
16. Click the second `text` block and type `http`.
17. In the My Blocks tab, click My Definitions, and drag a `call displayURL` block to the `then-do` section of the second `ifelse then-do else-do` block.
18. In the My Blocks tab, click My Definitions, and drag a `value result3` block to the `result1` socket of the `call displayURL` block.
19. In the My Blocks tab, click My Definitions, and drag a `call displayMessage` block to the `else-do` section of the second `ifelse then-do else-do` block.
20. In the My Blocks tab, click My Definitions, and drag a `value result3` block to the `result` socket of the `call displayMessage` block. Your `when BarcodeScanner1.AfterScan` block should look like the one in Figure 12.9.

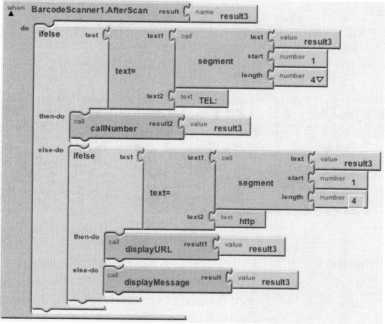

FIGURE 12.9

The completed scanning logic.

You have now programmed the application logic that determines what to do with the QR code. The entire code is shown in Figure 12.10.

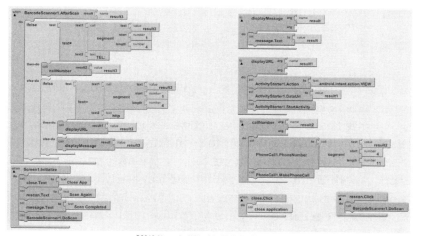

FIGURE 12.10

The completed application blocks.

THE TESTING PHASE

Now that your app is completed, download it to your phone by clicking the Package for Phone button on the main App Inventor screen. Test your app by scanning the QR codes in Figure 12.11!

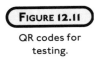

FIGURE 12.11

QR codes for testing.

ON-YOUR-OWN IMPROVEMENTS

While this app is completely functional, there are some limitations. For example, there are other types of data that can be stored in QR codes, such as contacts. As well, it is sometimes helpful to see what codes you scanned previously. To correct these shortcomings and practice app development, I recommend you complete the following exercises:

- Add the ability to store contact information retrieved from a QR code.
- Ask the user what they would like to do with phone numbers and links, such as saving or emailing them rather than just calling the number or opening the URL.
- Keep record of all data retrieved from QR codes and allow the user to scroll through past scans.

SUMMARY

QR codes offer an easy-to-use method for bridging the gap between the physical and digital worlds. Because of their easy-to-make nature, they have begun appearing in television ads, billboards, and all types of printed materials. Luckily, their widespread popularity means that they are well formatted, allowing you as a developer to create standard applications that can perform actions for the user, such as making a phone call if a phone number is detected. As you've seen, this task is not very difficult to understand, and can easily be done for all types of data. The result is a near seamless bridge between the real and digital worlds. In the near future, you will see more and more technologies like QR codes in advertising and technical applications to automate tasks.

Setting Up Your System to Run App Inventor

Before you start working with App Inventor, there are some steps you have to complete. These include preparing your system, installing App Inventor, and starting App Inventor. Instructions for these steps are provided in this appendix.

NOTE The information provided here is adapted from the text at appinventor.mit.edu/explore/test-your-system.html. This work is licensed under a Creative Commons Attribution-ShareAlike 3.0 Unported License, ©2012–2013, Massachusetts Institute of Technology.

Prepare Your System (Java)

App Inventor requires Java. If you already have Java installed, or if you are not sure, proceed to the "Java Web Start Verification" section. If you are sure you do not already have Java installed, follow the instructions on Oracle's Java Installation page (www.java.com/en/download/help/download_options.xml).

Attention Mac users: The Oracle Java page says that Java does not work with the Chrome browser on the Mac. This appears to be false. You should be able to use Java 7 and App Inventor on the Mac with Chrome.

Java Web Start Verification

To verify that Java Web Start is working properly, click the orange Launch button on the page at appinventor.mit.edu/explore/test-your-system.html to try to launch a program from the Web. This test should download and run a file (notepad.jnlp), which will create a window named "Notepad," where you can enter text. Depending on your browser, you might need to manually open the JNLP file after it downloads.

If Notepad does not run, then the test fails. Do not try to use App Inventor. Read on for possible solutions. If the test passes, then close the Notepad window and go on.

If the test fails, reasons might include the following:

- Your computer is behind a firewall that will not let the program download. (See your network administrator or IT department.)
- Your browser is not configured to use Java Web Start to open JNLP files. Fixing this might require creating an association between JNLP files and Java Web Start, or reinstalling Java.
- Your computer does not have enough memory to run App Inventor. It requires a Java heap size of about 950 Mb of contiguous memory.
- Your network proxy settings for Java need to be changed.

System Requirements

The system requirements for App Inventor are as follows:

- **Computer and operating system:**
  - **Macintosh (with Intel processor):** Mac OS X 10.5 or higher
  - **Windows:** Windows XP, Windows Vista, Windows 7
  - **GNU/Linux:** Ubuntu 8 or higher, Debian 5 or higher
- **Browser:**
  - Mozilla Firefox 3.6 or higher

 If you are using Firefox with the NoScript extension, you'll need to turn the extension off.

  - Apple Safari 5.0 or higher
  - Google Chrome 4.0 or higher
  - Microsoft Internet Explorer 7 or higher

According to some users, the Windows 8 operating system and the Google Chrome browser also work with App Inventor. However, these are not explicitly listed on the App Inventor website.

INSTALL APP INVENTOR SOFTWARE

Before you can use App Inventor, you need to install some software on your computer. The software you need is provided in a package called App Inventor Setup. Follow the instructions for your operating system to do the installation. Instructions can be found here:

- **Mac OS X:** appinventor.mit.edu/explore/content/mac-installation.html
- **GNU/Linux:** appinventor.mit.edu/explore/content/gnulinux-installation.html
- **Windows:** appinventor.mit.edu/explore/content/windows-installation.html

START APP INVENTOR

To work with the App Inventor, you must have access to the Internet and must have a Google account. To start App Inventor, go to beta.appinventor.mit.edu/. After you start App Inventor, you can start working on Chapter 1 of this book, "Introducing App Inventor." For more resources on using the App Inventor, or to teach or access tutorials, visit the following website: appinventor.mit.edu/explore/teach.html. Resources related to this book can be downloaded here: www.cengage.com/downloads.

INDEX